The Book of
THORLEY

Chronicles of a Century

BY THE PEOPLE OF THE PARISH

HALSGROVE

First published in Great Britain in 2003

This book is dedicated to Gladys Warboys.

British Library Cataloguing-in-Publication Data
A CIP record for this title is available from the British Library

ISBN 1 84114 211 5

HALSGROVE

Halsgrove House
Lower Moor Way
Tiverton, Devon EX16 6SS
Tel: 01884 243242
Fax: 01884 243325
email: sales@halsgrove.com
website: www.halsgrove.com

Frontispiece photograph: *Bert Bird with chickens at Hither Farm, 1930s.*

Printed and bound by CPI Bath Press, Bath.

Foreword

One day when I was with Rose Monk in her kitchen in Rectory Close waiting for Frank, her husband, to fetch me a cauliflower from his garden, she remarked that her neighbour, village schoolteacher Gladys Warboys, had lived in Thorley all her long life of nearly 100 years. And so the idea took root to write this book. Within days Rose, who is 86, had written pages of her own memories, covering all aspects of parish life. She talked to other villagers and word spread.

It seemed most propitious that we should launch the idea of *The Book of Thorley* on 2 September 2002, the occasion of Gladys' 100th birthday. Gladys had been a schoolteacher in Thorley Village School before she later married and raised four sons and a daughter in the village. Rose, Frank and I, with much optimism and Gladys' help, set about the task of identifying pupils in old school photographs.

Liz Eldred, the Thorley shepherdess, soon joined us, and with promotional help from church historian Bill Hardy, news spread even further. To my complete astonishment, our combined efforts have discovered some 60 former pupils of the Village School and a far greater number of relatives and friends, many of whom have living memories to share of life in Thorley.

The numbers of photographs and texts proffered have been threefold in excess of the capacity of the book commissioned. Consequently, we have been obliged to make selections, an unenviable task most reluctantly taken up until villagers suggested that we follow up this publication with a much less ambitious village

Gladys Warboys (née Eagling) and Rose Monk (née Stoakes) looking at school photographs, 2000.

School shop, 1940s. Among the children are Don Powell, Arthur Willis, Mary Monk,
Jean and Joan Hammond

album of omitted photos and texts to supplement these chronicles. Contributors should not therefore be too dismayed to find their photos missing or memories cut short, because these will follow as 'Chronicle Supplements'.

In this book the people of the parish invite the reader to walk with them around Thorley, as it existed within the wider parish boundaries at the turn of the century, and to hear stories of their youth. Thorley has suffered grievously from urban encroachment and boundary changes during the last century, and this book is offering us an opportunity to revive, on paper and perhaps for one last time, the traditional English Rogation Day ceremony of beating the bounds, when villagers would accompany the rector around the parish as he blessed the fields, and children would be given treats.

Compilation of the book could not be completed in time for publication on Rogation Sunday in May 2003, but the village went ahead with its planned celebrations for that day. After morning service in St James' Church, Revd Bob Payne, the newly appointed rector of Thorley, walked in the fields with the choir and congregation, and from noon until dusk a fête and barbecue were held on the cricket field. Local schoolchildren, Thorley Scouts, and one former pupil of the Village School, Albie Camp, enacted extracts from a pageant written and performed by villagers 52 years ago to celebrate the Festival of Britain. Visitors to the fête came from afar, and the day finished with a party in St Barnabas Centre, and with many renewals of old acquaintances.

The focus of the book is Gladys and the pupils of the Village School but, as you will see, the story of Thorley comes from the intertwining of the lives of all the people of the parish, be they gentry or worker, clergy or farmer, teacher or trader. This book is also a tribute to those who, sadly missed but much spoken of in recent months, have died since that first discussion in Rose's kitchen.

Sylvia McDonald, parish councillor, 2003

Contents

Right: *Twyford Mill, c.1900.*

Below: *Blanche Streeter* (seated left), *c.1900.*

Bottom: *Laying tarmac on Great Hadham Road. William Crabb (Frank's father) is on the far left, c.1905.*

Acknowledgements

This Book could not have been put together without the enthusiasm and encouragement, patience and shared participation of a great number of people. And it is to all of them, former pupils, Thorleyites, relatives, friends and local people alike, that acknowledgement is given. With special thanks to those included in the list of names below for their written and verbal contributions to the story of Thorley, and to the many others, individuals and groups, who made the Rogation Day village fête such an enjoyable occasion – in particular the cricketers and Scouts of Thorley, the wood band and Morris men, the jazz musicians and pageant children, and everyone joining in to help run stalls, raffles, races, games and pony rides.

Joan Abbotson, Anne Ashpole, Dawn Ashraf, Eva Ashwell, Geoff Ashwell, Alyson and John Bailey, Dorothy (Cissie) Banks, Bubbles Barker, Pat and Ian Bateman, Emma and Richard Bates, Penny and John Beer, Paul Bennett, Lilian Bentley, Pat Birch, Grenville Bird, Rene Bird, Graham Bishop, Joan and Joe Brace, Charlotte and Chris Bradley, Alison and Donna Bradnick, Ron Brett, George Brewster, Geoff Brewster, George Bright, Ina Bright, Des Brown, Stanley Brownridge, Pauline Burpitt, Albie Camp, Clara Camp, George Camp, Tom Camp (dec.), Clare Chapman, George Clark, Joyce Clark, Doug Collidge, Pam Coster, Ann Cottee, Norman Coulson, Ron Cox, Jill Cranwell, Maisie and Bob Crisp, Jean and Peter Cullen, Ann Curnow, Richard Doe, Angela and John Davies, Nan Davies, Phil Dedman, Nicole and Tony Drath, Sheila Dutton, Cicely Eadie, Liz and Dave Eldred, Maurice Elliott, Eileen Faulkner, Pam and Allan Finch, Chris Foreman, June, Simon and Lorna Fuller, Suzanne Gale, Sandy and Andie Gibbs, Emie Glasscock, Andy Graham, Coral Gray, Linda Greenwood, Joyce Griffiths, Doreen (Griff) Griffiths, Sandy and Roger Halford, Janet Hammond, John Hammond (dec.), Bill Hardy, Philip Hargrave, Geoff Harris, David Herbert, Sheila Hewitt, David Hickling, Hope Hill, Derek Hinge, Maurice Hockley, Tom Hunter, Eileen and Reg Jacobs, Deirdre and Peter James, Paul James, Betty Jennings, Marie, Beri and Saira Karim, Lawrence Karthauser, Teddie Kent, Rosina Kirkwood, Johnny Kitchener, Terry Kitchener, Simon Knight, Cynthia Knott, Molly Lambert, Peggy Lamyman, Wendy Linney, Robin Lumsden, Pat Martin, Sue Mascall, Sylvia and Mac McDonald, Carol Miller, Ann and Edward Miller, Rob Mills, Alison Mitchell, Roy Money, Rose and Frank Monk, Flossie and Vic Monk, John Monk, Margaret Morley, Jim Morton, Maura Newman, Mrs F.H. Osborne, Alf (Ossie) Osborne, Ethel and Bert Outlaw, Stella Owers, Vera and Ron Oxborrow, Nita and Sid Oxborrow, Terry Parsons, Dr Ian Paterson and Dame Betty, Revd Bob Payne, Molly and Tony Pigram, Ivy Pigram, Jack Phillips, David Philpott, Ian Pinder, Brenda and Bill Pleasance, Joy and Freddie Prior, Mrs B. Rawlinson, Trevor Reedman, Glyn Reedman, Carole and Anthony Robins, John Robinson, Jimmy Robinson, Peggy Robinson (dec.), Janet and Jimmy Rolph, Daphne Ruddock, Jean and Les Sage, Marjorie and Colin Sampford, Mary Sampford, Chris Saunders, Audrey and 'Ginge' Sayers, Colin Selwood, David Smith, Brenda Sortwell, Bryan South, Len Sparks, Andy Streeter, Patrick Streeter, Max Streets, Ann and Tony Swan, Peter David Teitz, Michael Teitz, Alan Threadgold, Jane and Richard Timmis, David Tinney, John Tinney, Violet Vale, Virginia Wade Bain, Jean Warbey, Gladys Warboys, Frank Warboys OBE, Peter Warboys, Charlie Ward, Stephen Warner, Paul Waters, Charles Watson, John Whalley, Barbara White, Compton Whitworth, John Wick, Mary and Roy Wilson, Edna and Mark Wolfson OBE, Jo and Peter Wood, Dorothy Wood, Len Wood, Philip Wood, David Wood, Philippa Woodall, John Wyllie, plus the girls in the church office and the tea ladies.

Gladys May Eagling, aged 3, 1905.

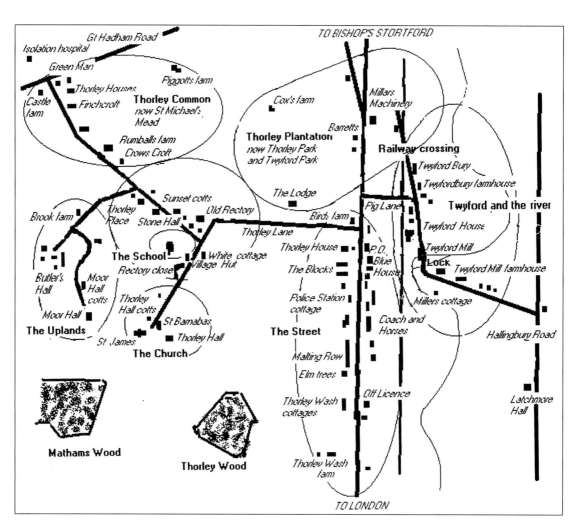

A schematic map of the buildings of interest in old Thorley.
Each encircled area tells its own story in a chapter of this book.

Beryl Frere in her pony and trap, with her sister Phillis Woodall's children Barbara, Bartle and Philippa
and their friend Pam Wolfson, c.1939. The gentleman with the dog is unknown.

Introduction

'I Often Go Back to Thorley'

Words from Virginia Wade Bain (née Jones), who spent the war years here as a child:

I clamber aboard the Greenline Coach, which leaves Aldgate in London for Bishop's Stortford. The driver has been asked to kindly set me down in Bird's Lane as near to Bird's Farm as possible. 'Will Mrs Wolfson meet me or maybe Pam or Ena?' London and the suburbs pass and then the magic begins. I try to catch a glimpse of the pale pink walls of Thorley House with its green shutters, dear house, so full of lovely people and lovely memories.

First I see the Coach and Horses, and now the lane seems more narrow, more leafy, ahh, there is the little Post Office on the right, almost opposite the gates of Thorley House. 'Stop driver, here we are, Bird's Farm', with its farm shop where Ena will take me at some time to buy the fresh eggs, buttermilk and cream (yummy). Pammy is there to meet me and usher me along with my little brown suitcase, mindful that there is no pavement!

Tom Camp is working in the garden; he lives in the house just inside the gates with his wife Vera and their young son Michael. Tom looks after the lawns, flower-beds and vegetable gardens. There are lots of fruit bushes, and Ena makes lovely blackcurrant puddings.

Miss Frere, from Twyford House, will come by on Sunday and we will go to church in her pony and trap. A bit scary, like being in a boat swaying from side to side.

Very slowly we pass the gypsy encampment with their colourful, painted and strange shaped caravans. Miss Frere says they are Romany. We arrive at lovely Thorley Church, just past the duck pond. Tom Camp sings in the choir. He has the reddest cheeks I have ever seen, like two shiny apples, and he is always smiling!

I remember crossing the fields to get to the brook, but first I had to get past the cows! Pam laughs and calls me a silly girl to be afraid of cows, and we cross the narrow wooden bridge with its high handrails across the River Stort. In the distance I hear the whistle of the steam train.

The church fête was often held in the field alongside Thorley House. That was always fun, the house bustling with people, food, toys and bunting. I remember Valerie, Coral and Dawn, who lived nearby, used to come to play. We would have tea parties under the huge willow tree on the lawn and walk Hero, the Scottie dog, in the cornfields.

A magical journey to a magical place for a child from war-torn London. It was a world of peace and tranquillity with green fields and the new tastes of fresh fruit and vegetables!

Of course Thorley has changed, but the warmth, magic and excitement of Thorley, as I originally saw it all those years ago, live on in my memory.

Thorley lies south of the market town of Bishop's Stortford and straddles the River Stort. Its footpaths, springs, fields and woods are all named. Its people were known as Thorleyites. In this book the reader will 'beat the bounds' in a figure of eight, starting and finishing at the Village School, where 101-year-old Gladys was schoolmistress in the 1920s and where many of those who have stories to tell were once pupils. Below we anticipate the route we will take, following a schematic map of Thorley's places of interest.

Old Thorley divides easily into seven encircled areas, each of these forming the basis for a chapter in this book. These 'chronicles' are of old Thorley, by which is meant the parish of Thorley as encompassed by the civil and parochial boundaries in force in 1900. The start of our walk, at the Village School (Chapter 2), is where most villagers' memories begin.

The first places to visit are Thorley Hall and the church (Chapter 6), along the lane from the school and then the several upland farms (Chapters 7 and 8), which are accessed by footpaths from the church and owned by one of the two prominent farming families, the Streeters and the Tinneys. The route follows Thorley Lane to return to the school, stopping at Thorley Place, Stone Hall and the Rectory (Chapter 9).

Passing the school the route continues eastwards along Thorley Lane to arrive at what used to be known as Bird Lane at the T-junction with Thorley Street. Towards the town along the main London–Cambridge road lies the Plantation area (Chapter 10), now within the town civil boundary. Across The Street, Pig Lane leads to the river, and Twyford (Chapter 11) lies alongside the Herts/Essex county boundary. Here there was a mill at the side of the river which at one time carried barge traffic to and from Bishop's Stortford.

The last area to visit is The Street. Behind the cottages and the Coach and Horses pub (on the east side) are meadows, allotments and the flood plain. Behind the cottages and Thorley House (west) is open farmland, with paths leading across the Valley fields back to the church. From there we return along Church Lane to the school, where our walk began.

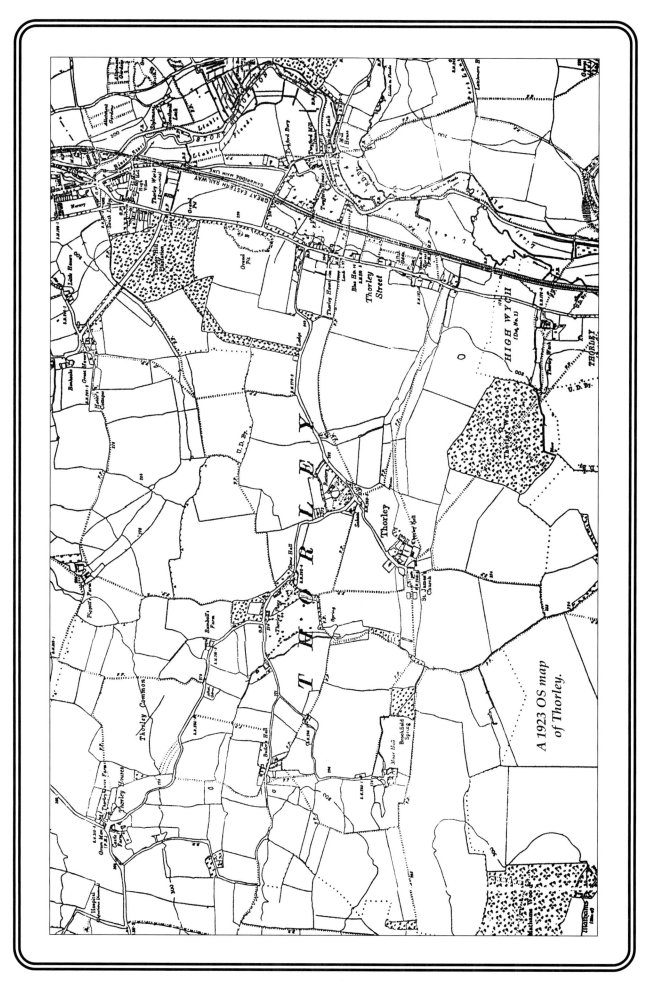

*A 1923 OS map
of Thorley.*

Chapter 1

The Story of Thorley and its People

Setting the Scene and Beating the Bounds

Discoveries from archaeological digs tell us about Thorley from prehistoric times. Excavations in the 1990s, prior to commencement of extensive house building on ancient Thorley Common, revealed evidence of prehistoric occupation from the Neolithic, Bronze, Iron and the later Roman periods. The earliest evidence discovered was of a burial of a 45-year-old Neolithic man found 200 metres north-east of Rumballs Farm. This grave, dated 2,900–2,750BC, is contemporary with the first phase of Stonehenge. Excavations 500 metres to the north of Rumballs Farm revealed a small farmstead from the late Bronze Age. The discovery of pottery dating from around 300BC indicates that the inhabitants of Thorley at that time were farming communities, raising cattle, sheep, pigs and horses as well as cultivating wheat and barley – all of which are familiar activities in Thorley within living memory.

Historical records provide further information. Small settlements existed into the early Romano-British era. An extensive enclosed-field system was identified, and deep ploughing in 1954 revealed a villa or farmhouse. The Catuvellauni tribe was known to occupy territory in the area, and a coin of Cunobelinus, a Catuvellauni leader, was found in Thorley. Local metal-detecting enthusiast, Tom Hunter, has also found pottery bearing a Roman name, which he has been able to identify from internet research.

The medieval village of Thorley, set on the eastern edge of the county of Hertfordshire, grew as scattered agricultural settlements. The Domesday Book and Ordnance Survey maps show us that Thorley remained without radical change through to the twentieth century. Thorley – or Thornley, Torley, Torlei, Thorle, Thorlye, as it has been recorded in various times and places – is believed to have been so named from the Celtic word Tor (stony or rocky hill) and Lei (meadow or pasture).

Living memory recalls how change in Thorley has quickened during the last 100 years. Before large-scale new housing in the 1970s and the 1990s transformed its rural setting and skyline, Thorley was still the straggling village it had always been, with its many footpaths leading importantly from one settlement to another. Its most ancient lane, Thorley Lane, leads from the Green Man public house shown in the top left-hand corner of the 1923 OS map of Thorley *(see opposite)* to Thorley Street, on the right-hand side. Thorley Street is a section of the old A11 London–Cambridge trunk road and runs parallel with the Great Eastern Railway and the Stort navigation canal.

A second map, of the central and oldest part of Thorley, shows how the parish has been severed by the recently constructed town bypass, which was built to serve the newest housing estate and Stansted airport traffic.

The parish of Thorley has always been small in terms of the number of parishioners. *The Gentleman's Magazine*, as early as August 1811, described Thorley as containing 'in 1801, 55 inhabited houses and 269 persons, and this year [1811] the population was found to be 313 and 60 houses.'

The scene at the beginning of the 1900s is set by a description given in the *Short Account of the Parish and Church*, written some time after 1923 by Revd J.E.I. Procter, rector of Thorley and rural dean of Bishop's Stortford. The original parish acreage was 1,527 of land and 9 of water, but in 1910 an area of 80 acres 1 rood and 24 perches in the north-east corner, containing 59 houses and 244 persons, was transferred to the civil parish of Bishop's Stortford.

Looking at population records and the 1901 electoral roll, it would appear that the 1910 civil boundary change would have left in 1911 some 347 persons and 83 houses in the civil parish of Thorley. The ecclesiastical parish boundaries remained unchanged, and in 1911 this population totalled 590 (inclusive of the 347).

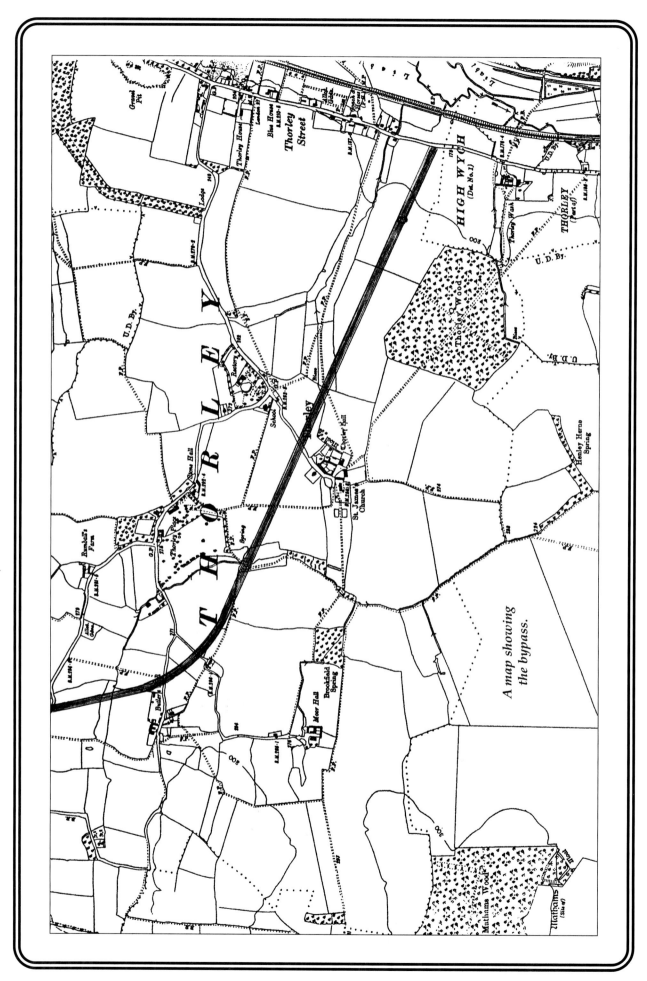

A map showing the bypass.

The north-east corner (see Chapter 10) was the most densely populated part of the parish. This covered the area east of the London Road centring on Twyford Road, where the 18 houses of Thorley Terrace used to be. An indication of how closely the boundary approached the town is given in Revd J.E.I. Procter's account when he writes of a trust deed pertaining to King's Cottages, the four cottages in South Road, Bishop's Stortford, nearest to the Thorley boundary, which were erected in 1910 by Admiral Vander-Meulen 'for the benefit of poor aged parishioners of Thorley.' A Revd F. Vander-Meulen had been the rector of Thorley before Revd J.M. Procter. *Kelley's Directory* of 1914, as well as Revd Procter's account, should be consulted by the serious scholar of Thorley history.

Discussions with parishioners and entries made in the Parish Council minute-books explain further the impact of later boundary changes on population. A boundary change in the 1930s took even more land from the parish of Thorley into the civil boundaries of the town, and the parish/town boundary then ran parallel with, but to the south of, Thorley Lane, following the line of Metropolitan Green Belt for some of the way.

Most of the land and properties in Thorley Street and Twyford used to belong to the Frere family. In 1946, all of the Twyford estate (on both sides of the London Road) was sold to Boyd Gibbins, a property developer, who then built the Twyford Park housing estate on the western side of the London Road (area now belonging to the town). On the eastern side, he sold the farms and land by the river in smaller plots, redeveloped the mill as apartments, and attempted to turn Twyford House into a hotel and restaurant.

Later, in the 1970s, the land farmed by the Tinney family in the Plantation area west of The Lodge in Thorley Lane (also an area now belonging to the town), was sold for further large-scale housing development; it then became known as Thorley Park. It lies adjacent to Twyford Park. Meanwhile, behind the housing of Thorley Park and Twyford Park, the rest of the Plantation area was continuously being developed, to the point where, at the time of writing, the houses and schools of the Thorley Hill and Havers Lane neighbourhoods complete the coalescence of town with village behind the eastern section of Thorley Lane. The new housing consequently greatly increased the population of the town, not of the village.

In the 1990s, much of the farmland and green belt land in the Uplands and on the Common was sold to the developers Countryside Properties for the purpose of even further large-scale housing development and a town bypass leading to the M11 and Stansted airport. This housing estate is known as St Michael's Mead and lies adjacent to Thorley Park housing. It covers all available farmland between the Great Hadham Road and the present delineation of green belt which protects the hamlets of Moor Hall and Butler's Hall. This completes the coalescence of town with village behind the western section of Thorley Lane. But here the result is a doubling of the population of the village because the latest changes in green belt and civil boundaries together conspired to locate one-third of the new St Michael's Mead housing within the parish.

In 1999, another change to parish boundaries, this time for purposes of local government administration at district level, gave yet more of Thorley's autonomy to the town, since all of the parish north of the new bypass has since been administered as part of Bishop's Stortford South Ward. A glance at the OS map with the bypass superimposed will show that, as a consequence, rural Thorley is now reduced to some 20 dwellings, around Thorley Wash, St James' Church, and the hamlets of Moor Hall and Butler's Hall.

What is interesting to observe is that over time the parish has 'lost to the town', in a manner of speaking, not only its ancient Thorley Lane which was its 'backbone' linking one settlement with another, but also its Old Rectory and old Village School and many of its oldest farmhouses and dwellings, as well as its 'name' and, increasingly, its identity.

On the other hand, however, the ecclesiastical parish of Thorley remains intact within its much wider and unchanged parochial boundaries, and now it increasingly reaches out to potentially very large numbers of worshippers on the new Thorley urban housing estates. Paradoxically, the village church is growing, while the rural village as a community is in decline and becoming lost in the suburbs of the town.

Landowning Families and Change

The well-being of an agricultural village community used to depend in large measure upon the influence of the prominent families. For the ordinary people of the parish, the certainty of provision of employment on the farms and the philanthropic activities of the ladies in the 'big houses' were dominant aspects of village life. Villagers mainly lived in tied cottages and were farm workers or domestic servants in the 'big houses'. The smaller farmers were often tenants of the larger landowners. The church was central to all activities and the ladies of the gentry and the farming families would host meetings and social occasions for the villagers. Then came the Second World War, heralding such unprecedented and widespread change that village life and the expectations of villagers took on a radical new aspect.

During the first half of the century there were four prominent landowning families in Thorley. These were the Frere, Streeter, Tinney and Patten families. The Freres used to own land and properties in Twyford and The Street and on both sides of the

London Road until the middle of the twentieth century. After the war the Frere estate was sold, and Miss Beryl Frere, the last member of the family to live at Twyford House in Thorley, moved to Latchmore Hall in nearby Little Hallingbury.

Peter Warboys recalls that there used to be ten working farms in Thorley in the 1940s, but there are now only three:

The three farms owned by the Freres have gone. Twyford Mill Farm and Hither Farm (known as Bird's Farm) were farmed by my Uncle Bert Bird (married to Mum's second sister Dot Eagling) and his brother Arthur Bird. Twyfordbury Farm, where my father, Frank Warboys, was born, formed part of Havers Farm, now within the boundary of Bishop's Stortford.

The fourth, Thorley Wash, on the borders with Spellbrook, was owned and farmed by Messrs Willi and Drury Patten, both bachelors, and later by Tony Kluysse until his death. The land has since been purchased to increase the acreage of the adjacent Tinney farmland.

Three of the four Streeter farms in Thorley, namely Castle Farm, Brook Farm and Rumballs Farm, were managed by Tom Streeter, from his Great Hallingbury farm, and the fourth, Butler's Hall, was farmed by tenant Reggie Newman and after his retirement by nephew Tom Seabrook. After the war, the managed farms were sold, and Tom Streeter's son, Andy, took over the farming of Butler's Hall, which he now manages from the family's farm in Great Hallingbury.

The last two farms are still owned by the Tinney family. After the death of John Tinney (grandfather), Thorley Hall and Moor Hall were farmed together as one farm by a partnership of brothers, Wilfrid and Edgar Tinney. Their foreman was Mr Ernie Barker, and later they had a manager, Mr Roy Money, resident at Moor Hall. They were the most advanced farm in the area, and the biggest single local employers.

The Frere family in particular had a remarkable impact on the whole village, and their disappearance after the war was widely felt. Two incoming families during those days were the Wolfsons, who moved into Thorley House in The Street, and Revd Sydney Robinson, who moved with his family into the Old Rectory. They appeared at the right time, and with optimism and vigour they took up Miss Beryl Frere's concern for the villagers, and they shepherded the village through two decades of change after the war. A community spirit held and all manner of activities flourished, as will be recalled in this book by the villagers who were the teenagers of those earlier years.

Changes were already being observed in 1937 by Canon Procter, as seen in his memorable last address to his congregation in Thorley Church:

Together we have seen many changes in the 55 years I have been privileged to reside in Thorley parish.

We have mourned three sovereigns and seen the abdication of a fourth, and have celebrated three Jubilees and three Coronations. We have seen men go out from the village to two wars, some to make the supreme sacrifice, some to return wounded. There have been some wonderful services in the church.

Changes and progress have been made in the world of science, progress which has provided not only the wireless and telephone, but also changes in the implements and in the crops seen in our own fields. The electoral rolls and parochial councils have also been instituted, that the church might be placed on a more democratic footing.

I am sorry to be going, because we have 'grown used to one another', and I should like to leave Joshua's message with you: Cleave unto God.

Dorothy Wolfson too recognised that change was continuing, when in October 1969 she wrote:

Much of course has changed since 1936 when we first settled in Thorley. At that time the Frere family lived at Twyford House and owned most of the hamlet lands, as well as Thorley House. Before the Freres many notables lived in Thorley and as early as 1700.

The Rapers are an old Buckinghamshire family of Norman descent. Matthew Raper, a bachelor, lived at Thorley Hall. John Raper lived at Twyford. Both these brothers were scientists, and at Thorley Hall and Twyford observatories were built. Matthew had a library built into Thorley Hall to hold all his books, maps, prints, engravings and mathematical instruments. It was he who planted Thorley Wood and laid out a formal garden with oval pond, and gravel walks with wide grass verges. Any rustic taking a shortcut across his garden, and detected from the observatory by Matthew, was ordered off by shouts from a 'speaking trumpet'.

Sir Richard Whittington (thrice Lord Mayor of London), was Lord of the Manor of Thorley, so it has been said, in 1400.

Lord Ellenborough, the famous 'Hanging Judge', owned much land in Thorley and in about 1800 used to preside at Hertford Assizes.

Geoffrey de Magnaville seems to have been somewhat of a rogue in King Stephen's reign – a disturber of the peace, pillaging Thorley lands. But, eventually cornered and wounded by Stephen's forces, his body in its coffin was hung on a tree in Temple Churchyard in London.

And now, in 1969, things are changing. The hedges and trees are fast being bulldozed and there are no longer barges on the Stort. There is a new rectory. But the Church stands, unchanged and cared for through wars and strife. The Thorley branch of the British Legion is stronger than ever, the Mothers' Union membership is increasing, the Women's Institute now has nearly 60 members, and recently four Scouts from the First Thorley Group were presented with their Queen Scout badges.

The footpaths are coming back following our fight over the years to keep the Rights of Way over Thorley lands. Our harvest festivals seem to be more lovely each year – and the bells of St James' still ring across the fields, calling the faithful as they have done in days of old. From Thorley House we see them; from the further fields we see the Church spire – a symbol of our faith and surely our hope for the future.

Our narrative continues with some brief accounts of the Frere, Streeter and Tinney families.

The Frere Family

In 1969 Dorothy Wolfson wrote:

The Freres are to this day a household word in Thorley. Laurie Frere, when at Oxford, became a fine oarsman and his college was Head of the River. He rowed stroke for the varsity. He did not pursue the profession of lawyer, as did his father and grandfather, but settled down at Twyford House to improve the house, farms, cottages and estate generally, and to exercise his natural talent for landscape painting. The Frere family consisted of Mr Laurie Frere, his wife Maud, three daughters – Phillis, Ursula and Beryl – and a son Bartle, who was killed in the First World War.

Rose Monk recalls:

Miss Phillis married Jack Woodall and moved to Highlands Farm in Leatherhead, while her sisters Ursula and Beryl carried on with the house and estate after the deaths of their parents, until Miss Ursula went overseas to do missionary work as a physiotherapist from 1946 to 1957 at Jane Furze Memorial Hospital in Pretoria. She was visiting Miss Beryl in Latchmore Hall in 1957 when she died.

Dorothy Wolfson continues:

In the First World War, as well as being a Special Constable, Laurie Frere worked as a foreman in a machine shop at Featherby's (now Millar's) where they made shell caps. In 1917 he started the National Savings Movement at Featherby's and in Thorley village.
The family's nursing interests must be mentioned. In about 1898, Laurie, Margaret and Ester Frere founded the Cottage Hospital at Rye Street in Bishop's Stortford, in memory of their father Bartle John Frere. Maud Frere, Beryl's mother, started District Nursing in the village.
During the Second World War, Twyford House became a maternity hospital home for evacuated mothers, some from the East End of London. Six hundred and ninety three babies were born there.

By happy coincidence, the whereabouts of Barbara

Above: *The Frere girls, Beryl, Phillis and Ursula, c.1905.*

Right: *Phillis Frere with her father Laurie in the 1920s.*

Right: Blanche Streeter, aged 85, with her great-grandchildren, c.1959.

Below: Tom Streeter dressing and weighing corn in Harp's Farm barn, late 1930s.

and Philippa, the daughters of Phillis Frere, have been traced, and they are very pleased to be contacted. Philippa has sent albums of photos from her home in France, and Barbara (now White) travelled from her home in Devon to revisit Pam, daughter of Cmdr and Mrs Wolfson, and Mark her brother, who came from London to open the village fête on Rogation Sunday in 2003.

The Streeter Family

Both Andy Streeter and brother Patrick recall memories of Thorley Place, the family home purchased by their grandfather George Streeter. Andy writes:

My Grandmother, Blanche, was born in December 1874, so by the time I knew her in the 1940s, she was a very gracious lady of some 60 years and had already been a widow for 15 years. She was the twelfth of 13 children of Sir Charles and Fanny Gold (née Gilbey) of Stansted,

so all her life she had lived near Bishop's Stortford.

I first remember her in the war – she was always very busy doing good work but also always had time for her grandchildren. Tom, one of her five children, was my father and he set up home in Great Hallingbury when he married my mother Nesta. We used to go to Thorley from there by pony and trap, or sometimes we even walked with me in my pram.

My memories of Thorley are connected with Thorley Place, my Grandmother's home where she lived with her unmarried daughter Pam Streeter until she died in 1966. My father, Tom Streeter, was always involved in Thorley affairs. He was a churchwarden at St James' and a councillor on the Braughing District Council. We always liked to go with him to look at the Thorley farms, mainly because we stopped off to see Grandmother, which was always a wonderful thing to do!

When my father died I became much more involved in looking after my Grandmother and the Thorley farms. The door of Thorley Place was never locked;

one used to go in and just shout to see which room she was sitting in and then chat to her until one had to leave for work.

After my Grandmother's death, the house was sold for an hotel, which was never successful. It was then empty for many years and was very badly vandalised, so it is nice to know that it has now been sold and restored back into a family home.

Thorley was very lucky in having the Revd Robinson as Rector for many years. He was a great friend. He often came to see my Grandmother, when their conversations were inspiring to listen to, very often on religion but also on many other matters. We went to Thorley Church most Sundays and I have very fond memories of it – all four of our children were christened there as well as several of our relations being buried in the churchyard.

After the departure from Thorley in 1963 of Tom Seabrook, who took on the tenancy of Butler's Hall Farm from his uncle, tenant farmer Reggie Newman, the Streeter family took back the farm and I have been farming it ever since. I still enjoy going to Thorley but it has changed so much. It does not quite have the same character as in the 1950s/'60s, but it is still a village and we are very pleased to be farming there.

The Tinney Family

John Tinney includes these lines in his account of his family's association with Thorley:

The Tinney family first arrived in Thorley in 1920 from a rented farm near Ongar. My grandfather, John Tinney, born 1868/9, moved with his second wife Fanny. His first wife Mary had died in 1914. John had four sons by his first marriage. The eldest three sons had moved away to their own independent farms at the time of the move. Two of these boys had served during the latter part of the Great War and fortunately returned home. My father Wilfrid was 15, and his younger brother Gordon, from the second marriage, was about three at the time.

Both Thorley Hall and Moor Hall Farm were auctioned together at the sale, which my grandfather successfully purchased. These have always been farmed together since that time. Some time later in the

1930s or 1940s my father and his older brother Edgar obtained the tenancy of Piggott's Farm. Some time in the 1950s the landlord sold the farm and the family were lucky to buy.

My father obtained the tenancy of Bentfield Bury Farm, Stansted, in 1929 and moved from Thorley. He married in Thorley Church in 1931. My mother was born in Havers Lane, the only daughter of Frederick and Mary French.

After my grandfather died in 1929, my uncle Edgar and my father ran the farm at Thorley and were able to buy out their brothers. In 1947 my uncle Edgar unfortunately died early. My grandmother occupied the house at Thorley Hall until about 1945 when she too died. Since that time the house has been continuously let. The house at Moor Hall has also been continuously let since 1920, except for a period of about 10 years from 1947 when our farm manager Roy Money and his family lived there. David, my son, was therefore the first Tinney to live in Moor Hall when he moved in about five years ago.

For a brief period of about 10 months in 1965/6 my late wife Judy and myself lived at Stone Hall prior to the move to Farnham Hall Farm when we became new tenants on the Hassobury estate.

Of course there are other established family names in Thorley. Readers may find interesting the list of key parishioners appearing in an extract from Kelly's Directory of 1914:

James Bertram Bull, Twyfordbury
Mrs Clark, Stone Hall
Laurie Frere, Twyford House
William Hartigan MD, Thorley House
Revd Canon John Matthias Procter MA (surrogate), Rectory
Revd John Edward Ingleby Procter MA (rector), Rectory
George Skelton Streeter JP, Thorley Place
Frederick Bird, farmer
Shadrach Brace, Green Man PH
William Chappell, beer retailer, Thorley Street
Alfred William Death, gardener to Laurie Frere Esq.
Wallace Augustus Evans, corn merchant, Blue House
Charles Fowler, farmer, Butler's Hall
Arthur Gilson, Coach and Horses PH
Kennard H. Kent, head gardener to G.S. Streeter Esq.
John Lawrence, miller (steam and water), Twyford Mill
Francis Newman, farmer, Moor Hall
Edward Raymond George Patten, farmer, Thorley Hall
Hannah Louise Patten Mrs, farmer, Thorley Wash
Daniel Reed, pork butcher [or as Rose Monk and others remember him, Lew Reed]
George Watson, assistant overseer and collector of rates [Gladys Warboys' grandfather]

Left: John Tinney with son David and his wife Sally exhibiting a field map, St Barnabas, 2002.

Field Names

The Streeter and Tinney families have both researched the field names on their farms and have maps showing old field names and boundaries. A supplement will follow on this fascinating topic, but meanwhile local people will perhaps be interested to read the field names shown on maps or in common usage.

Andy Streeter has listed: Hospital Field, Upper More, Further More, Hither Moor, Moor Ley, Harps, White Croft, Dark Croft, Crooked Shelter, Wood Field, Sheeps Croft, Halloways, Stocking Croft, Wisbeys, Finch Croft, Great Pasture, The Leys, Mares Ley, Lympsteads, Long Field, Spencers Pasture, Hoppet, Barn Field, Double Gate, The Keys, Leylands, Five Acres, Home Dale, Pound Home, Whitelands, Broomfield Spring, Brookfield, Hobbs Croft, Pond Field, Park Meadow, Starlings, Glebe, Eight Acres, Meadow, Sudricks, Little Sudricks and Stone Hall Meadow. Other names found are The Mead and The Pightle.

David Tinney has listed: New Mead, Reeves Croft, Upper Brooms, Lower Brooms, Miltons Close, Pond Field, Wood Field, Lower Thorley Field, Upper Thorley Field, Spring Field, Long Valley, Plowed Aldbury, Aldbury Mead, Alberry Arable, Alberry Pasture, Forberry Pasture, Bush Faire Croft, Hoppet Mead, Nightleyes, Little Valley, Hop Ground Mead, Mill Field, Church Field, Winches (or Wynches), Colsdon (or Coldson) Field, Henley Herne, Pear Tree Croat, Fourteen Acre Field, Clay Croft, Stable Ley, Kitchen Field, Mr Bull, Grove Pasture, Ox Croft, Vineyards, South Wicks, The Greate Moore Pasture, Little Moore Pasture, The Moore Pasture, Five Acre Moore and Mr White's Peece of Land. Other names listed are Great Field West, Great Field East, Barn Field, Mead Field, Mathams, Tin Shed, Sunset, Kitchen Field, Dicks, Rectory, Obery, Walnut Tree Meadow, Ingrams, Wood Field, Long Field Valleys, Marshes, Church Field, Top Wood Field, Pumpitt, Coaching, Han Lane, Mill Field, Bottom Low Field and Frank's Field.

Footpaths

Footpaths had names mostly associated with the names of the nearby brooks, streams or fields. One such name is Roley Croak (origin and spelling unconfirmed) which was the stream running through the meadows close by Twyford Mill in Pig Lane and presumably joining the river further downstream. The footpath that starts in Thorley Street alongside Post Office Cottages goes over the railway line and leads down to the river and across a bridge to Twyford on the other side. Both the footpath and the bridge take the name Roley Croak. Other names come from Saxon words, such as Dall, which is an Upland footpath alongside New Cottages, and Bault (or Baulk), which is a ridge route, such as the one

Mrs Thomas Streeter with her five sons, 1988. Left to right: George, Andy, Patrick, Nesta, John and David. The occasion was Andy's 50th birthday.

Above: *Rare wrought-iron pinch gate on Roley Croak footpath.*

Left: *Old yew tree in Thorley churchyard.*

Below: *Turkey oak at Twyford Lodge, 1986.*

there used to be from Stone Hall to St James' Church. An interesting gate, at the start of the Roley Croak footpath, was nearly lost in the 1990s when workers on the mains drainage system for Thorley Street threw it away as old iron. It is an old wrought-iron pinch gate curved to fit the shape of sheep.

Many parishioners recall their appreciation of the Thorley countryside, as can be seen from just a few of their comments offered in these excerpts. Sid Oxborrow begins:

When I think of 'Old Thorley' I remember the small farms, little fields, many of them with ponds for watering, the cart-horses and cattle, the tall hedgerows and the numerous elm trees. I remember the fields of wheat, barley and oats competing with wild flowers like poppies, cornflowers and thistles – unlike the much larger fields of today with their clinically clean crops.

Woods

Rose Monk and Bryan South remember:

Thorley Wood was outstanding for its beauty, and was a favourite walk leading from Thorley Wash Farm to the church. It was a picture with its graceful trees, and at Easter time the ground was carpeted with primroses. People outside the village would at that time come specially to wander through the wood. Schoolchildren used to play hide and seek (war) games in Thorley Wood and pick bluebells and cowslips. In Brookfield Wood, which we used to call Bluebell Wood and where bluebells grew profusely, the ground was covered a lovely colour blue. But little is left now as we remember it.

Albie Camp and Rose Monk recall:

At one time the three main woods in Thorley were in the charge of gamekeeper Frank Kinge, assisted by Ernie Hammond. Frank was responsible for keeping the rides clear of overgrown bushes, and also for the protection of the young pheasant chicks. There were always fears of poaching in those days. If a poacher was caught he would be given a heavy sentence.

Rose continues:

The spinney in that part of Thorley Lane that we knew once as Rectory Hill is very old and famous for its trees, especially for some rare American oaks amongst the English turkey oaks. It is pleasing to know that the spinney is under a preservation order. There is another spinney at the top of Bird Lane, but it now has a new road, Whittington Way, going through it. Lastly, there is the spinney or coppice at Thorley Place, which used to belong to the Streeter family and was well known for its lovely old trees.

Andy Streeter tells us that:

The gardens at Thorley Place were beautifully old fashioned – in the vegetable garden there was a wide border of flowers either side of the paths grown in the Victorian way and a very ancient mulberry tree which is still there today. The other part of the garden consisted of walks, rose gardens and lawns but now is completely covered by Premier Court Nursing Home. Beyond, in the park, were wonderful trees and at the bottom was a clear pond, which we used to swim in. Half the pond still exists alongside the new bypass.

Many villagers talk of Thorley Wood and the horror when it was destroyed by a farmer. This was Tony Kluysse, who had bought Thorley Wash Farm and Thorley Wood in the late 1960s. Perhaps Thorley can forgive farmer Kluysse now, after Freddie Prior, who used to work for Tony Kluysse on the farm, recalls:

I had a conversation with the ailing Tony Kluysse just before his death, when he admitted that taking down Thorley Wood was the one thing he really regretted doing, and he agreed with me when I told him that it was the worst day's work he had ever done.

It could be that the primroses of beautiful Thorley Wood live on, since Charles Watson recalls:

The gypsies used to go into the wood and lift all the primroses. They would come round to houses selling them, a whole root in each of the pots carried in cane baskets made of hazelnut. You'll see many of the gardens in Thorley Hill and Havers Lane still full of primroses every year.

On the Friends of St James' website it is recorded that:

In the churchyard to the south-west of the tower there is an ancient Yew Tree which has been dated as being at least 1,000 years old. In April 1991, firemen acted to save it from destruction by fire, possibly started by children in its hollow trunk. In 2001 its girth was measured at one metre from ground level and found to be 6.10 metres in circumference. Revd J.M. Procter recorded that its circumference three feet from the ground in 1923 was nearly 17 feet.

Liz Eldred, shepherdess, recalls that at Thorley Farm the tall elm trees stretched up into the sky and down the track to Thorley Wood, before they had to be felled owing to the spread of Dutch elm disease.

Barbara White, niece of Beryl Frere, remembers a 'particular holly tree in the gardens of Twyford House', while Peter and Jo Wood used to delight in their majestic turkey oak in the former grounds of Twyford House:

It stood alone in the middle of the lawns looking

magnificent, but sadly it was blown down in the hurricane of October 1987. We are trying to grow another one from it, but this will take a while yet.

Peggy Robinson (née Harris), who sadly died only days after the Rogation Day fête in 2003, remembered:

In Old Cottages, there used to be a tree of Cockrell apples, very small and very sweet, and in Butler's Hall cottages, there was a Warwick Pippin apple tree. Native bullaces, sloes and blackberries used to be all around in the fields and hedges.

Frank Warboys recalls that:

The Warwick Pippins and Victoria plums and green-gages we used to scrump as boys in the orchards opposite Sunset Cottages were delicious.

Ponds

Thorley Hall pond and Moor Hall pond are the most attractive in Thorley at the time of writing. Other ponds remembered, such as the ones that used to be at Meadow Cottage, Thorley Houses and in the Valleys field opposite the school, have long been filled in by farmers or new owners, and are only seen on old maps or in older paintings. The Streeters' pond at Thorley Place still exists but the new bypass goes through it.

Liz Eldred recalls childhood interests around the ponds of Thorley:

As children we used to go fishing in the local ponds, mostly in the pond by the church but also in the 'twin ponds' behind the church and the fish-pond down in Streeters' meadows, known as the park. The fish-pond use to be a swimming hole for the Streeter family, and my mother said there used to be a diving-board there as it was very deep. There is a spring nearby that ensures that it never dries up.

Our equipment for net fishing consisted of one of Mum's old stockings, fitted with wire onto a bamboo cane or suitable stick. We caught a wide variety of aquatic life, including great-crested newts. All were returned to the pond except for a few tadpoles. We progressed to fishing with rod and line, and spent hours fishing out roach and rudd from the fish-pond, which were also returned. The pond at Moor Hall yielded crucian carp, but these were more difficult to catch.

The fish-pond at Thorley Place.

Wildlife

Villagers will tell of birds and creatures often no longer seen today as farmland diminishes, but there are still rabbits, pigeons, foxes, muntjac and other deer – and badgers, as was much in evidence during the disturbances experienced at the time of field excavation and spinney demolishment for the new bypass.

Edward Miller:

Thorley Lane, just beyond Rumbles Farm, as it runs towards the Green Man pub, was bordered by high hedgerows, partly of hazelnut. This area was a haven for yellowhammers and to walk along there on a summer's morning was a joy.

Roy Wilson:

As a youth I became keen on ornithology. When out woodpigeon shooting along the hedgerows and in the spinneys at Thorley Hall Farm, I still enjoy observing the various bird species including songbirds. Unfortunately, I have noticed a decline in certain species over the last 40 years – particularly peewits, skylarks, English or grey partridges, and also house martins, swallows and swifts.

Weather

Rose Monk remembers the very cold year of 1947 and other years when particularly bad weather conditions occurred in Thorley:

One year in the early 1920s the snow-drifts were so high, even on the main A11, that the road was impassable between Thorley Hill and Bishop's Stortford. No traffic could get through, and a passageway was dug by local people. Managing to walk was very heavy going, and only possible by wearing Wellington boots.

Again in 1947 there was a very heavy snowfall, and high drifts blocked the lanes here in Thorley. At a neighbouring village, Bury Green, the Bishop's Stortford fire brigade was blocked in a snowdrift. A local village fireman, Albert Camp, spoke of three days trying to get through. Strangely, the roads were all blocked up, yet the fields were almost free of snow.

Bryan South:

In the awful winter of 1947, Ian Reedman and I sledged on the pond in the Valley opposite Thorley School, and had a lucky escape when the ice started to crack. The sledge was formed from the rockers of a rocking horse!

Jim Morton is bemused to recall that:

Newcomers living in St Michael's Mead, which was built on the fields my father used to plough, have often said to me: 'You don't get much bad weather round here then!' But I remember the early to mid 1950s, when Thorley Lane and the Great Hadham Road were blocked off with three to four feet of snow, taking a bulldozer a week to get through.

Bob Crisp, husband of Maisie (née Akers), also recalls the winter of 1963:

During this winter of heavy snow that blocked and cut off transport to Thorley Lane, Maisie's mother, Sarah, was taken ill and needed urgent hospital treatment. Mr Sortwell of Rumballs Farm, down the road from Fairview (home of Maisie's parents) was contacted and he turned out with a tractor, fixed a door to the tractor as a stretcher, used a mattress to make Maisie's mother comfortable, and transported her to London Road where the ambulance picked her up.

Penny Beer and Sylvia McDonald recall the snow-drifts of 1976:

Butler's Hall Lane used to lie well below field level and access was cut off from the hamlet for about a week. Penny had to ski across the fields to fetch milk and supplies for the hamlet. Sylvia recalled that young son James spent several days trying to dig out the lane, which began to look more and more like the Cresta run, with snow six feet high on each side that did not totally disappear for some weeks. The trees in the hedgerow gave the only indication of where the lane might be.

Rose recalls the time when Thorley was subjected to serious flooding:

There was one year in the 1940s when the River Stort burst its banks and flooded Pig Lane near Twyford Mill. I was working for Doris and Bert Bird down at Twyford Farm, and when I tried to get to work, Bert was on the other side of the flooded lane shouting for me to stop, because the water was too deep to cross. Likewise the road at Thorley Wash was flooded and also the main rail line.

There was also severe flooding in September 1968 in the London Road and Twyford areas, and this was when Revd Sydney Robinson came to the rescue of his parishioners by rowing a boat in the flooded lanes and offering assistance.

Above: *Moor Hall pond in winter, 1963.*

Right: *Floods in Pig Lane, 1940s.*

Tributes

At the turn of the century and during 2003 we have sadly lost a number of parishioners and others, who would have had stories to tell. For some we have photos. Saddest of all perhaps is that just as the new millennium was dawning, two tragic road accidents on the London Road took from the village both Laura Bateman, a young singer at only 19, and Bert Mingay, Thorley's 'paper-boy', well past his three score years and ten. Both were well known in the village; both were optimistic and cheery, both lived for what they loved doing; and both were unexpectedly taken. Also sadly missed by many is Tom Camp, well known and well liked all his life.

Tribute to Laura from parents Ian and Pat:

Laura was four years old when we moved to Rectory Close in September 1984 and it soon became clear that her great love was for singing which she had shown a flair for at nine months, when she hummed Frere Jacques in time with the local ice-cream van!

Hope Hill became Laura's surrogate granny and it was through Hope that Laura became one of the youngest members of St James' choir a few years later. She loved to sing solos and as her confidence and ability increased she was ecstatic when Revd Clive Slaughter presented her with the blue ribbon she had worked so hard for.

Laura suffered from numerous illnesses and had to have surgery on her eyes twice, but nothing stood in the way of her singing. Her determination and courage were tested repeatedly. Gradually her health improved and in September 1997 she went to Harlow College to take the GCSEs she had had to give up earlier. We must have been the proudest parents in Harlow Playhouse when she won an award for outstanding achievement a year later.

Laura wearing her blue ribbon.

A few days before Christmas 1999, Laura was asked to sing at a concert to celebrate 50 years of Amnesty International – a cause she felt strongly about. She sang the 'Pie Jesu' by Faure and we have never heard her sing so beautifully. On New Year's Eve Laura was knocked down, and two days later died in intensive care. Unlike some parents who lose children, we were all able to be with her.

We visit her grave in St James' churchyard and feel her close to us always.

Tribute to Bert from a newspaper customer:

The remarkable fact about Bert is that in 30 years there was only one week in which he didn't deliver his papers, and even then he sent out an elderly substitute so as not to let anyone down. He would make his rounds in Thorley on his bicycle, until his years forced him to drive his Austin mini – ever so slowly – instead. His accounts were written in pencil – ever so cramped and tiny – on the back of an envelope. He will be especially remembered during the seven or so horrendous years of disruption when St Michael's Mead housing estate and new bypass were being built. He would cheerily, and undeterred, lift his bicycle with its heavily mudded wheels over any obstruction impeding his access, because no one was going to make him let his Uplands customers down.

Tribute to Tom Camp from fellow school pupil Rose Monk:

I knew Tom throughout my school life as a quiet unassuming boy, who was popular with the teachers; as a strong lad he was very helpful in moving heavy things such as desks! He was good at singing, his voice was strong and he sang in the Children's Concerts held in the school. After he left school, he continued belonging to the Folkdancing Club and the Morris- and sword-dancing teams.

Miss Beryl Frere was our dancing teacher, and the 'Flowers of Edinburgh' and 'Gathering Peasepods' were among many of the tunes I recall that we danced to. In the winter time we danced in the schoolroom, and during the summer on the lawns at Twyford House. At one time I was a folk-dancing partner of Tom's. Although a large man, he was very light on his feet – not a bit like the blundering elephant, I thought he might be! They were the most memorable days, and Tom especially will always be well remembered.

Dorothy Wolfson with Vera and Tom Camp, 1960s.

Tribute to Percy from neighbour Anne Ashpole:

We first met up with Percy in 1964, who worked for Willi Patten and lived in one of Thorley Wash Cottages. Many times he regaled us with stories of how many mice he had caught, and he regularly 'weeded' his kitchen floor (this being brick on earth).

He has told many stories too about his experiences with Thorley Home Guard and how on one occasion during a night exercise they managed to crawl into the church pond! On another occasion, this group of 'gallant defenders' took the fire hose from the river across the railway line, but unfortunately they put the hose over the line rather than under it, with the inevitable result!

Percy Abra at the Coach and Horses on his 90th birthday.

He walked several times a week into Stortford to collect his shopping and pension, and was a familiar sight striding down the road lifting his stick to anyone who acknowledged him.

Successive landlords at the Coach and Horses looked after Percy as he grew older, and whilst Tim and Sharon Metcalfe were there he had his own seat in the pub by the fire in the front bar, known as 'Percy's patch'. He would frequently visit us at 8 Park View, and was also a regular visitor to Derek and Jane Cayford at Laburnum Cottage.

Life became increasingly difficult for Percy living in later years in his primitive caravan, and he died in hospital. He is buried in St James' churchyard overlooking Thorley farmland.

Tribute to Tom Hammond from wife Janet:

Henry Thomas (Tom) Hammond grew up at 4 New Cottages, the middle son of Len Hammond, horse keeper at Butler's Hall Farm, and wife Annie (Daisy). He had two brothers, Walter (Pimp) and Arthur (Ben) and two sisters Ellen (Nell) and Dorothy (Doll). After leaving Thorley village school, he was apprenticed to Hughes of Bishop's Stortford as carpenter and joiner. In 1939 he joined the Household Cavalry and served in the Royal Horse Guards Armoured Division, taking part in the D-Day operations. His battalion was one of the first to enter Brussels. He was wounded twice on active service. He remained in the Household Cavalry, riding in The Queen's wedding procession on his horse Dante, and he danced with Princess Margaret! He left the Army in 1953.

Tom Hammond, 1940s.

Others remembered and missed: Denis Prior, John Hammond, Jack Constable and Peggy Robinson, all died in 2003; Tom Hammond, Henry Jennings, Cissie Day, Kit Chappell, Paul Frain and Ron Brown, all died at the end of 2002; Jack and Gwen Harris, Jack Bird and Desmond Miller, all died in 2000/2001; Mick Hill, Mrs Lawford, Ernie Vale and Fred Owers, all died in 1995/1996; Ron Owers, Dolly Wick, Frank Crabb, Violet Jane Crabb, Vera Camp, Denis Monk, and Walter Hammond, all died in 1984–1992.

Left: *Jim and Emily (Cissie) Day, 1920s.*

Right: *Mick Hill, Thorley Hall Farm manager, 1995.*

Fred Owers, Piggott's Farm, c.1960.

Dolly Wick, Jack Bird, Ron Owers and Walter (Pimp) Hammond at Thorley Hall Farm, 1970s.

May They Rest In Peace

Chapter 2

School in Thorley

The Village School

We start our walk at the Village School. As Canon Procter recorded in his book, written in the early 1930s:

The school opened on 29 November 1875. It was built as a Board School for 100 children, at a cost of £1,500, with a residence for a schoolmaster, one Charles Buckham at that time. It seems unlikely that as many as 100 children would have attended at any one time.

Rose Monk recalls that:

There were once between 50–70 children attending the school, but over the years the numbers dwindled. After the Second World War there were only nine children left, and the school closed in 1947/8. The building remains unaltered and has become the HQ of the Thorley Scouts and Girl Guides group.

My earliest recollection, aged five, was of the head teacher Mr Morgan, a strict man who kept Sealyham dogs, in the girls' back yard, fenced in of course! Much yapping and barking went on.

Joyce Clark, who must be the oldest Village School pupil in Thorley, recaptures a school day in 1930:

It is 8.20a.m. I am now ready for school. My small case contains sandwiches for my dinner and an apple or an orange, and a small cake or biscuits for my lunch. I am waiting for the children who live further away.

At 8.30a.m. along they come. We walk the mile long lane chatting as we go, and we wait in the playground with the Uplands children until the school bell rings at 9a.m.

We then enter the school porch, boys and girls separately. The infant teacher (Mrs Smith) commences to play a march on the piano and we all march to our places. A hymn is then sung, prayers

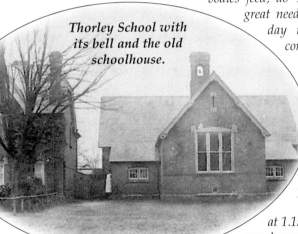

Thorley School with its bell and the old schoolhouse.

are said, and the register is called by the head teacher (Miss Hummerstone).

The first lesson of the day is always scripture. Arithmetic follows.

At 9.45a.m. it is time for our lunch break and at 10a.m. we are back at our desks. Then follow further lessons until midday, such as composition, dictation, reading and learning poetry.

At 12 midday it is dinner time and we commence by saying grace: 'Daily O Lord our prayers be said, As Thou hast taught for daily bread, But not alone our bodies feed, do Thou supply our souls' great need, Oh bread of life from day to day, be Thou our comfort, food and stay.'

At 12.30p.m. it is out to play in the playground if the weather is fine. During the summer we played in the Mr W. Tinney's field opposite the school. The boys loved playing cricket there.

The school bell rings at 1.15p.m. for us to go back to our classrooms. Then grace is sung: 'We thank Thee Lord for this our food, For life and health and every good. May manna to our souls be given, the bread of life sent down from Heaven.'

Then it is lessons again, history, geography. Each Tuesday and Thursday afternoon, the boys were taught drawing and painting, the girls needlework and knitting.

At 2.45p.m. another break for 15 minutes. One afternoon is given to games in the field with the head mistress. Then back to lessons until 3.30p.m. when school ended for the day.

In summer time after school we would walk through the park to Twyford House to learn to swim in the Mill Pool under the wonderful care of Miss Beryl Frere and this was great fun.

Mike Teitz, a wartime evacuee, also recalls days at school:

Thorley School stood in a small playground, next to

This picture: *The interior of Thorley School.*
Right: *Victorian postbox in the school yard wall.*

the schoolteacher's house. It had a 'little room' for the infants and a 'big room' for the older children. The big room was lit at each end by lancet windows, which, with the high ceiling, gave it a slightly ecclesiastic air.

Mrs Smith was a rather formidable lady – at least to a six-year-old boy. Every day, she bicycled a great distance from the other side of Bishop's Stortford on a creaky, upright machine. On arrival she would remove her high button gaiters, with a button hook that made a loud popping noise.

We learned to write by copying from the blackboard on to slates using thin slate pencils that made squeaky noises. Another never-to-be-forgotten part of our day was fraying. We were each handed a bundle of cloth scraps and shown how to pick them apart to create a pile of fragments of thread, which was then stuffed hard into cylindrical white cloth tubes perhaps three inches in diameter, then sewn up. We were told that these would be used to support the limbs of wounded soldiers in hospital.

In due course, we moved up to the big room with Miss Moorhouse. This was a very different place – almost a different century. Miss Moorhouse believed in learning 'by doing', as well as a thorough grounding in reading, writing and mathematics. And she did it all by herself in one room with children ranging in age from seven to fourteen years old.

With Miss Moorhouse we were never bored. Somehow, she managed to teach us all the usual things, while also ensuring that something interesting was always happening or about to happen. To teach reckoning and money, we constructed a shop, using empty packages and tins from home, creating signs, labels and prices, and buying and selling with money that we designed and made. We sang the old songs, accompanied by Mrs Smith on the piano. We also danced country dances; I was in awe of the older boys' sword dance with its circling and clashing of wooden

swords. At various times, we acted out historical episodes, creating costumes at home. One year I was David in the story of David and Goliath.

Art was another important part of our school experience. I don't know how she found the materials in wartime, but Miss Moorhouse always had us drawing, painting and modelling. I think my love of art comes from this time. Miss Moorhouse's philosophy included creating a school garden, where we dug and planted, raised chickens, and tended a goat. Miss Moorhouse would take us to the pond in the neighbouring meadow to examine newts and collect tadpoles, where we would slosh about and collect frog-spawn, hoping for it to turn into frogs.

We also learned to swim, taught by Miss Beryl Frere, who lived with her sister in the grandest house in the village, Twyford House. Beginners were placed in a canvas loop attached to a rope. Miss Frere would walk back and forth on a narrow bridge across the stream supporting the flailing would-be swimmer, calling out encouragement and instructions for the breast-stroke. Those who succeeded then moved to the millpond.

Thorley School gave me a wonderful education up to age ten.

Other pupils have similar memories to share. Frank Warboys recalls:

Mrs Smith was a character. In the winter she would stand in front of the coal fire in the little classroom and haul up her skirt at the back to warm her legs! She gave little pieces of fudge as rewards to those who did well in class. She often wielded a twiggy stick with which she regularly hit wrongdoers on hands and legs. She rode a big upright ladies' bicycle and wore long buttoned gaiters to protect her legs. She took quite a long time each morning to undo these buttons with a button hook. Miss Hummerstone, as a favour to my mother (who was remembered as a former teacher at the school), coached me for the scholarship examinations.

School milk came in one-third pint glass bottles with real straws. In the winter the crate of bottles was warmed in front of the big coke fire before distribution at morning playtime. We always seemed to be singing, sometimes hymns, sometimes folk songs; sometimes banging old biscuit tins for drums and beating triangles whilst one of the teachers played the piano. We also performed Morris dancing and country dancing. Besides the three Rs, we also had games, nature walks, plaiting and fraying, and art. I learnt there how to make pictures. That developed into a lifelong devotion to painting. In our playtime we skipped with ropes, ran wooded hoops, whipped tops, played rounders and in season played conkers with chestnuts gathered from the trees just outside the school gate.

Peter Warboys:

I remember we were encouraged to play at 'soldiers', and Miss Hummerstone would take the salute from the top of the fire-escape steps, erected to facilitate exit from the infant classroom through the window in the event of an air raid.

I have some classroom memories of sitting at a desk opposite the large fireplace and looking at a picture on the wall with an African thunderstorm scene which made a great impression on me, as I subsequently went to work in Kenya as a young man.

George Camp:

Mrs Warboys used to take a group of children into the meadow behind White Cottage to do some sketching. One day, they all sat down to sketch the cottage and Mrs Warboys sat in a cow-pat. She couldn't leave the children so she made a list of clothes she wanted and sent one of the older boys to fetch them from her mother. When he got back she had the problem of changing, so she said 'All you boys, look the other way!'

Albie Camp:

Thorley School had an open fire, which the older boys lit before starting school. It was used also to heat the black kettle ready for a hot drink during the day and the cups were lined up all ready. The toilets were outside at the rear of the school, and in winter sometimes the pipes were frozen up.

Sid Oxborrow:

I shall always remember my school days with particular affection, sitting in class silently at our lessons, with the big clock ticking away on the wall, with Miss

Hummerstone and later Miss Moorhouse sitting at her desk. In March I can recall the rooks noisily building their nests in the trees over the lane in the Old Rectory gardens.

At Christmas time we children would help decorate the school. A concert was held, a nativity play of course, and an excerpt [used] from a children's classic book, such as Treasure Island, when I recall playing the part of Blind Pew. At the end, parents and children sang carols, with Mrs Smith accompanying us on the piano, which was, as often as not, out of tune.

Village Schoolteachers

The head teachers, as already recalled, were first Mr Morgan followed by Mrs Smythe in the 1920s, Miss Hummerstone in the 1930s, and Miss Moorhouse in the 1940s. The infant teachers were Gladys Eagling in the 1920s, and Mrs David Smith from the 1930s until the school closed. There was also a Mrs Sutcliffe teaching in the 1940s. Two have a special mention here: Gladys Warboys (née Eagling) as Thorley's 'very own', and Miss Moorhouse as a remarkable and innovative teacher who would become an influential force in primary education.

Frank Warboys, eldest of Gladys' five children, recalls the family's long association with Thorley:

My mother's span of knowledge of the village goes back to at least 1905 when she was three and came to

**Gladys May Eagling,
aged 21, in Thorley, 1923.**

*Gladys Warboys on her 100th birthday,
with her four sons Frank, Cecil,
Peter, Michael and daughter
Barbara Orsbourne.*

*Left: Gladys and Frank Warboys on their
wedding day at Thorley Church, 1928.*

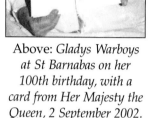

Above: *Gladys Warboys
at St Barnabas on her
100th birthday, with a
card from Her Majesty the
Queen, 2 September 2002.*

visit her grandparents George and Mary Anne Watson, who lived in the village from about 1895 until their deaths in 1924 and 1927. Aged 16 years, at the end of the First World War, she became a 'pupil teacher' and obtained teaching qualifications. She was appointed teacher at Thorley School in 1920, and as Gladys May Eagling she lodged with her grandparents, close to the school, at No. 1 Sunset Cottages until 1928, when she married local boy Frank Bertie Warboys from Twyfordbury Farm and moved next door to No. 2 Sunset Cottages.

Later they moved to No. 6 Rectory Close, nearer to both school and church, where she remained after her husband died in 1975. As her children grew up, my mother returned to occasional supply teaching to supplement the family income, and from 1953 to 1967 she taught full time at Great Havers Primary School, where she continued part time after retiring age for five more years until she was 70 years old. My father, Frank, was a keen gardener, a bell-ringer, chorister, and one of the Thorley Cricket Club's slow bowlers for many years.

Apart from her family Gladys has always had three major interests: Thorley Church, where she has been a regular worshipper for 82 years, starting when as a child she accompanied her grandfather who was a churchwarden; the village of Thorley and its people and history, about which she wrote a very readable booklet in 1985; and botany. Her children were expected from an early age to learn the names of all the plants that could be found in the fields, woods and hedgerows of the Thorley countryside.

Her family of five children, fifteen grandchildren and, to the time of writing, fourteen great-grandchildren are loyally devoted to her. She moved, reluctantly, a year ago into Premier Court Nursing Home, which was built about five years ago in the grounds of Thorley Place near her old home Sunset Cottages. Two of the highlights during early 2002, to take her mind off her

unwelcome new style of life, have been her 100th birthday celebration and the central part she is playing in the recall of memories for this book.

Gladys has an aura about her that has affected many people. Stanley Brownridge, headmaster of Great Havers Primary School, reveals that 'we have all learned a great deal from Gladys, who was the best teacher I have ever known.' Terry Kitchener, a pupil of Gladys at Great Havers School and now a local plumber, is pleased to recall: 'I remember her cheerfulness and friendliness all the time I have known her, and it has always been such a pleasure to be able to help her out.'

Daphne Ruddock, a chorister at the church, recounts a story typical of Gladys:

We were talking of 21st birthdays, and Gladys told me about hers. When her parents asked her what she would like to mark the occasion, she asked if she could have the money to take all her schoolchildren on a train (she knew that not one of them had ever travelled on a train). So it was arranged to take the children to a station somewhere along the branch line, where they found a good field in which to play games and eat her birthday cake. The joy of those children she treasures still.

Robin Lumsden and Sheila Hewitt recall moving into Rectory Close:

We both clearly remember the day we met Gladys. We were on the scaffolding in front of our house and we saw Gladys weeding in her garden and topple over. We rushed over to pull her to her feet, amidst quite a lot of giggling, and it seemed a very fitting way of meeting her. She has a very strong sense of fun and makes everyone feel welcome.

The other families in the Close helped us move in, inviting us to meals and cutting hedges, and Mike

Pupils and teachers in Thorley School yard, 1911. No names have been confirmed.

Hill, the farm manager, and his wife Hope, suggested that we could burn our hedgerow debris on the field, and that it would make a good bonfire on 5th November. A party was duly organised and neighbours brought fireworks, wine and huge trays of baked potatoes. Frank and Rose Monk brought Gladys round and she became the central figure of the party.

It was a cold night, and she sat outside with the rest of us whilst eating, drinking and watching the fireworks with much laughter and oohing and aahing. The evening was finished off in Thorley style with hymn singing. We all had a lovely time and she often mentions it. We both congratulate her heartily on her 100th birthday, and wish her well.

The following is an extract from a booklet written by Miss Edith Moorhouse:

My life at Thorley was a rich experience – the building was old but the rural environment was there to be exploited and this was added to by the keeping of small stock, rabbits, chickens and two goats, one of which was kidded. A tremendous amount of work arose from the small animal project; practical work in the making of frames, hutches and pens, academic work in reading about the health and needs of the animals, in mathematics weighing the amount of food necessary and measuring their growth in size and weight, in marketing and in recording in a range of ways, graphs, sketches and writing, life and death, but perhaps most important the sense of responsibility for creatures dependent in their case at certain times of the day, and every day, not just five days a week. It needed organisation if there was to be no neglect.

The farmers allowed the groups of boys and girls to work at many mathematical problems to do with volumes and capacity on the farms. We were informed if anything of interest was to take place, for example, when the first bulldozer arrived in the village to rip up a hedge between two small fields. An HMI had arrived at the School that day to find a note on the door to say where we were and he was delighted to find children learning in a real situation. Fields, hedgerows, the people, their work, homes, means of transport, the Church were to be explored and were a source of interest and learning. The wide age span, the ability, the speed of working, maturity varied so much that we found it necessary for some children to complete a piece of work, some others to start another activity, so that one would find children working at different aspects of some study and in a variety of places, in classrooms, cloakroom, playground, orchard, garden and in lanes and fields.*

Village School Pupils

Peter Warboys, who attended the school in the 1930s, lists the pupils he was at school with:

The most vivid memories are of my fellow pupils. These were mainly farm-workers' sons and daughters. Denis and Freddie Prior, Donald Powell, and Yvonne and Yvette Parrish from Moor Hall Cottages; Jean and Joan Hammond (twins) and their cousin Benny from Butler's Hall; Teddie Kent and Fred and Ron Owers from Castle Farm and Thorley Houses; the Browns from Thorley Street; Ron, Desmond and June whose father worked for the Patten brothers; Flossie and Cissie Hutchin from Hither Farm cottages; and Georgina and Margaret Brewster from Latchmore Bank cottages, whose fathers worked for Uncle Bert and brother Arthur.

Above: *Gladys Warboys and pupils in Thorley School yard, 1920.* The photograph includes: *Gladys* (standing far left), *Jim Day* (third row, ninth from left), *Beattie Stoakes and Emily (Cissie) Day* (sitting second row, third and fourth from left) *and Leslie Threadgold* (front row, third from left).

Right: *Gladys Warboys and pupils in Thorley School yard, 1923.* Left to right, back row: ?, *George Camp*, ?, ?, ?, ?, ?; middle row: *Jim Day*, ?, *Rose Stoakes*, *Gladys Warboys*, *Joyce Clark*, ?, *Jack Bird*; front row: ?, *Geoff Brewster*, *Sid Hammond*, ?.

Pupils in Thorley School yard, 1927. Left to right, back row: *Ron Brewster, Jack Harris, George Brewster, Sid Hammond, Frank Ganley, Joe Day;* third row: *Dolly Hammond, Joyce Clark, George Camp, Tom Camp, Dolly Camp, Violet Harris, Ada Hammond, Hector Prior, Rose Stoakes, May Saville, Alice Day, Cissy Camp;* second row: *Albert Camp, Gordon Barker, Harry Ganley, Ron Oxborrow, Audrey Harris, Hilda Akers, Clara Camp, Joyce Harris, Peggy Wright, Peggy Harris, Geoff Brewster, Phil Akers, Tom Hammond;* front row; *Jack Bird, George Clark.*

Pupils in Thorley School yard, 1932. Left to right, back row: *Sid Hammond, Joe Day, Ron Brewster, George Camp, Sonny Prior, Jack Harris, Tom Hammond, George Clark;* third row: *Peggy Wright, Peggy Harris, Dolly Hammond, Ada Hammond, Joyce Clark, Alice Day, Cissie Camp, Hilda Akers;* second row: *John Reed, ?, Audrey Harris, Maisie Akers, Clara Camp, Joyce*

Harris, Joan Brewster, Lilian Akers, Albert Camp, Ben Hammond; front row: *Geoff Brewster, Jack Bird, Gordon Barker, Bert Hammond, Phil Akers, Harry Ganley, Ron Oxborrow.*

Pupils on a school trip, 1946. 1. John Hammond, 2. Francis Herbert, 3. Ron Owers, 4. Mrs Gilson, 5. Colin Sampford, 6. ?, 7. Mrs Warboys (?), 8. George Black (?), 9. ?, 10. ?, 11. ?, 12. Cissie Hutchin (?), 13. Brian Sampford, 14. Mick Marns, 15. ?, 16. Barbara Warboys, 17. Miss Sutcliffe, 18. Sonnet Chappell, 19. ?, 20. ?, 21. Cliff Williams, 22. Michael Warboys, 23. ?, 24. ?, 25. Johnny Williams.

From outside farming were the Monks, Mary, Denis and John from Stone Hall. From Thorley Street were George and Ina Bright and Sid Oxborrow, whose fathers were railwaymen. There was also a gypsy girl Amy, who came for a short time and was mildly teased by the children because of her long skirts. We were enlivened by the arrival of evacuees early in the war, of whom George Black and his well developed elder sister Grace made a distinct impression. We went for games in the horses' meadow opposite the school, and used to sit by the pond discussing the facts of life, etc.

Pupils John, Mary and Denis Monk, 1940s.

This picture: *George and Ina Bright (now Kenward) in the orchard behind the school, 1939.*

Below left: *Irene Prior (née Chappell), winner and wearer of prize watch, c.1947.*

Below: *Gladys Warboys with former pupils of the Village School on her 100th birthday in St Barnabas, 2 September 2002. Left to right: Lilian Akers (now Bentley), Flossie Hutchin (now Monk), Jean Hammond (now Sage), Sid Oxborrow, Teddie Kent, Colin Sampford, Joan Hammond (now Brace), George Clark, Rose Stoakes (now Monk), Maisie Akers (now Crisp), Gladys Warboys (seated).*

Below: *Former pupils of the Village School outside St Barnabas, January 2003.* Left to right, back row: *Joan Hammond (now Brace), Teddie Kent, Ron Oxborrow, Des Brown, John Monk, Colin Sampford, Alan Threadgold, Sid Oxborrow, Len Wood, Philip Wood, David Teitz;* front row: *Coral Chappell (now Gray), Rose Stoakes (now Monk), Lilian Akers (now Bentley), Maisie Akers (now Crisp), Flossie Hutchin (now Monk), Jean Hammond (now Sage), Frank Warboys, Albie Camp.*

Chapter 3

Work and Worship

This picture: *Nathan Bird, ploughing with a horse.*

Inset, top: *Henry Clark, father of George, reaping in Thorley uplands.*

Inset, bottom: *John Kitchener, carting sacks of potatoes, Thorley Hall Farm, c.1946.*

Before walking up the lane to the church (Chapters 3, 4 and 5), we will recall memories of village life and events that had impact for all; stories abound about farming, cricket, war, amateur dramatics and families. There are too many for this book, so with a plea for readers' forbearance, we have included as many villagers' photos and memories as we can. The remainder will appear in our 'Chronicle Supplements'.

Farming

Rose Monk remembers farming at the start of the twentieth century:

In the early 1900s, when farming meant very hard work, many farm labourers were employed. Their wages were

low, but the advantages they did have were a row of potatoes grown for their own use in fields, and perhaps any rabbits they caught. Most farmers kept animals: cart-horses to pull the heavy carts, cows for milking, bullocks and pigs for market, and sheep. In those days ploughing was done by horse and plough; imagine the poor man trudging up and down the fields, wet or fine!

When the harvest season came round, in August/ September, the corn was cut by scythe or a binder, not by combine harvesters as in these days! The sheaves were stacked up in stooks, which were then carted away ready for the threshing machines. In due course the grain was carted off to the flour mills.

After the fields were cleared of the sheaves, the villagers, especially if they had chickens, went gleaning for corn. The farmer left one sheaf standing alone in the field while the corn was being cut, and when this was removed, the villagers were allowed to go on the fields to glean.

When less straw was needed for the horses, because tractors were taking over, the straw would be burned on the fields. This got rid of the insects and bugs living on decaying straw, and so these were not ploughed into the soil. Burning was banned in the 1970s because of pollution, and so now more chemicals need to be used.

September/October was the season for potato-picking. Local folk and travellers from outside the village were hired by the farmers for gathering in the potatoes. Working in pairs, the pickers were given buckets that they filled and dropped into wooden boxes. If the tractor driver was quick coming to a furrow, one had to be jolly swift picking up the potatoes! If the farmer allowed, we villagers could then go gleaning the potatoes that were left over on the field.

In those days the farmers, mostly in the autumn, held competition ploughing matches, with farm labourers ploughing for the best furrows. Ted Threadgold was said to plough the straightest and was a regular winner.

In more recent times the farmers began to use tractors. The first that the Tinneys had were Massey-Harris tractors, driven by Ted Threadgold, Ron Barker and Horace Barnard. The machines were not hooded, so the poor drivers in wet weather would have sacking round their shoulders to try to keep dry.

During the war years, 1939–45, farmers had to grow more wheat as part of the war effort, and common land went under the plough, including Thorley Common. The slogan at the time was 'Dig for Victory'.

Wendy Linney recalls:

When I was at Thorley Hall Farm, I was part of a group of ladies who used to help every year to harvest the potatoes. For the first few days you were as stiff as boards, but by the end of the harvest you had arms like weight lifters, and eighteen inch waists, from filling your baskets and tipping them into the boxes.

Michael Teitz, billeted in the hamlet of Butler's Hall, recalls his exciting life as a boy on the farm:

To a seven-year-old boy, a mixed farm offered endless excitement. When work was done and no one was around, we climbed the straw bale stacks in the Dutch barn, and jumped into straw piles. We helped with mixing pig swill and feeding it to the pigs, and we brushed the great cart-horses. Then there was the thrill of seeing the huge steam traction engine, pulling a threshing-machine, elevator, and bailer up the narrow lane and into the stack yard in late autumn. And when threshing began, the noise, spurting steam, whirling belts, and flying dust were irresistible. In the fields, it was exciting to ride on the mudguard of the tractor during ploughing. Len Hammond, who sadly

died of a mysterious ailment during those years, was a kindly man, who would let us ride with him.

Potato picking was arduous. The spinner, a strange piece of equipment with a large circular frame to which prongs were attached, would be towed down the rows by a tractor. It threw out the potatoes and assorted clods, rocks, and anything else in the soil. Each of us would have an assigned row or section, along which we would move, dragging our sack and filling it with potatoes. When the sack was full, it would be moved to a cart, where a record would be made. At the end of the day, we would be paid. By picking time, the potato plants would be mostly dried out and suitable for burning, so there was always a fire going. We would bury large potatoes in the hot ashes and wait for them to cook.

Even better was harvest time. Wheat was cut by a tractor-drawn binder, which produced sheaves that were thrown onto the ground as it circled the field, gradually reducing the standing grain. Groups of men would then pick up the sheaves and lean six or so of them against each other to make shocks or stooks. Stooking was really hard work, though nothing compared to knocking sugar beet. The shocks would be left to dry in the fields, creating an attractive place for boys to play war as well as small shelters in which we could hide and talk.

After a week or so, the corn would be collected, usually by horse and cart. The carts themselves were two wheeled and were each pulled by a single shire-horse. The cart would move down the rows of shocks, stopping at each one. On either side, a man on the ground would pitch the sheaves into the cart, where another worker would arrange them into a growing stack. Often a small boy would stand by the cart-horse's head, holding the rein near the bit, and leading the horse on when told to move.

Later a tractor replaced the horse. When all was ready, a rope would be tied over to stabilise the load, and the cart was 'driven away' to the stack or the Dutch barn. There, the sheaves would be pitched up to a skilled stacker who would create a stack that would later be thatched to keep it dry until threshing time.

Colin Sampford, who worked on the Tinney farms, reminds us:

When eventually the huge combine harvesters appeared on the farm, this made an enormous difference because many of the harvesting jobs we did were then rolled into one.

Tony Pigram, brother of Liz the shepherdess, remembers baling:

I started work on the farm at Thorley Hall, and my first job was filling in the well in Moor Hall yard with rubble. In 1967 I took over the baling, which used to be done by Freddie Cracknell, with myself riding on the sledge behind stacking bales. The

Left: *Pitching sheaves (possibly Harry Prior), 1940s.*

Below: *Stooking sheaves was tiring work in 1929!*

Bottom: *Reggie Newman with Henry Clark, twisting bands for thatching and trussing, Butler's Hall Farm, late 1920s.*

William (Pedlar) Hammond on steam plough engine, 1950s.

George Chappell, on a tractor hoe.

Above: *Bert Outlaw, on an early combine harvester, Thorley Hall Farm.*

Above: *Colin Sampford on a combine on Thorley Hall Farm, 1960s.*

Left: *Fred Owers baling at Thorley Hall Farm, 1977.*

sledge consisted of two long sheets of flat metal attached to a frame with a gap in between. These ran flat on the ground and as the bales were made they were stacked on the sledge. When the heap was big enough, an iron stake was usually thrust into the ground between the metal sheets and as the sledge moved forward the bales slid off. I did all the baling at Thorley Hall for 14 years, with John Hammond or my Mum, Doll, on the sledge.

Tom Camp talked about ploughing and sowing shortly before he died:

In the farming year there wasn't really much of a quiet time at all, because of all the ploughing that had to be done; I mean it wasn't done as quick as it is now, because it was all done by horses you see. They reckon a man could plough about half an acre a day.

Then of course there was all the other work to get on with as well. Where you've got livestock and that, you are always getting the straw in, and then there's all the manure to get out; that was all carted on the land and put in heaps, and then one or two of us had to come behind and spread it.

The crops were all hand hoed, before tractor hoes came in. I suppose there was anything between 14 and 15 people working on a farm like this, and eight horses.

The horse keeper was with the horses all the time. He had to get there early to feed them and groom them and keep them in good health. He used to work them in the fields as well, and I mean in those days, you didn't ride, you had to walk behind them and steer them to keep them straight across the field. And if you can imagine, when you've got a really wet season, it was really heavy going, because you've got all the mud building up on your boots!

We used to have competitions amongst ourselves to keep the straightest line. Ploughing was hard to keep straight; the ground had to be laid level and the furrows cut out cleanly; there was a lot more to it than people think.

The sowing was done in the autumn and spring. We used to do rotation. One thing we used to have was beans; you always got a good wheat crop behind beans you know, because it put the nitrogen in the soil. We used to grow a lot of clover and that sort of thing too, which you very rarely see now. There were different kinds of clover, Sandfine, Tripolian Clover and another one they used to call Cowgrass.

Tom's brother, Albert Camp, talks of their father working on the farm in the early 1920s:

My father, Alfred Camp, worked on the farm as horse keeper, starting work at 5.30a.m. He also used to thatch the stacks after they had been built with the sheaves of corn. He won prizes with his two horses for ploughing and how smart they looked! In winter fields needed to be drained and ditches cleaned out to stop flooding.

Grenville Bird, whose grandfather's brother used to work on the Tinneys' farms, writes about steam ploughing:

A regular sight on the farms around Thorley were the steam-ploughing engines, and my father often took me on the crossbar of his bicycle to see them working. They were owned by John Patten of Little Hadham, who was one of the last large-scale operators of these giant machines. They were at work around Thorley until 1960 when the business was wound up.

The engines worked in pairs, one standing at each end of the field; each engine had 800 yards of cable to drag the plough across the field. Appropriately, the engines were named in pairs, like Darby and Joan for example. Some years ago I did some research to find out how many sets were owned by John Patten and the engine names. The late Ernie Vale, for many years the manager of Piggott's Farm, was able to supply me with the information.

Alf (Ossie) Osborne, from a family of steam-ploughing men who worked for John Patten, and Charlie Ward, another steam-plough veteran, have many anecdotes to tell:

Steam-plough men worked in gangs of five, and would do dredging and pulling up trees as well as ploughing. They often worked long hours, from 5.30a.m. till 11p.m., earning up to £2 10 shillings a week. They would have to take circuitous routes on roads to get to fields because the engines were so heavy, and the engines had no brakes, only reverse gears as control.

The men knew all the ponds where they could fill up their engines. At the Green Man pub in Thorley Lane, where there were problems with springs in the cellars, they would stop and pump out clear sparkling water.

Tom Camp also talked about mechanisation and the accidents that happened on farms:

One of the things a lot of people did suffer from was bad backs. The people who used to load the lorries would wind the sack lift up to get the sacks on their shoulders. Then you carry them and put them on the lorries, but if they needed to go on the top, then you had to go up a sack ladder. The sacks would weigh up to 20 stone. You had to be strong, but it's like everything else, some of it was knack as well; it wasn't always the big chap that could do it. Clover seed sacks weighed 20 stone, wheat 18 stone and barley 16 stone.

You used to get accidents with the horses sometimes. I remember a horse bolting with a cart and as it came out of the gateway, the cart hit the gatepost and turned over, the horse with it. The first thing you do when you've got a horse that's gone over is you jump on the head to hold the head down because you've got all the harness to get unstrapped. This chap jumped on the head to hold the horse down and he started to undo the harness, when suddenly the horse flew his head up, threw this chap and hit me in the stomach and knocked me over backwards and knocked the wind out of me.

Rose Monk remembers an accident on the Pattens' farm at Thorley Wash, during harvest time when the thrashing engines were working:

A young girl, Florrie Eames, was playing in the field with other children and somehow got hit by the elevator. She was hit on the head and her sight was affected causing near blindness in later years. Florrie was the daughter of Police Constable Eames who lived next door to us, and she and my late sister Dolly remained lifelong friends.

Many villagers remember a fatal accident happened in Han Lane, when farm worker Peter Eldred was killed by one of the Pattens' steam engines weighing about 21 tons. He had sat down by the wheel to eat, fallen asleep and been run over.

Livestock

Tom went on to talk about keeping livestock:

Pedigree Essex pigs were kept in the barn opposite Thorley Hall Cottages. They were good pigs and were sent out for breeding, until they lost favour because they were

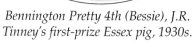
Bennington Pretty 4th (Bessie), J.R. Tinney's first-prize Essex pig, 1930s.

too fat. So they crossed them with the Large White to get a long pig that didn't get as fat. The old Essex pigs were what they call a 'fat stock' show in the market at Christmas. We had to wash them and scrub them, using soft soap, and they really looked a picture. We won quite a lot of rosettes and prizes.

After the pigs, the cows were kept in the barn until about springtime. Then they were ready to be driven to market. Just imagine, they had been shut in all the winter and when they got outside and saw all the green grass and that, they went nearly mad! We used to have to drive the cattle right down Thorley Lane and along London Road, that's if you could keep them on the road! If they saw a gateway, unless you got somebody standing in the way, they would make a bolt for it. We used to take two or three down at a time. We had to let them get close up to the shop windows because the street was narrow, but we never had a window smashed, 'cause they used to look at themselves in the window! I should think by the time we got them into market we'd run a lot of pounds off them!

Right: *Dave Eldred shearing sheep at Thorley Hall Farm.*

Right, bottom: *A Land Girl with the chickens at Bird's Farm, 1940s.*

Below: *Cows crossing Thorley Street from Twyford Park to Bird's Farm.*

Flossie Monk (née Hutchin), recalls the time when her father worked on Hither Farm and she lived with her family in one of the farm cottages next door:

My father, James Hutchin, was employed by Arthur Bird of Hither Farm [known as Bird's farm] to look after and tend to a small milking herd. Many times he spent all night staying with the cows as their calves were born. After morning milking, the herd was led from the milking barn, down Bird Lane, across the main road into the park to graze, and in the afternoon led back again for afternoon milking.

In winter they stayed in cowsheds at night, and in better weather in a field at the back of the farm. Chickens also roamed free in the yard or on part of the field that was fenced off.

Liz Eldred, shepherdess, has many tales of sheep:

The sheep year began in autumn when the rams were put in with the ewes. Suffolk (black-faced) rams were used up until the mid-1980s when Texel (white-faced) rams were gradually introduced, the first of which were Oscar and Oliver. All Suffolk rams for some reason were known as Charlie-boy.

Lambing took place in March/April up until 1980 when 'earlier' varieties of ryegrass were grown for combining. Then the lambing date was gradually moved to early February. The lambs would be turned out at three to four days old when lambing was early, but they would not go out into the fields until they were least a fortnight old, as the weather was less kind in February. Lambing is a time of very little sleep and a lot of hard work – but I loved it! Then came sheering. My father and brother Tony used to shear all the sheep, using shears powered by an old Lister engine, which could prove temperamental at times. Later, electric motors were used, but the method of shearing was the same – just not so noisy!

When the sheep had been shorn it was my job to roll up the fleeces and put them into wool 'ticks' or very large sacks, which had to be sewn up ready for collection. It looks so easy when an expert does the job, but believe me it's not!

Dipping was the next job. It used to be done in a 'dip', which is a concrete-lined pit about five feet deep with a slope at one end so that the sheep could walk out. This was filled with water and the sheep dip mixed in. Next, every sheep had to be manhandled and put into the dip. This was a two-man job when it came to ewes, but lambs could be managed by one person. Later, a new dip was put in – the sheep were supposed to walk in and walk out, but someone forgot to tell them that!

My earliest encounters with sheep were with the orphan lambs Dad would bring home to be revived in front of the kitchen fire. When Dad retired in 1972, I took over as shepherd. There were about 300 sheep in the flock. This was gradually increased to 400 and at lambing time, with the flock, there would be about 1,000 animals to look after in a good year. I was shepherd at Thorley Hall for 27 years until I was made redundant in the year 2000 and the sheep were sold; devastating, but at least we missed the nightmare of foot-and-mouth disease.

Dorothy (Doll) Wick (née Hammond) dipping sheep, 1970.

Dick Wick feeding sheep in the field behind Thorley Cottages, 1950s.

Two millers outside Twyford Mill, 1900s. Mr Sampford, Colin's grandfather is on the right.

Milling

Grenville Bird remembers that Twyford Mill was still working at the start of the war. He recalls being taken for a walk along the tow-path from Stortford and seeing sacks of grain being lifted up into the mill.

Rose Monk recalls that fascinated villagers used to watch the large water-wheel that turned incessantly. After the sale of the Twyford House estate, Boyd Gibbins converted the mill into flats for private residents.

Church Services and Sunday School

Joyce Clark draws a picture of a typical Sunday in Thorley in 1930:

At 8a.m. the rector, the reverend Canon Procter, celebrates a Holy Communion Service, and then opens the Village School at 10a.m. for the Sunday school children.

It is 10.45a.m. The church bells [only three bells at this time] are ringing (Come to Church Come to Church) calling the people to the morning 11a.m. service. The Sunday school children are walking up the Hall Road (as Church Lane was known) in twos with their teacher (Mrs George Chapel).

At the church the boys who are in the choir go to the vestry to put on their surplices, the rest of the children sit at the back of the church in pews, which are prepared for them.

At 11a.m. the bells cease. The rector walks up the aisle to the vestry. The organist (Miss Eccles) commences to play and the now assembled choir walk down the aisle to the choir stalls. The service is led by the rector and is taken from the A and M Prayer Book.

Depending on the Sunday in the month, different parts of the Holy Communion Service and litany are read. Psalms are sung. Lessons are read by the Lay Reader (Mr C. Kirk) and the sermon is preached by the rector, who ascends the pulpit and always begins with a text from the Bible.

Some of the Sunday school are allowed out before the sermon. Sometimes the sermons are so long one could not help but doze off!

The service ends with a hymn and a blessing. The choir then returns to the vestry while the organ is played.

Sunday school is reopened by the rector at 3p.m.

At 6.00p.m. the bells are ringing again for the 6.30p.m. service, which lasts about an hour.

Then everyone goes home. In the distance the clock on Twyford House chimes 8p.m.

Joyce remembers that her first teacher at the age of five was Miss Carrie Watson, Gladys' aunt. In Sunday school, children had to learn part of the catechism in the Common Prayer Book, then the collect of the day, parts of the Gospel and Epistle, as well as

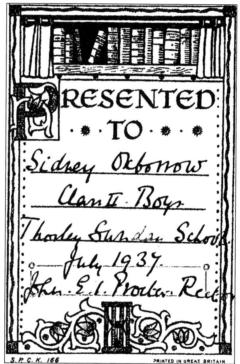

a hymn. They were given stamp books for good attendance, and if a child had good marks for the lessons at the end of the year, one would be presented with a prize, usually a prayer book or a bible.

Margaret Morley describes the problems 50 years later of finding a suitable home for a growing Sunday school:

In the 1980s and 1990s the Sunday school was moved several times, from St James' Church to Church House, thence to the Scout Hall, to two portacabins temporarily installed outside the churchyard wall, and finally into the St Barnabas Centre. In the 1980s there were between 14 and 18 children attending Sunday school, and some 12 babies and toddlers being cared for in a crèche. During the 1990s these figures had increased to over 30 Sunday school children and 20 small children in the crèche. But we had nothing to offer the over 11s, until the Pathfinders started up in the small Church Room in the churchyard. In 2002 the numbers are still growing, more groups and activities are starting up for the young, and planning for further change of usage for agricultural barns is in progress.

Frank Warboys remembers that the church featured heavily in his family's life:

The church was a focal point of our family life. Mother was a devoted churchgoer, Dad a member of the [men and boys only] choir. Great-grandfather Watson had been a Thorley churchwarden in the early 1900s. Granny Eagling was a church organist. Grandfather Warboys [was] a Thorley church sidesman. Going to church twice each Sunday and to Sunday school was part of the family tradition. Dad used to clip the grass on the family graves regularly and often took us with him.

Edward Miller recalls:

As a member of the Youth Club it was expected that you would attend Holy Communion at 8.00a.m. on the first Sunday of the month, and in 1954 four of us young men from the Youth Club were appointed as Servers. So whatever the weather you rode your bicycle up Thorley Lane, parked it under the yew trees and went to your duties; and because the stoke hole in which the coke boiler was located was prone to flooding, the church could be very cold on a Sunday morning in the winter.

A Sunday school presentation to Sidney Oxborrow, 1937.

Festivities

Frank also recalls the festivities that invariably were associated with the church:

I remember the Harvest Festivals and Christmas services. Canon Procter used to have a Friday night Harvest Festival service for all the farmers and farm workers of the village. This was always packed and the singing vigorous. Christmas with the church lit by oil-lamps and candles was much more mysterious. I can remember hiding below the pew's book rest beside my mother.

Edward Miller:

As youngsters aged 13 or 14, how we looked forward to the Festival services at Easter, Christmas and Harvest Festival. For these services a coach would be run in the evenings, picking up at the 'White Posts' at the bottom of Thorley Lane to help parishioners get to church, cars being far less common in those days. Harvest Festival evensong was always full to overflowing, and the church, decorated from top to toe with sheaves of corn, vegetables, fruit and flowers, was a joy to behold.

Youth Club members would join with members of the church choir and other folk to sing carols round the parish in the days before Christmas. A choir of up to 20 people would sing on four or five consecutive evenings, assembling at 7p.m. to sing round the Uplands, Thorley Street and Twyford, the Bishop's Avenue/Twyford Park estate, Thorley Hill and adjoining roads. We mostly rode our bicycles from point to point whilst some went in cars, and we covered a large area each evening, with the rector knocking on the doors for donations to the church

funds until 10.00p.m. These were very happy evenings and on each evening we would always be invited into one or two houses for drinks, sausage rolls and mince pies. I have particular memories of the singers being welcomed in by Mrs Wolfson at Thorley House and by Mrs and Miss Streeter at Thorley Place.

Church fêtes were very traditional, and venues were the gardens of Thorley House, Thorley Place, the Rectory, or in the old Village School yard or Valley field. There were always plenty of sideshows including hoopla, coconut shy, bowling for a pig, crockery shy, treasure hunt, etc., and when you had done all this you could have tea, sandwiches and cakes provided by the ladies. The church fête was a highlight of the year and often opened by a well-known personality.

Church socials were also very popular and were held in the Village School. One of the best would be on New Year's Eve when the rector would be the Master of Ceremonies conducting an evening of party games and dancing with great enthusiasm. Imagine the rector calling for 20 or so men to volunteer for an unspecified game. Having volunteered, you were then told to take your shoes off and place them at the far end of the hall – whereupon the rector would mix up some 40 shoes and then invite the participants to race to the other end and be the first to return wearing their own shoes. It was mayhem but created much laughter.

Bell-ringing

The bells of St James' have lifted the spirits of many a Thorleyite. Tom Camp, who died in 1999, left money for a new bell to be purchased, but sadly the twelfth-century church tower has been found too weak to support the extra weight. It is recorded in a church magazine article:

Thorley Fête in Thorley House gardens, 1965.

Left: *Revd Sydney Robinson with Thorley bell-ringers outside St James', 1950s. Left to right: Fred Warboys, Peter Warboys, Cecil Warboys, Colin Sampford, Reg Hayden, Henry Newman, Revd Sydney Robinson, Cyril Kirk, Walter Prior, Jimmy Foreman, Freddie Bird, Frank Warboys, Tom Camp, Daphne Hayden.*

Right: *Revd Sydney Robinson with Thorley church choir outside St James', c.1968.*

The bell tower of St James the Great contains six bells, three of which date back to the seventeenth century. Two more were added in 1937 in memory of the Procter and Frere families when all five bells were adapted for full circle ringing, the original three being set up for chime ringing. A sixth treble bell was added in 1946. The total weight of the six bells is over a ton, safely installed on a massive oak frame.

Canon J.E.I. Procter, in his church guide from the 1930s, writes:

The gleaning bell was rung at 8a.m. and 6a.m. at harvest time to signify when villagers were allowed on the fields to glean, but villagers have not heard this bell and tell of another custom, which is the removing of a single sheaf left standing in the field.

Edward Miller:

Several of the girls and boys from the Youth Club were

taught to ring the bells by the tower captain, Tom Camp. He had endless patience and got us to the stage of ringing quarter peals of Grandsire Doubles. I can remember Tony Swan, myself and Jean and Joan Lee being four of Tom's pupils. The great bell-ringing family of the parish was the Warboys family. But Tom was remarkable, and in November 1999 a 'Full Peal' was rung at his funeral.

The Choir

Singing in the church choir has long been very important in the life of many villagers, particularly Gladys Warboys. Edward Miller recalls that his parents attended St James' Church from 1946, and when the rector built up the church choir his mother, Carol Miller, was one of numerous ladies of the parish who joined. In 2003 the church choir is attracting younger membership from a wide congregation.

Chorister Chris Foreman with parents Elsie and Jimmy, 1950s.

Chapter 4

Leisure and Sport

Football

Rose Monk recalls that football matches were played in the field next to Brook Farm, and Bryan South, the Wood brothers and Maurice Hockley recall playing a football match against the Spellbrook boys in the field by the Roley Croak. Roy Money, farm manager for the Tinneys, recalls that Thorley had a very good football team, and that he still has his medals from the football team of 1951/2.

In the 'Sawbridgeworth Diary' section of the *Herts and Essex Observer* of 24 November 1994, there is a picture of the Thorley team of the 1950s. The writer reports that he played in goal with a broken finger throughout the 90 minutes.

Hockey

Rose recalls that in the early 1920s Thorley had a hockey team of young men in their teens or early twenties, who played on a field near Butler's Hall. Her brother George Stoakes and Frank Warboys senr were members of the team.

Cricket

Cricket was a passion in the past for many Thorleyites (and it still is), stirring so many memories of such wide interest, that this topic alone justifies the additional publication of a Chronicles Supplement. With apologies to contributors for ruthless omissions and curtailments, we include what we can in the hope that everyone has been given mention.

Starting from the early 1900s, Frank Warboys recalls:

My maternal great-grandfather, George Watson, played cricket in Thorley. My father was also a stalwart of the club. He played for the village team from his teens until he was 58. The cricket club membership was a reflection of almost all the village families.

Maurice Elliott reminds us that 'in most of our lives

Thorley football team, 1950s. The picture includes: *Reg Mansfield, Bill Bye, Ron Oxborrow, John Robinson, Jim Robinson, Phil Akers, Les Collidge, Chris Newman, and Bill Hampton.*

Thorley hockey at Butler's Hall, 1920s. Pictured on the back row are: *Frank Chappell (second from left) and George Stoakes (far right).*

there are single events or passages of time which later you realise were something special', which is how he begins telling his story of cricket in Thorley. In the following excerpt he recalls:

Right: *Thorley cricket team with Brutus, 1949.* Left to right, back row: *Bert Bird (umpire), ?, Phil Akers, Harry Warboys, ?, Maurice Elliott;* middle row: *George Brewster, Frank Warboys, Geoff Brewster, Fred Hatchett, ?;* front row: *Colin Trigg, Brutus the dog, Arthur Rayment.*

Left: *Thorley team with Epping Forresters (EF) at Brook Farm, early 1950s.* Left to right, back row: *Rick Shaw, Lionel Shellard (captain), ?, ?, Gordon Barker;* second row (standing): *EF, EF, EF, EF, Ernie Adams, Geoff Brewster, Fred Hatchett;* sitting on

bench: *Bill Wood, EF, EF, Ron Oxborrow;* front row: *EF, EF and Brutus, Phil Akers, Les Collidge, Jim Robinson, Peter Doyle, EF.*

Thorley cricket team and the Herts and Essex Observer *team (HE), 1957.* Left to right, back row: *HE, HE Tony Chancellor, Maurice Hockley, Colin Perry, HE Derek Eden, Tony Kluysse, George Brewster;* middle row: *HE Denis ?, HE John Keeble, Michael Warboys, John Robinson, Bill Monk, Bill Pleasance, ?, HE Ben Armitage;* front row: *Tony (Fritz) Fuller, HE Bill Pratt, HE Bill Hampton, Jim Robinson, HE Peter Brown, HE Josh ?.*

Right: *Thorley cricket team, 1979.* Back row includes: *Rob Mills, Jim Suggett, Peter Cavill, Glenn Collins, Sid Haddow;* middle row, left to right: *Andy Bell, Alan Wrentmore, John Challis, Rick Letchford, Simon Parker;* front row: *Jonathan Neville.*

It was just after the Second World War and men came back from the war to link up with friends. The Thorley lads came back, added a few local friends and formed a club.

The opening attack was normally the Brewster brothers, George and Geoff, and they were quite a combination. The big hitting continued with Arthur Rayment, the local blacksmith, and Harry Warboys.

Peter Doyle invariably opened with Phil Akers. Peter was a class batsman at this level and indeed went on later to play at a much higher grade. Phil Akers was an extremely thoughtful player. His fielding was extremely sharp and he was always on the prowl. Heaven help anyone in the field who was not concentrating!

Supporting these openers were a number of steady bats. Fred Hatchett, one of life's gentlemen, always managed a few runs and people like Frank Warboys senr helped stabilise the middle order. Ron Oxborrow reckons that Fred Hatchett was the outstanding fielder, usually fairly close in at mid-off he would field the ball whilst running flat out and return it over the top of the stumps time and time again.

On Sundays the side had the boost of Gordon Barker. He was a quick scorer and was a great source of encouragement to us, the youngsters, in the side.

One of the largest characters in the team (weddings and funerals, etc. permitting) was the rector, Sydney Robinson. He usually fielded close in where he would pass his comments to umpires, batsmen, and bowlers alike. On one occasion one of the opposition asked me 'Which one is your vicar?' When Sydney was indicated, the player's mouth opened wide – 'I can't believe it!' he said.

Now we come to the players who often saved the situation. Ron Oxborrow was one – he had great 'stick-ability'. He would often hold up one end whilst the big hitters came and went. Ron and I were often numbers 10 and 11 in the order but on odd times we opened the innings... very frustrating to the opposition.

Ernie Barber, who was the wrong side of 50, played for a couple of years, and Jim Argent was a good spin bowler when he could play. In the same category was Jim Day – to me as a sixteen-year-old he looked an old man, but he probably was only 40. He used to turn out with his flat cap and could do all kinds of wonders spinning the ball.

The club was lucky to attract a number of cricketers with a good record. Maurice Hockley was a good bat and wicket-keeper.

Then there were the boys. All very young but keen... the Robinson brothers Jim and John were good all rounders, Colin Trigg could 'bowl a bit', Colin Sampford played a bit despite his tender years, and others included Alan Summers, Mick Marns and Michael Warboys.

I've tried to remember all the names. Peter Doyle reminds me of a good batsman/wicket-keeper called Les Collidge, but I think he must have left before I joined.

Directly after the war when the club started up, the local farmer Tom Streeter played and also Reg Sibley, but once the team was on its feet they dropped out.

One special team we played was the Epping Foresters with whom we had all-day matches – home on Whit Monday and away on the August Bank Holiday. Vera Oxborrow used to score and the teams always partook of a lovely salad lunch.

But it was the Brewsters, Peter Doyle, Fred Hatchett and Phil Akers, who made the side tick, add a dash of Harry Warboys and Arthur Rayment and you could see why Thorley was an interesting side.

We were well served by our umpires, Mr Bert Bird, Mr Albert Brewster senior, and Sonny Gilson. There were obviously back room girls and boys, Vera Oxborrow, Audrey Doyle, Hilda Brewster and several others.

Andrew Streeter recalls his father's gift to the parish:

Tom Streeter, my father, died in 1962 and in his Will he left the cricket pitch to Thorley Parish Council, so that the inhabitants of Thorley could continue to play cricket for ever. Nobody at that time would have thought that Bishop's Stortford would grow and surround this peaceful ground with houses. I now have the honour of being President of the Thorley Cricket Club.

Maurice Hockley adds to Maurice's story and recalls helping to transform Tom Streeter's meadow into today's cricket ground:

The cricket team became for me a major pastime in my late teens. The pitch was no more than a rough meadow at that time and presented some challenge to the group of young enthusiasts who made up the team. In phases the wicket went from cement track with a matting surface to real grass, and the pavilion from a used shed to a permanent structure. Many of those who struggled in these efforts can be seen playing in the match between Thorley and the Herts and Essex Observer team (HE).

Rob Mills, chairman in the 1970s, adds to Maurice's recollections:

Introduced to the club by watching my father, my recollections can now cover the best part of four decades. On my early visits, unlike now, there seemed to be just a small pool of players available, namely Colin Perry, Pat Blaney (wicket-keeper), Jim Robinson, Bernard Shepherd, John Robinson, John Challis, Derek Clarke, Keith Robinson, Bob Mills, Ron Oxborrow, Selwyn Hutchin, Ivor Bush, Peter Cavill, Norman Coulson, Dave Pearmain and within a few years Paul Hutchinson (chairman in 2002). All were characters and they certainly seemed to have more victories than defeats, but then the memory does play tricks.

45

Peter Cavill was a wonderful servant to the club as groundsman. He was also club captain for many years and a fine all-rounder, recording the unique feat for a 'Gannet' in scoring 1,000 runs and taking 100 wickets in a season. He was tragically involved in a horrific car crash in the early 1980s which resulted in him never playing again. Norman Coulson was a fine left-arm seam bowler and in the right conditions was almost unplayable.

The late '70s early '80s saw quite a change as we struggled to raise teams, the club probably becoming too insular despite the increase in the population as the local landscape changed from the fields to houses.

Norman Coulson, former captain and secretary, recalls these landscape changes and other upsets of the '70s, such as positioning the pitch and pavilion to miss the underground pipe supplying the town's main gas supply. He then goes on:

One important feature of the club over the years has been its long and proud association with the old families of Thorley. It has always numbered amongst its presidents, vice-presidents and chairmen members of the Streeter, Tinney, James, Robinson, Brewster, Knight, Newman, Warboys, Maslen and Fuller families, together with many others.

Paul Hutchinson, chairman in 2002, adds to this:

It is indicative of family traditions and the nature of village cricket that, following on from Bob Mills, who started his playing career at Thorley in 1964, both his son (Rob) and his grandson (Robbie) have become club stalwarts, both playing for the club and preparing the pitch and mowing the outfield. It is to their credit that the pitch and ground are considered to be among the finest in the area.

John Davies, secretary in 2002, recalls:

Living as I do on the boundary line has its drawbacks. Every year there is a 'Cracked Tile' award for the player who has hit the most sixes in a season. Needless to say that the cracked tile has come from my roof.

Thorley Cricket Club continues to thrive and at the time of writing has two sides on Saturdays playing league cricket, as well as a side on Sundays playing friendly matches against local villages. Looking at the fixture list for the 2003 season the club will still lock horns with many sides who have been opponents for over 50 years.

On Rogation Sunday 2003, the club was pleased to follow early tradition and host the village fête.

Hunting, Shooting and Fishing

In earlier years, the hunt would meet at St James' Church and follow the hounds through the parish woods and farmland, on occasion meeting outraged opposition – even in those days, it must be said – from dwellers in cottages in their path, such as Mrs Lawford. Nessie Streeter was a very keen member of the hunt, and in the days when cooks and parlour-maids were employed to work in the 'big houses', the Streeter family would play host to the huntsmen in Thorley Place; later on, the pubs would take over this role!

Farmer Tom Streeter, of Thorley Place, had an artistic leaning, as can be seen from hunting illustrations he drew and sent to Revd Sydney Robinson.

Liz the shepherdess, whose antipathy towards fox hunting as a cruel means of fox control is well known locally, writes about the family fox:

We had a fox named Kedgee for 14 years. She would chew everything, so we had to banish her to a large enclosure in the garden, but she would still come in and spend the evenings with us. She would walk on a lead, and we roamed all around the village, much to the

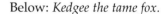
Left: *Hunting sketch by Tom Streeter.*

Below: *Kedgee the tame fox.*

Oh! the silly hunting man
will be in trouble if he can.

But the foxes love the sight
of him in such a sorry plight.

astonishment of any strangers we met. She got on very well with all our other animals, and the chickens used to wander around her run. Her best friend was Sam our ginger cat who used to go into her run and help himself to her food, and the rest of the cats treated her as one of their family. Foxes don't make good pets but it's an experience I wouldn't have missed for the world.

These days, however, there is more local interest in Thorley in shooting woodpigeon and rabbit in the fields, and angling from the tow-path on the river. Roy Wilson recalls:

When out woodpigeon shooting at Thorley Hall Farm I would occasionally call in at the farm to glean information from Mick Hill, the farm manager, and in earlier days would be given a box or two of 'Min of Ag' pest control cartridges. At that time I used to own rather large yellow labradors as retrievers, but Tessa, my present dog, is a first cross from Black Polly, belonging to Amanda James at Brook Farm.

On one occasion, while pigeon shooting, I observed a fox running through the ewes which were heavy in lamb, obviously 'reviewing the situation'. When it came within range, rightly for some, and wrongly for others, I shot it before it returned while lambing was in progress, knowing full well that nearby Mathams Wood had an abundance of the red beasties.

I knew this because Mick had asked me to have a look at a nearby field of winter wheat which was being devoured by rabbits. Some we shot with rifle and shotgun, but we then put down three dozen snares, and all that was recovered were tufts of rabbit fur in the snares, as the foxes were having a field day!

Peter and Deirdre James used to suffer quite heavy turkey losses at Brook Farm due to foxes over the years. Whilst shooting at adjacent Rumballs Farm, I accounted for a couple of bushy-tailed marauders, one of which was the largest dog fox (being so well fed!) that I had ever seen.

'Ratting' in the pig barn (now St Barnabas) could be a problem. Electronic/ultrasonic gadgetry was not considered a suitable solution, and poisoned bait could only be used in limited areas. Dave, the stockman, and I agreed to tackle the problem in the evenings using small calibre .177 air rifles fitted with torches, as these horrid little rodents are at their most active at night. There was little or no activity at ground level, most movement appearing to be on the beams which ran parallel between the top of the walls and the beams at the base of the corrugated metal roof. We shot literally hundreds, possibly thousands, some of which had

burrowed into large 12" and 14" square roof timbers to breed.

Jack Phillips:

The river was another great interest, and my friends and I used to spend hours down the Roley Croak fields and fishing in the Stort. It was then a very clean river and held stocks of fish, which latterly has not been the case, unfortunately – one more instance of how standards have been deteriorating in many ways.

Swimming

Miss Beryl Frere was a remarkable lady from the family that lived in Twyford House. She taught every one of the children of the village how to swim!

There is no one who does not speak of learning to swim with Miss Beryl, and of the enjoyment they had as children swimming in the river near the matchstick bridge and playing in the fields through which the Roley Croak stream ran alongside the Twyford House grounds. They all remember too the freezing cold of the mill pool water.

Group of girls by the river and Roley Croak bridge.

Brenda Pleasance and Peter Warboys are just two to tell the story:

Miss Frere made sure that all the village children could swim by giving us lessons in the river that ran through the grounds of Twyford House. We were started in shallow water, held in a rope sling from a footbridge, and graduated to swimming in the mill pool proper which was very deep, but had on one side a ledge normally about a foot under the water. Miss Frere used to say 'icebergs today' as she stood on the ledge in her waders. At that time the river ran under the working mill and into the freezing-cold mill pool on the other side, and we could sit on the ledge where the water rushed out.

It was particularly fun to try and swim against the current created by the mill-wheel when the mill was working. Boys had to change in the boot room in the old servants' quarters, but the girls had a larger room upstairs. We were sometimes joined by the Wolfson children, Pam and Mark from Thorley House, who changed on their own in the garden.

We graduated to swimming on our own in the River Stort from the Roley Croak bridge. There was an old bridge support from where we could dive into the water and swim across the river. If you did not have a swimming costume, Miss Frere would knit you one, which got a bit saggy when in the water!

Children were encouraged to enter competitions, and they won awards.

The swimming team, 1930s. Left to right, back row: Albert Camp, Ron Oxborrow, Tom Hammond, Geoff Brewster, Phil Akers, Jack Bird, Gordon Barker, Bert Hammond; middle row: Dolly Hammond, Dorothy Camp, Peggy Harris, Miss Beryl Frere, Joyce Harris, Clara Camp; front row: Maisie Akers, Audrey Harris, Hilda Akers.

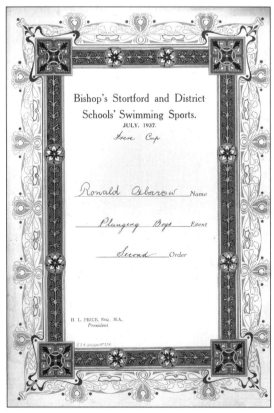

Bishop's Stortford and District Schools' Swimming Sports.
JULY. 1937.

Frere Cup

Ronald Oxborrow Name

Plunging Boys Event

Second Order

H. L. PRICE, Esq., M.A.,
President

Award to Ron Oxborrow for Plunging Boy event in Frere Cup, 1937.

The Frere girls on the ledge, Twyford mill pool, 1924. Left to right: Phillis, ? and Muriel.

Right: *One of the Frere family swimming in the Twyford mill pool.*

Thorley folk dance group. Among those pictured are: *Tom Camp* (fourth from left, back row), *Mrs Travers* (far left, sitting), *and Doris Brett (née Saville)* (ninth from left, sitting).

Left: *Thorley School sword dance, 1930s.* Left to right, back row: *?, Sid Hammond, George Brewster, Tom Hammond;* front row: *Bert Hammond, Phil Akers, Jack Bird, Geoff Brewster.*

Left: *Thorley School Morris dancers, 1930s.* From back to front, left column: *Gordon Barker, Phil Akers, Geoff Brewster;* right column: *Bert Hammond, George Clark, Jack Bird.*

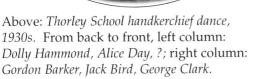

Above: *Thorley School handkerchief dance, 1930s.* From back to front, left column: *Dolly Hammond, Alice Day, ?;* right column: *Gordon Barker, Jack Bird, George Clark.*

Right: *Morris dancing at Hockerill, 1938.* Left to right, back row: *George Pavitt, Tom Camp, Bill Doe;* middle: *S.A. (Nibs) Matthews;* front row: *Phil Akers, George Brewster, S. Parlett.*

Dancing

Miss Beryl Frere taught folk-dancing in the villages around Bishop's Stortford. She had the ability, rare in the 1930s, to get men involved in folk-dancing, and Bishop's Stortford and Thorley each had men's Morris teams within the folk-dance groups. There are many accounts from villagers who remember being instructed in Morris and sword dancing by Miss Beryl and practising on the lawns of Twyford House, and later meeting up with other groups in competitions.

One of Miss Beryl's protégés was the renowned Nibs Matthews, who recalls the start of it all in this extract reprinted by kind permission of the editor of *English Dance and Song*:

I was in the Holy Trinity Church Choir, and the organist used to play piano for the folk-dancing on the same evening as the practices. We would have an early practice so that the organist could go and play. We used to play hell, banging on the door and running away, until one day the teacher Miss Beryl Frere got hold of two of us. We sat in the hall and watched the dancing. I had two uncles there, so why they didn't clip me over the ear I don't know! She asked me to come along, so the next week I went. I was a boy dancing with adults. That was the start of it, in 1932 or '33.

Drama

Music and drama always featured strongly in the school, and pupils remember dressing up for performances.

Thorley Amateur Dramatic Society (TADS), having been founded by Revd Sydney Robinson in 1946/7, performed a variety of very good shows, usually in the school classroom. Productions included *Thorley Follies* in 1947 and 1948, *Cinderella*, *Ladies in Retirement*, *Aladdin's Cave*, *Wasn't it Odd*, *Dick Whittington*, *Such Things Happen*, *It's in the Air*, and *Dangerous Corner*. A sizeable trunk of dressing-up clothes must have been amassed! Edward Miller recalls:

My mother, Carol Miller, was in TADS and the shows they put on gave wonderful entertainment. The annual pantomime was a great favourite with the parishioners. Revd Sydney Robinson always played a leading comic role, for example 'Widow Twankey', in the colourful and laughter-filled pantomimes. The stage in the Village School was small but the cast managed very well. Muriel Newman, wife of farmer and churchwarden Reggie Newman, was the capable accompanist on the piano.

There was always a very happy atmosphere at the village shows, and I remember sitting at the front on a row of cushions watching my mother playing Cinderella, with Pam Finch (née Wolfson) as Prince Charming and Revd Sydney as Buttons.

Andy Streeter, recalling memories of his family, says that his unmarried aunt, Pam Streeter, who lived with his grandmother in Thorley Place, was a very talented artist and loved flower arranging and amateur dramatics. They used to enjoy watching her play in productions at the Thorley Village School.

Music

Playing musical instruments and singing figured in everyone's way of life in the village, be it organ and choir in church, or piano and singing at home and in school. In postwar times, with the advent of radio and recordings and American influences, the youth of Thorley would meet in the Working Men's Hut to enjoy music and dance of different kinds.

In the 1970s, music teacher Mac McDonald held summer holiday music schools for local children in the old Village School (by that time the Scout Hall). On the occasion of Gladys' 100th birthday he put together some musical entertainment to launch the idea of this book. He tells us:

When asked to provide some music, I thought it would be appropriate to invite two former pupils, Stephen Warner and Suzanne Gale, to join me in performing

Above: *Thorley School percussion band, 1938.* Left to right, standing: *Lily Akers, Donald Powell, Teddie Kent, Sidney Oxborrow, Frank Warboys, Jean Brewster, Flossie Hutchin;* seated: *Dennis Prior, Jean Hammond, Margaret Brewster, Joan Hammond.*

Above: *Anne Miller and guitar trio (from left) Stephen Warner, Suzanne Gale and Mac McDonald) performing for Gladys Warboys' 100th birthday, St Barnabas, 2002.*

Left: *School drama enacted in the field across from the school, 1930s.* Left to right, back to front: *Hilda Akers, Tom Hammond, Clara Camp, Albert Camp, Joyce Harris, Ron Oxborrow, Peggy Harris, Gordon Barker.*

Right: *School drama enacted by the pond across from the school, 1930s.* Left to right, standing: *Ron Oxborrow, Albert Camp, Gordon Barker, Donald Powell, Maisie Akers, Lilian Akers, John Reed;* sitting/lying: *Audrey Harris, Ben Hammond.*

Left: *Cast of* Ladies in Retirement, *c.1950.* Left to right, back: *Betty Brewster, Maurice Wenn (?), Frank Warboys junr, Carol Miller, ?, Mrs Partridge, Bob French, ?, Pamela Streeter, Jimmy Foreman, Muriel Newman, Elsie Foreman, Revd Sydney Robinson;* front: *?.*

Right: *The cast of* Cinderella, *c.1953.* Left to right, back row: *Molly Bird, ?, Elsie Foreman, Thelma Gateley, Jimmy Foreman, ?, Geoff Brewster;* middle row: *Betty Brewster, Muriel Newman, Hedley Dellow, Pat Briers, Pam Wolfson, Carol Miller, ?, Cecil Warboys, Joan Hammond, Lilian Akers, ?;* front row: *Molly Hammond, Fred Hatchett senr, George ?, Revd Sydney Robinson, Maurice Wenn, Bob French.*

Left: *TADS dinner in the school hall, 1957.* Picture includes: *2. Clarrie Lambert, 5. Barbara Warboys, 6. Revd Sydney Robinson, 12. Jimmy Foreman, 13. Chris Foreman, 16. Mary Williams, 19. Fred Ball, 20. Elsie Foreman, 21. Brenda Perry, 22. Molly Lambert, 23. Muriel Newman.*

the Thorley Suite that I had written in 1972, based on a Danish fairy tale 'The Land of Youth', for the summer workshops I used to run. We also accompanied soprano Anne Miller (Edward's wife) who, although unaccustomed to guitar trio accompaniment and with only minutes of rehearsal, nevertheless sang beautifully for Gladys two of her favourite hymns, 'Just As I Am' and 'All Things Bright and Beautiful'.

Stephen Warner recalls helping with the annual workshops:

Every year we used to have about 30 children of various ages and abilities attend the summer school – and 30 guitars to tune! The memory I have of these weeks is one of all the children busily working away at pieces in all available spaces ready for the end of week concert that parents and friends always enjoyed. We played arrangements of all sorts of pieces from Bach and the Beatles to original compositions by Mac. It was very pleasing to perform the Thorley Suite again for the launch of this book.

Shopping and Tradesmen

Before the days of cars and out-of-town supermarkets, people used to walk or cycle, or send children, to the farms and small shops run by villagers. Tradesmen would call from outside the village, on their bicycles or in horse-drawn carts, or later in vans, to collect orders and make regular deliveries. Thorley at one time had a Post Office, an off-licence, a café and a pork butcher's shop.

Peggy Robinson (née Harris), who lived in the Uplands, recalled:

Springham, the grocer's from Green Tye, would come to Butler's Hall on Mondays for orders and return on Wednesdays to deliver the orders. Connie Symes, the greengrocer, was well known for her monkey nuts. Several bakers used to make deliveries. Newmans, from Newtown Road, and Barkers were bakers who came with horses and carts, while other bakers like Hardinge & Barge, Paveley's from Hockerill Street and Mascall's used to deliver on bicycles. Buns were 1d. each, and Bill Mascall from Sawbridgeworth would deliver fish as well as Betta biscuits sold at 3d. a packet. Their strawberry creams and orange creams were lovely!

Edward Miller, who lived on the northern boundary of the parish, recalls:

There were three shops in London Road: these being Thurley's Post Office and grocery shop at the junction of Twyford and London Roads; Barrett's, the grocers at 136 London Road, which was a well stocked shop on the site occupied by Dawn's Stores in 2002; and Price's, a smaller grocery shop at 158 London Road.

I didn't often go into Thurley's. Mr Thurley seemed a rather solemn man, but Barrett's, run by Jimmy and Elsie Foreman, was a busy and popular shop. Jimmy and Elsie sang in the church choir and performed with the Thorley Amateur Dramatic Society. Jimmy, who had a fine voice, would sometimes break into song in the shop.

As children, on our way home from school, we used to visit Price's, where the shop was the front room of a bungalow, to buy a drink of lemonade or cherryade. You simply went in, rang the counter bell and asked for your penny drink. This was poured into a small glass, perhaps about a sixth of a pint, and enjoyed while passing a few words with the white-haired Mrs Price. The other thing I remember getting there were Victory V gums, because they were cheap (but not very nice!).

Chris Foreman, whose parents ran Barrett's, tells us:

My father, James, managed the shop for the owners Mr and Mrs Barrett, who lived in Sawbridgeworth, until 1961 when he died aged aged 56. His wife (my mother) Elsie bought the shop and ran it until 1978 when she sold it to Dawn Ashraf (née Prior). My mother died aged 85 in 1994. Mum and Dad were both in the church choir and belonged to TADS.

From 1961 to 1965, I used to do a postman's round on a bicycle and went to many of the village addresses. I can remember many of the characters of the village.

At Christmas time after the war, my parents and I would join the villagers and go with Revd Robinson carol singing for three nights around the Twyford Park estate and The Street and the Uplands. On those occasions, I remember Mr Kirk who lived at The Lodge, Jim Knight (a Commander in the Navy) at Harringtons, and in Rectory Close the Williams who were related to Bill Seabon the road sweeper, also Ernie Warman, Bubbles Barker and the Monks. In the cottages were the Wicks and John Clark. In Thorley Farm lived either the Saunders or Geoff Sparrow, and in White Cottage was Horace Barnard with his little dog. In Sunset lived the Chappells and the Barkers, and in Stone Hall there was a tall upright man, Cyril House, who was married to Daphne Tinney. In Thorley Place I remember old Mrs Streeter, and in Thorley Place Cottages there were her gardeners Mr Brewster and Mr Gilson. In the cottage on the corner were Violet and Frank Crabb, and the Sortwells at Rumballs Farm. But the Newmans were the highlight of the occasion, because there you got mince pies and hot toddy. Then there were the Whalleys at Castle Farm and Mrs Monk Jones at Thorley Houses. In The Street I remember the Averys at the Blue House, the Wolfsons at Thorley House and Tom Camp of course.

Paul James, Thorley's postman at the time of writing, also knows many of the villagers. He recalls:

Above: *F.G. Warboys with his milk float outside Twyfordbury Farm, 1920s.*

Left: *Jim Foreman at Barrett's corner shop, 1954.*

Above: *Herbert Monk with a Model-T Ford lorry, outside Stone Hall, c.1930.*

Right: *Chimney-sweep Dai Griffiths, early 1950s.*

I was one of the many local children brought into the world by midwife Nurse Simonson, who died in 2002 at age 101 in Premier Court Nursing Home, and I remember Gladys Warboys from when I went to school at Great Havers. I've been on the post since I left school in 1963, and I was a telegram boy for three years. I remember one night when I was going to a football match having to take a telegram that had just come in late to Farnham. I went like mad on my push-bike that night! I remember Fred Owers living in Claypits Cottages, opposite the allotments where my Dad had two plots. I used to walk around the lanes as a kid and go to the Green Man with Dad. Over the years I've picked up letters from different houses to post for people or redirect. Sometimes they were left out for me under a weight on a window-sill, and I used to take round the letters the Beers wrote when we were fighting against the development, so I've got to know a lot of people.

Doreen Griffiths (Griff), who came to live in the Blocks when they were first built, was married to a charismatic man known to all, who was the chimney-sweep, before working at the telephone exchange.

Frank Monk has stories to tell of when his father, a woodman living at Stone Hall, used to transport villagers' furniture when they moved from one cottage to another in the parish. Peter Teitz remembers that Mr Monk's lorry had brass hub-caps.

Transport

Rail, road and river transport used to be of immense interest, particularly to the rural children. As Rose says, 'It's amazing how the times have changed!' Nowadays, the noise never stops in Thorley Street, traffic exceeds speed limits with impunity, villagers risk their lives crossing the road, commuter trains hurtle by crowded and trying to make up time, and Stansted airport aircraft are overhead low and loud. Only the river is silent, but alas is not without litter.

Rail

As told by Philip Wood and Maurice Hockley, the railway from London to Cambridge was constructed during the 1850s. The heavy freight traffic began to decline in the late 1960s but until then a succession of steam-hauled, then diesel-hauled, goods trains were often observed from favourite line-side locations at the Firs or the Roley Croak. These were the days of 'locospotting', and they spent hours on this hobby.

In the late 1960s a freight train named 'The Lea Valley' derailed outside neighbouring Spellbrook, leaving packs of frozen chickens scattered by the side of the line.

Electrification came in 1959 and the steam-hauled local trains from Bishop's Stortford to Liverpool Street were replaced by a new generation of electrical multiple units (EMUs). In the early days, however, there were many failures, so it was steam to the rescue! Philip and Maurice often observed EMUs being towed away for repair. Philip and Maurice continue:

Friends and I used to hang out by the Matchstick Bridge over the River Stort, and when we heard the sound of the last regular steam parcels train leaving Bishop's Stortford, we ran up to the Roley Croak crossing to savour the sight and sound of steam that we thought would be lost for ever. Since that time, however, special steam trains like the 'Britannia' and 'The Duke of Gloucester' in 1993 would arrive at Bishop's Stortford for a weekend of steam. 'Britannia', a class of locomotive that was a regular to the Thorley area in the 1950s (along with the superb Sandringham class), returned in 1995.

Rose Monk recalls:

With steam trains the carriages got smoky and sooty if the windows were left slightly open. They were drop-down windows. When we were youngsters in The Street the Royal Train came through, when Her Majesty Queen Mary and King George V were travelling to Sandringham. We ran down to the railway crossing to see the train and luckily enough we saw the Royals through the carriage window – most of us vowed that we did, but the train was travelling fairly fast! The Queen was wearing as usual her hat which was always a togue.

When my own two youngsters were little, after

This picture: *A steam engine in Thorley, 1959.*
Right: *An outing to Clacton in a charabanc, July 1924.*

visiting my parents' home in The Street, we timed it to leave at about five o'clock pm, so that we could walk up to the iron gate where the allotments still are, and get a good view of the latest train, the Fenman, travelling to East Anglia. It was thrilling for my young sons.

Road

Rose also has very clear memories of the road traffic on The Street:

The buses that I first remember were open-top double-deckers, running from Epping to Bishop's Stortford. It was nice riding on the top deck when the weather was fine. Then came the low-deck National Buses, also running the same route, and competing with them was a smaller type of bus, brown in colour, called the People's Bus, running between Bishop's Stortford and Hertford. When my grandfather was staying with us in Thorley Street, his jacket sleeve got caught in the door, and thereafter our family nicknamed the bus the Pincher bus! The double-deckers still remained on the road, but only eventually ran only from Harlow New Town.

Then the Acme coach service started up between Bishop's Stortford and Victoria, London. One could buy a return ticket for about 1 shilling and 6 pence in the old money. A rival coach service, the Green Line, ran from Bishop's Stortford first to Liverpool Street and later to Aldgate, but the fare was slightly dearer – 1 shilling and 11 pence.

Then there was the charabanc, a low coach, that would do a day's excursion trip to the seaside. One of the summer treats for all the villagers was a trip to Clacton-on-Sea.

The roads in those days were nowhere near as busy as now. Very few Thorley villagers, apart from farmers and professional people, owned a car. Our neighbour, Policeman Reed, had a motorcycle side-car before he had his first Baby Austin Seven car. At weekends, we would see groups of about 50 cyclists riding through The Street. They were cycle-racing clubs from London, and they would meet up for refreshments at the Blue Café.

How different it used to be, when we children could play without fear in the London Road. We could spin our tops, play ball, trundle hoops – boys mostly with iron hoops and girls with wooden ones! Now and then we would hear a distant rumble, in time to scuttle on to the side when John Patten Steam Engines, usually two of them, would trundle

through The Street! The drivers with sooty black faces always gave us a friendly wave!

Jack Phillips remembers the London Road traffic. He says that steam engines used to travel up and down before the combustion engine became the menace it is today. Horses were still used to a great extent by local traders, and he remembers that they used to water them in what used to be called the horse pond at the junction of Southmill Road and London Road.
Edward Miller recalls that:

As children from the northern side of the parish, we went to school in town and caught the double-decker bus that used to turn round at the White Posts near Bird's Farm to pick us all up. We paid a fare of one penny and used to enjoy seeing the conductor pull the ticket from the ticket 'rack' and 'ping' it in the silver hole-punching machine attached to his belt.

George Bright says that there used to be double-decker gas buses that ran from Epping to the Bricklayers' Arms. It would be a journey of one hour and twenty minutes, but they would never stop at Thorley because they were always full up. They would invariably slow down on the incline at the Coach and Horses. The conductor would have to get out and run behind to the trailer which was hooked on the back, which had a retort on it full of red-hot coke that generated the gas needed to run the bus, and he would poke up the coke to keep the bus moving.

River

Many villagers recall the heavy cart-horses pulling the barges along the river tow-path. Sid Oxborrow and Rose Monk remember that:

The river was very busy when used by the horse-drawn barges that used to come up the Stort, laden with timber for William Hughes' timber yard. Two men were always in the team, one leading the horse, the other steering the barge. Nowadays only houseboats are seen on the river, and the lock gates are rarely opened. Rose remembers that one of their summer treats as a family was on a houseboat. She remembers too when the swinging bridge down by Twyford, which has now been replaced, really did swing!

The Streeter family's bull-nosed Morris outside Thorley Place, c.1925.

Brenda Pleasance (née Hockley) recalls:

The Roley Croak stream ran down the side of our garden in the Blocks in Thorley Street to the railway crossing via a twitchel alongside the Post Office garden, and then on to the river where we swam and where we could also paddle in the stream and have family picnics. The river was then kept quite clean because it was used as a waterway to transport goods and was therefore dredged frequently to ensure a clear way for barges.

Maurice Hockley adds:

Dredging cleared a central channel for navigation but introduced a danger for swimmers, as the floor of the river bed often contained a step. There was almost a tragic accident on one occasion when my mother, a non-swimmer, went into the water to rescue my sister who was being dragged down by a friend Valerie Chappell who had lost her footing.

The river was otherwise another playground for boys, especially for fishing for minnows which were kept in glass jars but always died within a few days. Frog-spawn was another annual collection process and it was usually found in the same place.

Brenda and Sid recall:

If a barge came along while we were playing by the river, or perhaps swimming under the bridge at Roley Croak, we would hurry along to Twyford Lock in Pig Lane to see the lock gates being opened and closed to let it go through, and sometimes we followed it to the next lock at Southmill. We used to watch for the lock keeper to cycle from Spellbrook to the lock at Twyford, because then we knew that a barge was coming.

Edward Miller tells us:

Just across the field from us was the boat-house at Southmill Lock from where very good rowing boats could be hired. From Southmill Lock my father or uncle would row the family up the delightful stretch of river to Twyford Lock where the water lilies used to grow.

Southmill Lock is the location from where Robin Dromard of Pig Lane runs his canoe club at the time of writing for children and adults.

Allotments

There used to be allotments in Thorley in several locations: across the lane from the cricket field, by Stone Hall and the fish-pond, along Thorley Lane behind Brook Farm and opposite Rumballs Farm, and in Thorley Street alongside the railway line. The 'big houses' such as Twyford House, the Rectory,

Thorley Place, Thorley House and Thorley Hall all had kitchen gardens, and the ordinary people of the parish all had plots somewhere for growing vegetables – which became a necessity during the war. Only the allotments in Thorley Street alongside the railway line remain in 2003.

Frank Warboys recalls that his father had three plots in the field opposite the cricket field and grew almost all the vegetables and fruit the family needed, including potatoes, carrots, swedes, parsnips, peas, lettuces, runner-beans, cabbages, cauliflowers, Brussels sprouts, onions, shallots, rhubarb, gooseberries, black, white and red currants, raspberries and strawberries. His mother used to bottle much of the fruit for winter use and salted down some of the crop of runner-beans. Potatoes were stored in sacks under the house stairs. As the eldest child, he did much of the necessary digging! Nearby plot-holders were Horace Barnard and Nathan Bird.

Maurice Hockley recalls that:

Most fathers in what was known as the Blocks in Thorley Street Estate tended the allotments by the railway. Thus we grew healthy on organic produce before we knew what the word meant. Albert Brewster, living next door to the allotments had two or three plots joined up and was always there. Percy Hockley (my father), Bert Bright (the railway signalman next door), Ted Shorter (next door on the other side), and Mr Dedman (who lived opposite) were all avid gardeners. I always enjoyed the potato harvest, seeing how many each plant produced, and the laying out to dry and the sacking process.

Scouting and Guides

Frank Warboys recalls the wartime Scout troop in Thorley:

During the war years and the incumbency of Revd G.R. Harding-Wood, a Thorley Scout troop was formed. Scoutmaster Astle ran the group which paraded on Monday evenings in the old schoolroom in a corner of the churchyard. Astle later had an assistant 'Scoutmaster', Miss Cooper. Activities ranged from tracking, fieldcraft, field cookery and – important in the war years – identifying aircraft types. The troop disbanded after the war.

Reg Jacobs, Scoutmaster for many years, recalls the history of the 1st Thorley (St James) Scout Group, in excerpts from an article for the church magazine:

The group was formed in January 1956 by the Rector, Revd S.E.F. Robinson, Cub Mistress, Beryl King and Scout Master, Peter Steggles. By March 1957 the group comprised 19 Cubs and 15 Scouts.

The first camp was at Marble Bridge Farm,

Thorley Cubs in the Scout Hall (formerly the village school classroom), early 1950s.

Left: *Scout leaders at camp, 1958. Left to right: ?, Revd Sydney Robinson, ?, Peter Steggles, Mr Pleasance, Jim Morton.*

Below, inset: *Jim Morton raising the flag, 1958.*

Left: *Jim Morton (left) and Peter Steggles.*

A group of Scouts, 1958.

Siddlesham, West Sussex, with equipment borrowed and transported by lorry. By the next year the parents' committee had raised enough money for their own equipment.

During 1960 John Bishop (1st Class Scout and Silver Cord) helped at the wedding of Princess Margaret and Mr Armstrong Jones. By 1961 the group had moved into the Scouts' own hut, which was previously the Thorley Working Men's Club and Village Hut.

In February 1965 the County Commissioner, Melville Ballsillie, presented four Queen's Scout certificates and badges to Michael Camp, John Charlish, David Loveday and Richard Robinson, and in 1967 the Scouts uniform changed from shorts, khaki shirts and BP hat to long trousers, green shirts and the beret. The old Village School was opened as

the new Thorley headquarters in April 1975.

In the early twenty-first century there are 200 members, and there is a long waiting list. The group has one Beaver colony, three Cub Scout packs, two Scout troops and a Venture unit. In May 2002, 1st Thorley Scout Group entered a tableau with a pirate theme on a decorated moving vehicle in the Bishop's Stortford carnival, and won first prize.

With great enthusiasm, Thorley Scouts organised the barbecue at the Rogation Sunday village fête in 2002 and the proceeds were donated for renovation of the Village Hut, now the Venture Scouts Hut.

After the Scout group, there soon followed the formation of a Girl Guides group, with Jo Wood from Twyford Lodge and Anne Lofts from the Old Rectory becoming presidents for the eastern and western areas respectively. For a number of years both Mr and Mrs Wood and Mr and Mrs Lofts hosted Girl Guide activities in fields at their homes.

Women's Institute party in the Village School, 1949/50. Pictured are: 1. ?, 2. Bessie Darnell, 3. Sarah Hammond, 4. ?, 5. ?, 6. Margery Clark, 7. Muriel Newman, 8. Mrs Gateley, 9. ?, 10. Hedley Dellow, 11. Dorothy Wood, 12. ?, 13. ?, 14. Connie Williams, 15. Mary Monk, 16. Mrs Pigram, 17. Alice Pateman, 18. ?, 19. ?, 20. ?, 21. ?, 22. ?, 23. Molly Hammond, 24. Cecil Warboys, 25. Mrs Warboys, 26. Molly Bird, 27. Mrs Bert Bird, 28. Elsie Foreman, 29. Vera Camp, 30. Michael Camp, 34. William (Pedlar) Hammond, 35. Yvonne Gover, 36. Ena ?, 37. Betty Brewster, 38. ?, 39. Bubbles Barker, 40. ?, 41. Bert Bird, 42. Jimmy Foreman, 43. Ernie Barker, 44. Ellen Brewster, 45. Mr Sargent, 46. ?, 47. ?, 48. ?, 49. Gordon Barker, 50. ?, 51. Dorothy Hammond, 52. Jean Hammond, 53. Joe Kimber, 54. ?, 55. Joan Hammond.

Above: *Youth Club members.* Left to right: *Elizabeth Somerville, Sue Clark, Sheila Taylor, Diana Martin, 1950s.*

Left: *Working Men's Club darts team in the Village Hut, early 1950s.* Left to right, back row: *Dick Clark, Gordon Barker, Michael Nelson, Jim Day, Herbert Brewster;* front row: *Ron Oxborrow, Harry Brewster, Jim Knight, George Clark.*

Clubs

After the Second World War, the arrival in Thorley of Revd Sydney Robinson brought to the village perhaps an air of adventure into new horizons. He arrived at a time, just as war ended, when lives had been turned upside down. He was, as Miss Beryl had been, full of energy and impetus for good in the village. In a word, wherever the action was, there also was the Reverend. Wartime children were now teenagers, and this became a time of fêtes, amateur dramatics and fun. New groups and clubs were formed, often inspired or facilitated by the new church rector. The 'new ladies' appearing at that time, especially Mrs Wolfson in Thorley House, were there to support him in new ventures. Thorley's Festival of Britain programme of 1951 list the village activities going on that time:

Thorley badminton club; Reggie Newman, D. Miller, Roy Money.
Thorley British Legion branch; Revd Sydney Robinson, C. Sargent, Arthur Bird.
Thorley cricket club; Revd Sydney Robinson, Phil Akers.
Thorley band of change ringers; Revd Sydney Robinson, G. Newman, Tom Camp (captain).
Thorley amateur dramatic society (TADS); Jim Foreman, H. Dellow, Molly Bird.
Mothers' Union; Marjorie Robinson, Mrs Foreman.
Thorley Men's Club; Bert Bird, Fred Hatchett, Reggie Newman.
Women's Institute; Mrs B. Bird, Mrs D. Partridge, Gladys Warboys.
Thorley Football Club; Revd Sydney Robinson, P. Briers, Ron Oxborrow.
C of E Children's Society; Dorothy Wolfson.
Church Missionary Society; Mrs G. Watts.

Society for the Propagation of the Gospel (Jane Furze); Beryl Frere.

After the closure of the Village School, the old schoolroom and the Village Hut became the venues for club activities and gatherings such as socials, whist drives, Mothers' Union meetings, parties and wedding receptions. The British Legion, Thorley branch, also met in the Village Hut.

Dorothy Wolfson tells us of events in Thorley House:

In 1944, Thorley Women's Institute came into being, and we formed our first committee in the drawing-room of Thorley House. Later the Women's Institute Choir came there regularly for practice. Each year our church fêtes have been held in the garden, as well as fêtes in aid of the C of E Children's Society's Thorley Branch, of which I was secretary for many years. There have been Scout rallies and jumble sales also in the garden and the house, and the first Thorley tennis club also started on our lawn.

Tony Pigram recalls joining the Youth Club:

Mr Warboys and Jim Knight (Simon's father) ran the Youth Club. I started going when I was 15 or 16 years old, with friends Martin Sortwell, Johnny and Cliff Williams, Barbara and Sheila Taylor (who lived at Meadow Cottage), Sue Clark, Elizabeth Somerville, Angela Simpson, Jacqueline Barker, Pauline Harris, Richard Robinson, Michael Warboys, Hilary Smith, Terry Eley [sic], David Hale and John Morell, to name a few.
Michael Warboys formed a skiffle group, Johnny Williams played tea chest and broom handle, I had a guitar, and someone else played washboard and

thimbles. The Youth Club was held in the old hut which was then the Working Men's Club. I would go at 5 o'clock to light the 'tortoise' stoves that heated it, ready for a 7 o'clock start. We had a billiards table and dartboard, a record player, and a rota for tea making. We would bring our own records to play. Youth Club 'socials' were held, with some of our mothers helping out, including mine and Bubbles Barker.

Bubbles Barker recalls that a group of villagers, including Hilda and Geoff Brewster, Mary and Roy Money, Carol and Desmond Miller plus her and her husband Gordon, started a badminton club.

Children's Pastimes and Ghosts

Many villagers recall how they kept busy as children, starting with Tony Pigram:

I can remember riding Nobby, the last cart-horse at Butler's Hall, in the Mead, and I also used to catch newts in the pond in the Pikle. On Sunday mornings I used to go ferreting with Ben and Pimp Hammond, instead of church! The ferrets were Pimp's.

When the threshing tackle was working in the stack yard, we used to go over there with sticks after the rats and mice that ran out of the stacks. Dr Wallis from Bishop's Stortford would pay us for the rats – it was popularly believed that he used to eat them.

While still at school, Johnny Williams and I would go and help look after Mr Knight's pigs at Finchcroft. He used to go in his car and collect waste food (offal) from Hutley's in Hallingbury and fish heads from Hanks in Bishop's Stortford. We would ride in the back seat with the full buckets on our laps to stop them spilling!

I remember that my brother John Wick used to climb the beech tree in the church yard and sit up there for hours reading.

Sid Oxborrow:

At harvest time the grain stacks were built. I remember particularly those at Thorley Wash Farm, and others behind high elms in Thorley Street. Later in the year the threshing tackle would arrive. The stacks would disappear, and as they did, we boys with our sticks would chase the fleeing rats and mice.

When the shooting season started, one of the game-keepers, Frank Kinge or Ernie Hammond, would come to the school playground on a Friday afternoon, recruiting boys as beaters for the following day's shoot. I remember those often very cold November mornings, meeting at Thorley Hall Farm. We were given a stout stick each and our instructions. We were told, I remember, to walk in a straight line, not walk round anything in our way, be it a ditch full of water or the most dense of thickets and, of course, make as much noise as possible. At noon, or thereabouts, we had a break and were given bread and cheese, and ginger

This picture: *A group of children in their Sunday best outside Post Office Cottages, 1940s.*

Right: *Molly Bird leaning on a gate at Twyford Mill Farm, 1938.*

Bottom, inset: *Philippa Woodall in Walnut Walk, 1937.*

Left: *At Hayter's fête on the field behind the Coach and Horses, 1950s. From left: Len Wood, wife Hilda May, Bryan South, David Wood and cousin Pat Crocker.*

Below, inset: *Beryl Frere with protégés Sally Brewster, Malcolm Morris and Lawrence Karthauser at Latchmore Hall, 1950s.*

Far right: *Alan Threadgold with Great Gran Alice in 1941.*

Bottom right: *Leslie Threadgold with dog, early 1930s.*

Below: *Sarah Georgina and William John Hammond with twin daughters Joan and Jean, outside Old Cottages, early 1940s.*

beer or lemonade. At the end of the day we were paid up with a half-crown plus a rabbit (if we were lucky) to take home for the pot.

Brenda Pleasance:

At harvest time we all went out into the fields to glean what we could after the farmer [Mr Bird] had finished. The gleaned corn was used to feed the chickens that we depended on for eggs and also for making wheat wine which was very potent! Also, as the corn was cut, those men in the village that had a gun would wait for the rabbits to run out and shoot them; this made a welcome addition to wartime rations.

Rose Monk:

When my sister Beatrice and Winnie Barker (née Candy) were working for the Procters at the Old Rectory it was nothing for them to walk the two dogs Trixie and Betty on Sunday afternoons around Thorley footpaths, wet or fine, finishing in Thorley Wood, and if Frank Kinge was in the keeper's hut there, they would join him and his helping hand, Ernie Hammond, for a welcome cup of tea!

Edward Miller:

At harvest time I worked on Reggie Newman's farm at Butler's Hall. These were tremendously happy times, although hard work. At 12 years old the pay was one shilling per hour, going up a bit each year. My first 'pay-packet' was £1.16s.0d. (36 shillings) and I will never forget the thrill of receiving it. It seemed an enormous sum of money.

One job was to follow round setting up the sheaves into stooks to ripen off. This was back-breaking work and the secret was to set a steady pace. Then, perhaps in the middle of August, came the 'carting' phase, with loads being brought from the fields to the farmyard for making into stacks. After first being on the stack as middleman, the one who turned the sheaves the correct way for the stack maker, my regular job became that of unloading the cart loads of sheaves into the elevator. I loved this work. High on the load, throwing the sheaves crossways into the elevator to avoid damaging the ears of corn at the head of the sheaves.

I shared these good times with friends such as Reggie, a true gentleman and churchwarden at St James', Claude Mitchley, Cecil Warboys, Brian Sampford, Albert Clarke, Pimp, Ben and John Hammond and the foreman, Tom Seabrook (Muriel Newman's nephew).

Anon of Thorley recalls strange goings-on:

This is a true account of something that really happened, albeit some years ago.

Just like any lads of our age, my friends and I used to lark around in the lanes. So there we were, on a pleasant

autumn day walking through the Thorley countryside when, out of the blue (sky, that is) stones started raining down around us but not actually hitting us.

This happened on many occasions, sometimes by the River Stort, where we gathered in the evenings, or walking along a road in Thorley, and even when cycling home. When the stones hit the road, it was with such force that they broke into small pieces, but if any did happen to touch me, they felt like feathers. They never caused any injury to me or my friends, and we nicknamed our invisible but apparently harmless assailant the Goblin.

In addition to the raining stones, I had two further 'other worldly' experiences which we also attributed to the Goblin. The first was that, on more than one occasion, I found myself covered from head to foot in what can only be described as slime. I could be travelling in a car, just walking along, or once, as I remember clearly, I emerged from a public telephone box soaked with the stuff. The other odd happening was when some friends and I were in a spinney and, it being a cold evening, had a brazier going. The brazier was burning red hot and, as I turned away to gather some more fuel, it took off and went flying away through the trees. The Goblin also threw stones at me in places further afield, such as Derbyshire and Scotland.

These occurrences, both home and away, went on intermittently for some 18 months and then stopped as suddenly as they had begun. I was obviously puzzled by all this, but I can honestly say that I was never frightened... What do you think?

Jim Morton, brother of Margery Sampford, reports a strange hearsay story:

In January 1956 Thorley Youth Club had an outing to Finsbury Park Empire, and Peter Armstrong, who had just moved to Much Hadham from Thorley, rejoined his friends for the outing. Peter had a motorised bicycle, and on his way home along the Great Hadham Road, which was quite dark and lonely, he had got as far as Exnalls Cottages when he saw a plane coming towards him which was on fire. It came right overhead and crashed into a field behind Jobbers Wood. The extraordinary thing was that there was no noise at all, just an eerie silence, leaving him shocked, to say the least. Next week at the Youth Club he told his friends about his experience.

After a few enquiries, Win Barker, who had lived for many years in Chrysanthemum Cottage until her death in 1994, was able to verify what Peter had seen. She told him that her husband, Ron, had died in 1956. During the war years he used to do fire-watch duty. One night he was on duty as usual and Win thought she would take him a thermos of drink. The time was round about midnight, and as they were standing talking, a German plane came overhead, on fire, and crashed into a field behind Jobbers Wood. Win said it was exactly how Peter had described it.

Chapter 5

National Events

Red-Letter Days

Villagers recall how the people of Thorley enjoyed the happy occasions of national and royal events in the twentieth century.

Sid Oxborrow and Frank Warboys recall the silver jubilee:

In 1935, to celebrate the silver jubilee of King George V and Queen Mary, a fête was held on Thorley cricket field. Tom Streeter presented all the schoolchildren with commemorative jubilee mugs, a bottle of ginger beer and an orange. There were races, competitions, food and a huge bonfire. One of the main prizes of the day was a pedal tricycle, which [Frank recalls] was won by his brother Peter, about which he remembers being envious!

Rose Monk continues the story:

At the death of King George, Edward the eldest son would naturally have become the next king, but before the coronation and crowning he abdicated, and so his brother, the second eldest son of King George, came to the throne as King George VI with his wife, Elizabeth. Their coronation in May 1937 was celebrated throughout the country. Thorley village held an open-air celebration party on the cricket field; luckily it was a fine and sunny day. There were sports, a flower and vegetable show, and a roundabout for the smaller children.

Dorothy Wolfson recalls the Festival of Britain, June 10–18, 1951:

In 1951, after the Second World War, we organised a pageant in the garden of Thorley House to celebrate the Festival of Britain – the biggest event up to that date, for practically everyone in the village took part in it. We attempted in tableau form to give the history of Thorley from 1051–1951, and on a perfect June day, in the Festival of Britain year, it proved an enormous success. As a result we were able to raise a large sum for our 'Welcome Home Fund' for the returning servicemen and women.

Rose continues:

With the failing health of King George VI and his eventual death, his eldest daughter became the new Queen Elizabeth II.

The coronation of The Queen took place in June 1953. The day was disappointingly wet for the huge procession held in London. Most of the royal carriages were covered in, but one carriage was open topped, with the colourful, smiling Queen of Tonga waving to the crowds.

Here in Thorley the day was celebrated with the villagers being invited to go to the school, where a large screened television was rigged up. At that time not many people owned televisions. Some of the villagers of course heard the programme at home on the wireless. Incidentally the very first radio programme I heard was on earphones. It was a news bulletin, way back in the early 1920s.

Vera Camp and other villagers served refreshments since it was a three-hour programme, and so many people turned up to the tea that a second sitting had to be arranged. The children's tea was held in the Village Hut, which had been decorated for the occasion. All the children received a coronation mug.

Margery Sampford (née Morton) well recalls coronation day, as this marked the beginning of her courtship with Colin:

It was a miserable day (weather wise) and Colin had a motor bike so he took me home after the party. The week following, a Coronation Sports Day was held in the Valley Meadow. It was organised by Mr B.C. Mitchley and Gordon Barker, and over 100 children took part in the events. My brother, Jim Morton, then aged 12, won the obstacle race and his prize was an alarm clock which is still working to this day. In the evening a 25-foot-high bonfire was lit and there was a fireworks display.

Memorial service for Her late Majesty Queen Victoria, February 1901.

Festival of Britain pageant in Thorley House, 1951.

Joyce Griffiths remembers that she was working at the Snap factory in Twyford Road and helped make the coronation streamers, party hats and crackers that went all over England. Doug Collidge and Pamela Finch (née Wolfson) were fortunate to see the coronation procession at close quarters as it passed by them in Piccadilly. Doug worked at the Western Union Office, and got to work before 6.30a.m., before the route was cordoned off, and was given permission to leave his desk just in time to see Queen Salote of Tonga pass in her open-topped carriage. He remembers the day was particularly wet and hers was the only open carriage in a long procession.

Pamela was also in position, in a hotel overlooking Piccadilly, and says that 'what I remember of Her Royal Highness was that she looked so grand and pretty but quite pale due, my father thought, to the weight of her crown.'

On 5 June a special service was held at the Church of St James the Great, with the presentation of a new flag of St George. The parade was led by Hector Darnell and the standard bearer was Gordon Barker. The rector, Revd Sydney Robinson, addressed the congregation:

Today we have made a new beginning in the dedication of this St George's flag. It is the symbol of Christian faith and of Britain's greatness. It will be a constant reminder of the coronation.

World War Memories

Every Thorley household has wartime memories, actual and hearsay, of bombs dropping, of family members away from home, and of 'carrying on'

regardless of disruption and hardships. Those with memories today were children or young adults then, and they can recall the fear and excitement of those years and the changes that afterwards influenced their way of life and expectations. Nothing was ever the same again. Rose Monk, whose fiance, Frank, survived the Japanese prisoner-of-war camp and, as she says, 'luckily came home to us', writes:

One day, my friend Joan and I were in Sawbridgeworth when the siren sounded the air-raid warning. Some soldiers were standing outside The Gate public house. We did not know where to go, and they made us go round to the back of the pub where there was a dug-out trench. We stayed there until the all-clear. A dog fight between our Spitfires and German fighters was going on high in the sky, and we hoped the German planes were fought off.

After dark, all lights were blacked out by putting dark curtains or shutters on the windows. If anyone was out in the dark and using a torch, the light had to shine on the ground, and lights on vehicles were dimmed. Everyone was issued with gas masks that we carried in a cardboard box and slung over our shoulders; these were a protection in case of a chemical war attack.

Food rationing was in force, every household was issued with Ration books. Dockets were for household goods, such as utility blankets and sheets in dull colours; furniture was plain and wooden, and clothes had no style. Women in war work mostly dressed in trousers, and this has stayed the fashion in the present age.

The Warboys brothers Frank and Peter, who lived in Sunset Cottages near the Village School, recall wartime happenings. Frank begins:

Dad hired a battery radio in 1938 and we all heard Chamberlain's solemn announcements, and after listening to him, we crept into the garden and hid. We dared not go far in case there was an air raid or the Germans suddenly came! Not for many months did the sense of foreboding subside. It took real air-raid warnings and bombs actually dropping for us to realise that we were a small target and the Germans were not particularly interested in us.

Dad hired a radio again a year later and we listened with trepidation as the events leading up to September 1939 unfolded. When it became clear that war was coming, fear of air raids was the primary concern of every family. Dad dug a big hole in the garden at Sunset and fashioned a rudimentary air-raid shelter from wood, bricks and earth in an effort to protect his family. He also made wooden blackout boards for window protection. When war actually came, Dad managed somehow to acquire a radio permanently. It had two huge batteries, one 'dry' high-tension battery about eight inches by eight inches by two inches and one low-tension 'wet' acid accumulator which he had to take to work to recharge regularly.

Peter goes on:

I particularly remember the day in 1939 that war was declared, when I was nearly eight years old. I stood at our shared front garden gate with our next door neighbour 'Uncle' George Chappell and watched the fighter planes with black and white wings as they circled overhead. These were locally known as Debdens from their base near Saffron Walden.

There was one particular raid in which a stick or line of bombs was dropped about 200 yards from our house across the cricket field and on towards Bishop's Stortford. The deep craters filled with water and were highly dangerous. One plane crashed near Butler's Hall and another in the river meadows. The sky was also lit up one night by incendiary bombs dropped on Millar's factory and the timber yard. We had wooden shutters on our kitchen window, the only room used in the evening, and no lights were allowed upstairs. Towards the end of the war the V1s or doodlebugs were most frightening as one listened for their engines to cut out and the flying bomb to fall to the ground. The nearest one fell near Exnalls Farm about two miles away as the crow flies while we were outside the church one afternoon, and it sounded as though it was in the next field.

Troops occasionally visited the village on manoeuvres and dug gun emplacements in the first Valley. The area to the west of the village by Mathams Wood became an airfield, the perimeter fence running behind the paigle meadow, with a pillbox in the fence, and an ammunition dump in the spinney at Henley Herne spring. We used to watch for any activity at the airfield from the top of the straw in the Dutch barn at Moor Hall. Also the American planes used to come over very low as they took off from Stansted with their heavy bomb loads.

Frank, at age 13, started a diary, giving a child's perspective of family life during the war years. These few excerpts will remind others of those years:

Thursday Sep. 3 1942: Today the war has been going on for three years. I decided to take five [home bred] baby rabbits to market. They fetched one shilling and seven pence each. I went to Long Field today to 'drive away' for Uncle Bert [Bird].

Sunday Sep. 13: Today Michael [his youngest brother, born 30 July 1942] was christened at 4p.m. Present were Mum and Dad, me, Peter, Cecil, Barbara, Molly [Bird], Miss [Pam] Streeter, Auntie Dot [Bird], Uncle Bert [Bird], Mr [Cyril] Kirk and of course the rector [Revd GR Harding Wood] and Michael.

Thursday Jan. 14 1943: Today when I woke up the wind was shrieking round the house and the rain lashing on the windows... Mum came up with a cup of tea, put the black out up and lit a candle... Later I took Muff [a rabbit he had bred] to the market. On the way I saw that the river was flooded and the lower part of the field in front of Uncle Bert's house [Twyford Mill Farm] was flooded three feet deep. In the afternoon I went to collect the money for Muff. I was handed a 10 shilling note!

Monday Jan. 18: Last day of my Christmas school holidays. Last night there was terrific gunfire over London. It started about 8p.m., about ten minutes after our siren went. The firing was incessant for about two hours; shells, gun flashes and flaming onions filled the sky over London way. This was evidently a reprisal for our raid on Berlin. 8.30pm... we have just had another one and a half hour alert. We could hear planes heading towards the Midlands.

Thursday Jul. 29: On Sunday July 25 at 8a.m. I went to my first communion. I remember the Bishop had said that we should probably live to the year 2000, and it was not so much the first communion as the last, which mattered.

Thursday Oct. 26: The siren has sounded eight nights running.

Monday Nov. 8: On the way down to Twyford we saw some Italian prisoners of war working in a field of sugar beet. They were singing lustily and Joan [Brewster] who was also working there said that they had been singing all day... There has been an air raid almost every night lately.

Thursday Nov. 11: Mrs Streeter came round this morning selling poppies. I bought a three pence one.

Sunday Apr. 23 1944: Mum and Dad went to a parochial church meeting. Dad was voted onto the parochial church council, and so were Tom Camp and Mrs Wolfson. Today is St George's Day. It has been proclaimed by the Archbishop of Canterbury and York as a national day of prayer for the second front. We had special prayers and appropriate hymns and psalms, and we sang God save the King in the service.

Thursday Apr. 27: When tea was finished, I went down to Mrs Hadaway's [the village shop] to get Dad a packet of cigarettes.

Sunday Jun. 4: Peter and I went for a walk down to Ann Lane Spring. When we were nearly there, we suddenly saw on the Blounts Farm airfield a terrific sheet of flame combined with a huge volume of smoke and then the sharp crack of an explosion. Tonight we learned that it was a plane which had crash-landed with a load of bombs which blew up. It gave us quite a fright. If I hadn't had my best clothes on, I would have lain down flat.

Monday Jun. 19: Now that the second front has started, the Germans are sending over a new weapon which they have invented – a pilotless plane. It is believed that they are jet propelled. They are sent mainly over London. We had a 10 hour siren alert the other night because of these things about. I felt quite bad when I first heard them.

Sunday Jul. 23: The doodlebugs are still pretty bad. They don't seem to be able to do much about them except shoot them into the sea. When so many come over, it is impossible to shoot them all down.

Peggy Robinson (née Harris), who lived in the Butler's Hall hamlet, also remembered the bombs and planes that came down in the fields of the Uplands farms:

A spitfire was shot down in Double Gate, and a pilot from the Commonwealth killed. Parts of it were in the pond for a long time, and Tony Pigram dug up bullets at the crash site. Wreckage was found by Pimp and Ben Hammond when they were cutting the field with a binder, and John Hammond and Albert Clark, who were setting up stooks, found a wheel from the plane.

A bomb fell on the field later to become the cricket field opposite Thorley Place, which meant that school was closed and there was a prolonged holiday for the Uplands children, while the 'Lowlands' children went to school temporarily set up in Thorley House.

A bomb also fell on Double Gate, near Fairview Cottage, where Joan Hammond and her Mum were potato picking. The Army came to detonate it the next day.

Later there was a doodlebug that landed at Exnalls Farm.

Children would rush to the scenes of air crashes to fish out of the wreckage any trophies they could find, like shrapnel, blood on a parachute, etc. Pamela Finch's godmother and son once went inside the cockpit of a Heinkel bomber that went down on Hatfield Heath.

Albie Camp, whose family also lived in the Uplands in Moor Hall Lane, recalls the night when he helped his father put out the fires:

During the early part of the Second World War, the Army were in Mathams Wood. They had pillboxes on the outside in case of the enemy. One night early in the 1940s a bomb was dropped near Moor Hall Cottages. The Germans had dropped a Molotov basket of incendiary bombs which lit up the sky for miles away. My father woke me up to help him put the fires out, in case the Germans came back again.

Villagers in The Street and Twyford also recall war stories. One villager is Maurice Hockley:

I can remember sleeping in the shelter in the front room. The first Christmas present that I can remember was made in wood by George Brewster who was lodging in the house for a while during the war, with his wife Win.

At the age of four I can recall a doodlebug passing overhead in daylight and, with other children, vainly attempting to track down its landing place. I can also recall the sky full of planes and gliders, presumably on their way to assist the invasion of Normandy.

There were frequent convoys on the A11 with tanks rolling on their tracks (no carriers). American GIs were much in evidence, offering gum and sweets to the children.

Harvest time held a compelling fascination for me as a child and, during the latter stages of the war, there was frequent friendly contact with German POWs who were deployed in the fields. The children, generally innocent of the ravages of war, had no fear of these 'foreign' soldiers and were at ease in their company.

Bryan South (whose uncle used to be responsible for taking POWs to work on the Thorley farms), Len Wood, Ian Reedman, Brenda Hockley and other youngsters in the Blocks recall the same events:

Ian's mother, Mrs Reedman, was given responsibility for keeping the pump going when the wind didn't blow enough to keep the windmill going during the Second World War. She had a precious gallon of petrol to get the generator going when necessary. On one occasion she mistook it for paraffin and took it to light a fire in the bedroom. She was often seen dashing up to the windpump to put the belt back on the generator when it had slipped off. She would also invariably run out into the road when she heard troops going by to give them cups of tea – often in her bare feet.

When a German plane crash landed in a field at Thorley Wash, everyone in the area rushed down there. It broke up into three parts, and Bryan and Len later used to play on the inflated tyres. Evidence of the wreckage can still be seen there, since an oily patch shows through when the field floods.

A pillbox shelter was built in the field at the corner of Pig Lane and London Road, and an anti-aircraft gun was mounted on the grassed area between Burleigh Road (Proctors Way) and London Road.

Molly Bird, who lived with her parents in Twyford Mill Farm, remembers that her mother took pity on the German and Italian POWs working for her father and would make them rabbit stew. One of them never forgot and when he went back home after the war he sent them a sewing workbox he had made for her mother and some slippers for her.

Edward Miller, who lived on the northern boundary of the Birds' farm, recalls:

I remember especially the fear caused by the warning siren and the relief of the 'all clear' siren – heard from within the Morrison shelter, and the fear of seeing a 'doodlebug' heading westward, to crash at Exnalls Farm in the spring of 1945, I believe. Then there were the tanks awaiting repair, which were parked in the gravel-pit grounds, in the area where the Boys' High School is now, and seeing them being driven to Featherby's (as Millar's Works was then known) for repair, ridging the road with their heavy tracks as they moved along.

Mary Sampford, in Old Police Cottage next door to the Stoakes family, remembers when a bomb landed in the allotments opposite. They thought it hadn't gone off, but it had exploded under the ground. It cut off the water-supply to the cottage and they had to walk a quarter of a mile to get to a pump. Rose's parents, sister and her baby son, who were living in The Street at that time, were evacuated until it was safe to return.

Flossie Monk recalls the bomb on the allotments:

My father was a keen gardener of vegetables and proudly kept his allotment completely weed free, but the bomb targeted his allotment (not the others alongside full of weeds and seedy grass), and blasted his cauli-flower and cabbages out of the ground and they landed in a heap, upside down with stalks in the air. It was an amusing family story, but my father was very annoyed!

Ron Oxborrow, of 2 Thorley Street, near the Coach and Horses, remembers when a bomb dropped in Joyce Harris' garden next door (Rockdale) and didn't explode. Mrs Hudgell, who couldn't easily get about, lived with her niece in a nearby cottage, and so Charlie Harris put the old lady in his wheelbarrow and ran with her down The Street, to what destina-tion no one knows!

Wartime plane crashes in the area, both German and British, have since been officially documented, and copies of these records have been kept by John Monk, Rose's brother-in-law, in his extensive files about events in Thorley, and also by Ian Pinder. These records include the shooting down of a Heinkel at Thorley Wash on 19 September 1940, the crash of a Junkers with a full bomb load on board on the Great Hadham Road on 16 October 1940, the crash of a Spitfire at Butler's Hall on 5 October 1941 (pilot survived), the crash of a Spitfire north of Sawbridgeworth on 3 June 1943, and the crash of a Mustang also north of Sawbridgeworth, on 24 November 1943.

Wartime Work and Evacuees

Rose Monk heard that in the First World War the village people were called up for war work on the land and for work in a nearby factory. Women and girls knitted woollens for the soldiers in khaki-colour wool to match up with their uniforms.

Jack Phillips has earlier memories of Twyford House in the First World War:

During the Great War, the women of the village used to gather with their children at the home of Mr and Mrs Frere whilst their husbands were away serving in the Forces. I remember vaguely these gatherings and remember too how, when I was particularly objection-able, my mother used to tell me she would get Mrs Frere to deal with me. I never really understood what that action might have been, as my impression had always been that Mrs Frere was quite a nice lady and no real threat.

Rose continues her story:

The Second World War is, however, more clearly remembered. The call-up was of all young people from the age of 21 years, even up to 40/50 years of age. We villagers had to register. People working already in factories were exempted. Our local factory was Millar's. Some people were called up for the Land Army, which was most important because the land had to be tilled and sown to help the food crisis. Young men and women were also called up for the Services in this country or abroad.

The job I did during the war for the war effort was at HA & D Taylors in the Maltings, as it was known in those days. Now the building is Triad in South Mill Road. We, the workers, were young girls, married or single, and we replaced the men who were called up for the Services. The work consisted of turning the barley, using wooden forks and wooden spades. The barley was coarse-grained when first brought into the Maltings, and eventually it was transferred to the kilns and was roasted. The barley was then bagged up and went to the breweries and consequently into beers, mainly lager beer.

Many of the beers were for the Forces, but some, however, was made into the malted milk and Diamalt that we women were issued with, these being very nutritious. We had to wear a special type of string-soled canvas boot. All told, the job was hard work.

Villagers recall that the Frere family helped very actively helping with the war effort. Molly Lambert (née Bird) recalls that Twyford House was used as a maternity home for expectant mothers, mostly from London, and some 693 babies were born there during the wartime period. Pig Lane became known locally at that time as Pudding Lane. Beryl Frere used to billet the mothers and babies on the farmers around, and Molly remembers her mother taking some of them in.

Brenda Pleasance (née Hockley) recalls a visit to Premier Court Nursing Home:

When I visited Sister Emma Simonson, who was a midwife at Rye Street hospital and delivered my son, we realised that she actually worked at Twyford House as a midwife during the war and knew the Wolfsons and the Misses Frere very well. Sister Emma died last year [2002], aged 101, a year older than Gladys Warboys, whose room used to be opposite.

Sandy Halford recently met a wartime 'baby':

On our recent trip to Sydney, Australia, we looked up an old classmate, Chris Pacey, from my husband's school in Snaresbrook, last seen in 1958. To our surprise he told us that he had been born in Twyford House in Pig Lane. This coincidence was even greater when we told him we lived in Pig Lane, and he was impressed to see from a photo we had how grand his birthplace had been.

Pam Finch (née Wolfson) and Alan Threadgold recall:

Beryl Frere was the billeting officer, carrying out a task needing much time and sympathy, and when she left Twyford House to move into Latchmore Hall (says Pam) she asked me to take over her work. Miss Beryl (says Alan) wrote to his father in 1940 that his mother was one of the most popular billets she had, and she had also written that '600 more [evacuees] are coming in tonight.'

Rose Monk recalls the fate of evacuees:

It was sad for the children evacuated from the cities. Some woe-begone youngsters coming from the cities to the country, and into an entirely strange environment, found it difficult. My parents' evacuee was a little girl called Gladys; she was so shy and became very lonely, so the people of the WVS sent her to a family where there were more children.

Villagers remember other evacuees, and so far those brought to mind are: Cathy Black, who stayed with the Wright family in Thorley Street; the Camino family, who stayed with Mrs Tucker in the Blocks; Rita Teitz and Joyce Parkin, two girls also staying in the Blocks, with the Wood family; and Virginia Wade Bain, who stayed with the Wolfsons. There were several reports of fatalities of evacuee children. At Easter in the 1940s, two girls cycling from Epping stopped at Thorley Wash Farm and waved to squaddies on a passing train, one of whom randomly fired across the field. Tragically his stray bullet killed one girl. An evacuee schoolgirl called Murray was killed in a road accident at the junction of Thorley Lane and the A11, possibly in 1940, when she was sent home to Burley Road to fetch her forgotten gas mask.

For two evacuee children, Thorley holds special memories, as a Chronicles Supplement will fully recall. Peter Teitz tells us:

I had never seen the country before. I stayed first with Mr and Mrs Wood, but Mrs Wood wanted someone to help with the washing for the Streeters, so I went to stay with Mr and Mrs Sampford in a beautiful cottage near the mill. Then I went to Thorley House and stayed with the kind of people I had never met before, and then to Mr and Mrs Barker, whose only son had magnificent toys. Finally I went to Mr and Mrs Clark with my brother.

Michael Teitz writes from California:

During the early years of the war, my sisters, Betty

Left: *Virginia Wade Bain at Thorley House, 1951.*

Above: *Evacuee Cathy Black, with Les Threadgold (on left) and Fred Wright, air-raid warden, 1940s.*

Right: *Evacuee family Heather, Rosemary and Myrtle Camino, with Mrs Tucker at No. 1 Block 1 (now 2 Highland Road), 1940s.*

Left: *Pam Wolfson (on left)* with *evacuees Betty and Millie Teitz, 1940s.*

Right: *Bomb crater on the cricket field, with view of Thorley Place, 1940s.*

and Mil, and my brother, Peter David, and I were evacuated from the Blitz in London, but of how we first came to Thorley, I have no recollection. My brother and I were with the Wolfsons for a while at Thorley House, before going to live with Albert and Annie Clark at Butler's Hall Cottages.

The period at Thorley House showed me another world, one in which there were large and beautiful gardens, and above all safety. I would go into the vegetable garden to talk with Tom Camp, who showed me how to catch rats – and what to do with them – and who took me up into the apple barn, with its rows of apples laid out for storage, none touching the other. He was an understanding man and kind to children. My stay there must have been during winter, for I remember waking up one morning to snow, and seeing Mark, Pamela, and David rolling a huge snowball around the lawn.

Mr and Mrs Clark treated me as their own. We would hear about war on the BBC news, to which the Clarks would listen twice a day, conserving their scarce radio batteries. We would see headlines in the Daily Express, which Mr Clark read every day after tea. For a while, though, the only direct manifestations of war were the fighters taking off from the temporary airfield near Sawbridgeworth and from Stansted airfield. One day an unexploded bomb landed in the cricket field, not far from the school. Eventually, it was detonated, and of course we all went to look at the site of the filled-in crater. The underlying chalk had been thrown up, making a white circle in the field. We looked for bits, but couldn't find anything.

Every so often the war would come very close. One day, there was a great explosion and we learned that a British fighter had crashed and exploded in a field near Butler's Hall, near the cart track to the Green Man. The place of impact was blackened and rough. We looked for pieces of wreckage, of which some fragments were still to be found, and sadly my brother found more than that under a clod of earth. I did not look.

One morning, we all listened to the news of the breakthrough at El Alamein. Somehow, I sensed a turning-point, perhaps from the expressions of the grown-ups. Monty became our hero.

Then, we began to hear about the V1s, the flying bombs or 'doodlebugs', which were landing on

London. We learned how they looked and worked, and what to listen for – the dying 'putt putt' of the motor, followed by silence then the explosion. One afternoon, the concept became reality when I was in the field in front of Butler's Hall Cottages. I heard that distinctive motor sound, knew what it was, and saw the shape – squat, with stubby wings and the distinctive motor above the fuselage – very low and seeming to come directly at me. A fighter, firing its guns, was chasing it. I simply stood there as it went almost overhead. The motor did not cut out and it crashed somewhere beyond the Green Man. As I ran in afterwards, Mrs Clark said that I looked 'white as a sheet'.

Not long after, while in another field, for the first time, I heard a different sound – a dull thud, followed by a rushing sound, something like a distant train. It was a V2 rocket landing almost 30 miles away in London. In the weeks that followed, we heard that sound often. Then, one morning, alone on the way to school, just before the Warboys' house, I heard the most tremendous sound. Out of the west, travelling towards Holland (though I did not know it at the time), came a huge fleet of Dakota transport planes pulling gliders. Every plane and glider had distinctive black-and-white stripes across its wings as a recognition device. Never before or since have I seen such an air fleet. I stood and watched it in awe, realising that something very important was happening. Now I know that it was the second wave going in to Arnhem for that ill-fated attempt to cross the Rhine in a bold stroke that would block the V2s. Many of the men in those planes I saw would never return.

During the later years, too, we began to see new people. The Americans, always generous with gum, would throw it to us from trucks as they went in convoy past the Green Man. We learned to ask, 'Got any gum, chum?' At Christmas one year, they gave a great party for children in Bishop's Stortford. Italian prisoners began to appear to help with the harvest, and we talked with them at length. My opinion of Italians was shaped by British attitudes towards their fighting quality, but I certainly liked them as people who would talk with children.

Finally, VE Day arrived and it was time to leave Thorley. Things were supposed to return to normal.

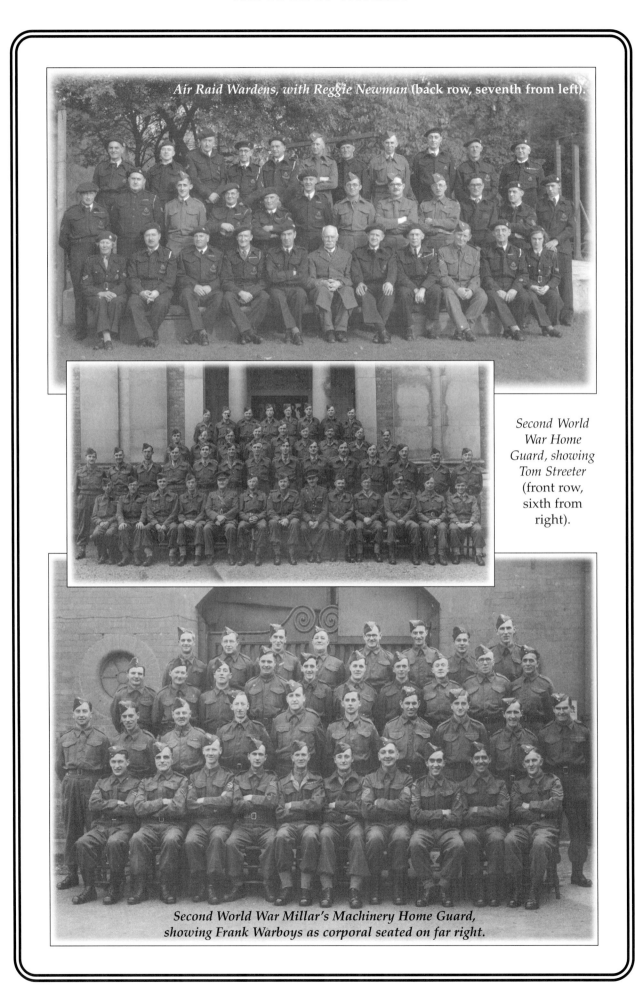

Air Raid Wardens, with Reggie Newman (back row, seventh from left).

Second World War Home Guard, showing Tom Streeter (front row, sixth from right).

Second World War Millar's Machinery Home Guard, showing Frank Warboys as corporal seated on far right.

The National Home Guard

The National Home Guard (Dad's Army) was crucial to the confidence of citizens across the country. Bob Crisp recalls some of those who joined up:

When the last war, 1939–45, broke out and the Home Guard was formed, Jim Akers joined and became a member of the Platoon that used Twyford Mill in Pig Lane near to the Frere mansion. At 15 I joined the Home Guard and was sent to the Mill to join up with Sgt Field's Platoon to train with Jim Akers, Tom Camp, Jack Bird, Mr Briers from the Coach and Horses, Frank Kinge from the Tanners Arms, Dick Abbot, Mr Sampford, Mr Rutland, Mr Brewster, Mr Pritchard and Mr Searle who worked in Edwards Mill. Other names I can't remember. Captain Tom Streeter was our commanding officer.

As time progressed the Home Guard improved and became more army efficient. Tom Streeter became Major Streeter and Company Commander. Home Guard HQ was held in Oxford House, White Posts, B/Stortford.

Sgt Field became in charge of Admin at HQ, Sgt Searle became the Sgt of my platoon, Lt Buzz (he was a bank manager) became C/O of our Company.

Jim Akers became Sgt Akers and moved to the HQ at the Drill Hall, signal section, B/Stortford, together with Lt Wilson (from Wilson's tobacconist in Bridge Street) an ex-Naval man and signals expert. The Home Guard had transformed from Dad's Army to quite an efficient force capable to assist regular Army units and disaster areas if required. I enjoyed every moment of it, it stood me in good stead when I was called up at 18 years old and found I had been well trained in the Army's ways.

There was an incident when incendiary bombs were dropped around the church in Thorley and the Home Guard patrol that night, which included Jim Akers and Frank Kinge (gamekeeper), assisted in putting the incendiaries out and preventing them from exploding and causing damage to the church. Also if an invasion had occurred the church spire would have been used by Jim Akers and the Home Guard signal section to receive messages.

Thorley Place, the home of Tom Streeter's family, allowed the Home Guard to use a room for the nightly guard that patrolled Thorley Lane from the Green Man to London Road (Thorley Street).

Casualties of the First World War

In an article in the church magazine it is recorded that at St James the Great Church there are two tangible reminders of those servicemen who died in two world wars. On the north nave wall in the church there is a memorial commemorating the names of those who made the sacrifice. A total of 20 servicemen are listed as having fallen in the First World War.

In the church archives is an account hand-written in 1919 by the rector, Canon J.E.I. Procter, detailing all those men who went from Thorley to take part in the 1914–1918 conflict. Each of the 103 servicemen has a page to himself with a record of where he lived, what

Memorial to those who served, 1914–19.

Peter Chappell, bearing Thorley's British Legion Standard in celebration of the amalgamation with the Bishop's Stortford branch in 1993. Col Vean is to the left of the flag.

Left: *George Sampford, 1917.*

Right: *James Akers.*

his pre-war employment was, which regiment he joined, where he saw action and the cause of this death – wounded, gassed, hospitalised, died in action or of his wounds. Often there is a transcript of the letter that the senior officer wrote to the next of kin telling of the circumstances of the soldier's death.

Of the many young Thorley men and women who joined up to fight in the Second World War, we have the space to publish only a selection of photographs.

In the First World War, two Thorley men were given awards for bravery. As recorded in Canon Procter's notebook, Major Charles Clark, of Moor Hall Cottages, was one of four brothers, all of whom died in action or on return from service. He went to Gallipoli on April 25th 1915, where he won the Military Cross for fixing wires and getting a message to headquarters. He was the first to land and almost the last to leave at the evacuation of the Peninsular. He was killed in action at Bienvilliers-au-Bois on 25 April 1918.

As reported in the *Herts and Essex Observer* of December 1983, Peter Chappell, of Thorley Street, who served in Kitchener's Army at the Battle of the Somme, died aged 89 without divulging to his family or Royal British Legion friends why he was awarded the Military Medal, one of the top bravery awards.

This publication can make mention of only a few of the fathers or sons of Thorley families who served in the First World War, some of whom died in action. Such brave men include George Harris, Hugh Harris, Arthur Threadgold and Bartle Frere; photographs of others appear above.

Pilot officer Leslie Threadgold (second from left) with his aircrew, 1940s.

Casualties of the Second World War

In the same article in the church magazine it is recorded that on the north nave wall in the church there is a second memorial commemorating the names of those who served and fell in the Second World War. The two men who died were George Reedman and Percy South. Percy died as a prisoner of war in Japanese hands and George fell in Tunisia.

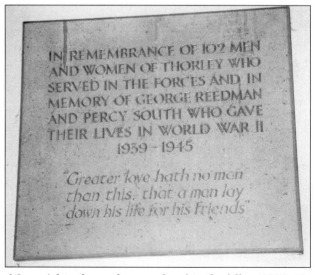

Memorial to those who served and to the fallen, 1939–45.

Right: *Tom, Clara and George Camp, 1940s.*

Phil Akers, RAF, 1941.

Above: *Henry Frank Monk, 2nd battalion Cambridgeshire Regiment, 1940s.*

Right: *Hilda Akers, WAAF, 1940.*

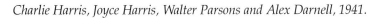

Charlie Harris, Joyce Harris, Walter Parsons and Alex Darnell, 1941.

Peggy Wright, 1942.

Stella and George Reedman with son Ian, 1940.

Ron Oxborrow and Spot the dog, 1940s.

Above: *Percy South with nephew Bryan on a motorbike, 1940.*

Right: *Frank Crabb accepts the British Legion banner from Revd Sydney Robinson, with Gordon Barker on the left.*

The Thorley Branch of The British Legion

David Philpott, in an article for the church magazine recorded that the Thorley branch of the British Legion was formed by a group of ex-servicemen living in Thorley in 1947. It contained four ex servicemen from the First World War: Jim Akers, Arthur Bird, Peter Chappell and Hector Darnell. The officers of the Thorley branch were Dr Patterson, president; A.F. Knight, chairman; K.E. Cook, secretary; and A.W. Bird, treasurer. Founder members included Charles Harris and Frank Crabb, and also Revd Sydney Robinson.

In its heyday there were over 100 members and they regularly paraded with the standard from the old school to St James' Church on Remembrance Sunday. Annually, thousands of pounds were raised through local collections for the Poppy Appeal. In 1971 the branch was granted a new Royal British Legion standard. This was presented to Frank Crabb in St James' Church by the Thorley branch padre, Revd Sydney Robinson.

Dwindling numbers caused the Thorley branch to disband in 1993. The last officers were David Philpott, president; D.V. Castle, chairman; J.A. Challis, secretary; D.M. Hickling, treasurer; and there were four branch members: R.E. Oxborrow, K.E. Cook, D. Miller and F.C. Lee. The branch standards have been laid up either side of the War Memorial in the church. Wreaths of poppies continue to be laid each November at the memorial by surviving members of the Thorley branch.

Left: *Thorley British Legion at the dedication of the War Memorial.* Pictured are, left to right: *Frank Monk, Frank Crabb, Phil Akers, James Akers, Fred Hatchett, Gordon Barker, Ron Oxborrow, Peter Chappell, Andrew Clark, Bert Bird, 'Sonny' Gilson;* front: *Arthur Bird and ?.*

Below: *Nibs Matthews at Twyford House, 1934.*

Claims to Fame and Infamy

Over the centuries, Thorley has produced its saints and sinners, or associations with the well known. Here we recall names from the last 100 years.

Sir Ivone Kirkpatrick identified and interrogated Hitler's deputy, Rudolph Hess, in Scotland in 1941. He rented Sparrow's Nest in Thorley Street from Commander Wolfson for three years during the war. Pamela Finch (née Wolfson), then 12 years old, remembers what happened:

During the night a big black car came up the gravel drive at 4a.m. and officials took off Mr Kirkpatrick. Violet, his wife, came to see my mother in a very distressed state. Neither knew where he was or what had happened. After three days he came home again. The news of Hess' crash-landing was all over the papers and my mother told me what had happened. Evidently he was the only man in Britain who could have identified Hess.

Kirkpatrick had been First Secretary to the British Embassy in Berlin from 1933–38, where he had met Hess. Churchill asked the Lord Chancellor, Lord Simon and Kirkpatrick to pose as psychiatrists when they interviewed Hess after his peace flight crash-landed in Scotland. Hess died, aged 93, in Spandau prison, Berlin.

Nibs Matthews *(above)* was director of the English Folk Dance and Song Society until retirement in 1985. Sidney Alfred Matthews (Nibs has no idea how he acquired the famous nickname) was born in 1920 in London, and grew up in Bishop's Stortford. Miss Beryl Frere, of Twyford House, recognised that Nibs was a natural dancer and he was soon having private lessons at Twyford House, where, accompanied on the piano by her mother, she would teach him Morris jigs. She also taught Nibs to swim, lifesaving, and later to drive a car, whilst her father taught him to row and scull. From this beginning Nibs went on to dance, teach and demonstrate all over England and in America.

Harry Roberts is still in prison for the crime of killing three police officers in London in 1963. He was caught in Thorley, which he had known as a child evacuee in wartime. Although villagers had noticed him as he walked openly about the village, shopped and travelled on the bus into town during the 95 days he was on the run and camping in Thorley Wood, no one had recognised him. Some had jokingly wondered if the bearded, untidy man seen about could have been the wanted man. He was captured almost by chance, when a local petty crime of theft was being followed up, and gypsies in the area, who were under suspicion, indignantly posed the question 'why couldn't the culprit be the strange fellow camping out in the wood?' A newspaper item, published in July 2003, reports that the parole board refuses to consider release, and that he has attempted to escape from prison 22 times over the past 37 years.

Arthur Negus was a television personality and expert on the BBC 'Antiques Roadshow' in the 1980s. Andy Streeter recalls the dismantling of Thorley Place on the death of his grandmother:

It was extremely sad when the contents of the house were sold by the famous firm of Bruton and Knowles in a two-day sale on 14th/15th July 1966. The catalogue was put together by the well-known television personality Arthur Negus, who was a partner in the firm at the time. He was a most charming and knowledgeable man.

James Frain is a young actor of talent having already become known in films and on television. His first screen part was in 'Shadowlands', starring Sir Anthony Hopkins, in the 1990s. He was brought up as a teenager in Butler's Hall, the eldest of eight children. The family is mourning the premature sad loss through illness of his father Paul, whose ashes are interred in the graveyard of St James' Church.

Canon John Matthias Procter and sister Miss Procter, with Mrs G. Streeter, (seated) holding eldest daughter Patience Mary, 1900.

Canon John Edward Ingleby Procter, 1924.

Chapter 6

The Church and Thorley Hall

Thorley Church (with no lych-gate), 1906.

We go first to the ancient church of St James and then to Thorley Hall, once the seat of the lords of the manor of Thorley.

St James the Great

The church and hall are both set in the middle of farm fields, barns and tied cottages. As written in Revd J.E.I. Procter's *Short Account of the Parish and Church*:

The Church of St James the Great dates from Norman times. The Chancel and Nave were built in the thirteenth century in the Early English style, but the Norman Font and Doorway suggest that the church existed at least as early as the twelfth century.

The Tower was added in the fifteenth century. Outside the Western Door is a Holy Water Stoup and the church contains three remarkable fourteenth century stepped sedilia, or priests' seats. In 1855 the church was thoroughly restored, chiefly at the expense of Mr Bartle John Laurie Frere of Twyford House, and at the same time the old Norman font, of Bethesden marble, which had been used as a horse trough at Thorley Hall, was returned to the church. At the south-east corner of the Nave is a list of rectors of Thorley from 1327, with the names painted on oak panels and given to the church by Mr George Skelton Streeter.

Thorley people give this description a personal touch. Grenville Bird begins:

Any visitor to Thorley church a few years ago couldn't help but be aware that pigs were reared in the nearby barn that has now been transformed into St Barnabas Centre. The smell coming from the pig barn is one I always associate with my earliest memories of Thorley church. Another early childhood memory is my grandfather showing me the stocks which stood in Thorley churchyard by the wall near the cart path. I must also mention Boris, the church cat. The black cat was always around to greet worshippers as they entered the lych-gate, and usually managed to get itself into wedding photographs. Boris was very much part of the church scene until he met with a bad end; he was savaged by the hounds as the hunt rode by. To this day it is held that there is always a black cat to be seen around the church.

Jack Phillips continues:

The lych-gate of the churchyard was made by Mr Alfred Currie, a skilled joiner, employed by Walter Lawrence of Sawbridgeworth. I remember watching him working on the gates at his home in Twyford Road. The gate was erected on behalf of Mrs Procter and her children in 1921 in memory of her husband, Revd Canon J.M. Procter.

Liz Eldred:

My Nan, Daisy (Annie) Hammond, used to clean the church for 2/6d. a week. No vacuum cleaners or 'miracle' polishes in those days, just hard work and elbow grease! The floor would be swept right through, the grates in the floor black-leaded and polished, the stone floor 'whitened', the pews and pulpit polished with wax polish, the hassocks beaten and brushed, and the brasswork made to shine. I can remember her telling me she used to fill the font, and before the days of piped water she used water from the pond nearby. She said it was holy water because it had come from heaven as rain.

Rectors

From 1883 to 1909 the rector of Thorley was Canon John Matthias Procter, who was very active in the community life of the parish. He played in Thorley's cricket and draughts teams, and judged the annual ploughing matches. He was also a prolific poet and hymn writer who more than once submitted his work to national celebrities, journals and newspapers.

From 1909 to 1937 his son, Canon John Edward Ingleby Procter, was the rector of Thorley, having been curate from 1890 to 1909. He too had a sincere sense of spiritual and social responsibility. Some time after 1923 he wrote his *Short Account of the Parish and Church*. Frank Warboys recalls that he often seemed:

Three reverends: Revd Sydney Robinson, Revd Alan Cole, Revd Clive Slaughter.

... remote, austere and authoritative, in spite of which he was kind. He owned Sunset Cottages [my home] and I suspect he was gracious about late rent payments when our mother and father were having financial difficulties.

Peter Warboys tells us that 'Canon John Procter was much revered, and as children we were told during the war that there was no doubt we would win as Canon Procter had said that Right must prevail.'

Between 1937 and 1946 the rectors were Revd Norman Ashby and Revd G.R. Harding-Wood, who were less popular. The 'doomsday' style of Revd Harding-Wood had a particular effect, and as Christmas neared Peter Warboys remembers praying that the 'end of the world' that the rector spoke about would not happen before Christmas.

From 1946 to 1979 the charismatic and energetic rector of Thorley was Canon Sydney E.F. Robinson, an ex-RAF chaplain, who arrived in Thorley and brought with him a different style of involvement in the community. He was a dedicated and tremendously popular rector, tireless in his work at St James'. He organised church fund-raising events to finance the conversion of the oil-lamps to electric lights (1947), to replace the boiler (1957), to restore the roof covering (1959), to install a new floor (1962) and to renew the spire (1966).

From 1980 to 1986, the rector was Revd Alan Cole, who in 1983 instigated the formation of the Friends of St James the Great and headed the project to run the Thorley Christian Centre in Thorley Park.

From 1988 to 2002 the rector of Thorley was Revd Clive Slaughter, who was in situ during the impressive conversion of the old pig barn into the new place of worship, St Barnabas. This was only made possible by the generous gift of Jean Papworth, owner of Stortford Park.

The first Thorley rector of the twenty-first century is Revd Bob Payne. On Rogation Sunday in 2003 he conducted a special service in St James' and revived the 'beating of the bounds' tradition to give a splendid start to the celebration.

Revd Sydney Robinson

Reggie and Muriel Newman, of Butler's Hall, wrote of Revd Robinson when he retired:

Sydney Robinson first came to Thorley when, as a young RAF padre, he was told by the Bishop of St Albans that there was a vacancy in the parish of Thorley. He walked from Bishop's Stortford station to the Old Rectory, borrowed a bicycle from a Land Girl and arrived at Butler's Hall, where Reg, one of the churchwardens, gave him lunch and introduced him to the church. He was inducted as rector in July 1946.

With a natural sense of humour, he quickly endeared himself to his parishioners, both in the church and in all the village clubs and societies of which he very soon became an active member... Ever with a mind for his church, the rector invited members of TADS to volunteer to sing in St James' and as a result round about 1950 the church choir was revived to continue under his direction with much success to this day.

He was a founder member of the Thorley branch of the Royal British Legion... and for the youth of the parish he formed a youth club, which held its meetings in the Village Hut and ran for several years from 1953 offering a varied programme to its members. The youth club members, with members of the church choir, much enjoyed the carol singing which the rector organised for the week preceding Christmas. No matter what the weather, all parts of the parish were visited.

A very notable achievement... was his founding of the Scout Troop and Cub Pack in the early '60s... A keen sportsman, he was a successful cricketer in the village XI, and enjoyed tennis and bowls and in more recent years... croquet. His presence here over 33 years has enriched the life of the parish.

Friends of St James'

Philip Hargrave, chairman of the Friends of St James the Great at the time of writing, records:

Our association was formed in 1983, at the instigation of Revd Alan Cole, under the chairmanship of Compton Whitworth, Parish Council chairman, who lived in Moor Hall, to assist the rector and parochial church council in maintaining and beautifying the church and churchyard, by raising funds through the organisation of events and membership subscriptions.

The first major project was the construction of a new north wall for the churchyard, which was completed in July 1986 when Revd Alan Cole placed in the wall a time capsule containing a record of how the wall was built, some coins and a copy of the parish church magazine.

The next landmark was the event in August 1987 that became the first of the annual Festivals of Flowers and Music held during the August Bank Holiday weekend. A total of £2,000 was raised towards an appeal for funds to carry out restoration of the font, stained-glass windows and the tower. The twelfth-century font has a turbulent history. Other projects have included a new kissing-gate, lightning protection, a new weather-vane and window restoration. The Friends website is a means of spreading information about the church, its activities and history to families who have moved away.

The Church Graveyard

As Revd J.M. Procter records:

In 1888 the 3rd Lord Ellenborough, landowner and Lord of the Manor, gave land that had been used as a stack-yard for an extension to the churchyard on the south side. Earlier, in about 1860, three dilapidated cottages towards the north-west corner of the churchyard were pulled down, and the Church Room built in their place by Revd Vander-Meulen. Near the south wall are the stocks and whipping post, which used to stand near the junction of Clay Lane with the London and Cambridge Road [and are now in Bishop's Stortford Museum].

Above: *The village stocks, which have been moved to Bishop's Stortford Museum.*

Left: *The Victorian schoolroom in a corner of the churchyard.*

Over the centuries, many Thorley families have been buried in St James' graveyard, and there are probably many Thorleyites like Gladys' son, Frank, who could say: 'If I stand in Thorley churchyard with my son and one of his children, there are six generations of the family within a stone's throw.'

There is not enough space to recount many family histories here. However, four gravestone pictures will recall a range of Thorley names from the recent past.

The gravestones of, clockwise from top left: *Revd Sydney Robinson (1915–90); Ursula Laurie Frere (1898–1963) and Beryl Laurie Frere (1901–75); little Rosie Loveridge (1954–57); Dorothy Wolfson (1890–1983).*

The Field Behind the Church

Ann Swan recalls, with feeling, a particular place and time in Thorley:

My parents Emily (Emmy) and Jimmy Loveridge and I lived in the field behind the church... in our caravan, from the mid-1930s to the late 1960s, along with my sisters Lena and Hilda and my brothers Fred and Nathan. Dad worked Thorley Hall Farm all the year round doing a variety of jobs. Mum, myself and my sisters would go to Coggeshall hoeing beet and pea picking and return to Thorley late July/early August to help out with harvest and potato picking. I met and married my husband Tony at Thorley. He worked at the farm as a tractor driver.

At the western side of the churchyard, next to the kissing-gate, a marble angel watches over the grave of little gypsy girl Rosie Loveridge, my niece, who died in 1957 aged three years. She was the granddaughter of Jimmy and Emmy.

Liz Eldred recalls:

Emmy used to call on my Nan for a cup of tea. She would always buy pegs from her and the wonderful roses she made from crêpe paper and wax. My Mum still had some of her pegs in use up until she died in 1990. Jimmy looked after the pigs at one time. I remember once he hung up his jacket and the pigs ate it!

Thorley Hall

Thorley Hall has a long history over the centuries, but here we must focus on most recent times.

Many villagers recall their associations with Thorley Hall and the farm. Rose Monk writes:

I have early recollections of working at Thorley Hall as a domestic help, employed by Mrs Tinney (senr), widow of John Tinney. The Tinneys had a large family of sons, Masters Reginald, Edgar, Arthur, Wilfrid, and Gordon (by second marriage). Each Christmas

Mrs Tinney had all the family at the house on Christmas Day, together with their families – a joyous day for them, but a working one for me!

When the shooting season came round, on a Saturday, most of the local farmers came in after the shoot for their meal in the hall kitchen. When they all left my job was to clean up – more muddy boots, I can assure you! The tips came in handy though!

Wilfrid married Dora French from a family of butchers and Edgar's daughter, Daphne, lived for a while in Stone Hall with her husband, Mr Cyril House.

Tom Camp recalled, in his own inimitable style of speaking:

Above: *Thorley Hall, 1834.*

Below: *Thorley Hall, 1965.*

Thorley Hall and stack-yard, 1911.

The moat around the hall used to come right up to the road, it's all been filled in. It's said that originally it used to go round the church as well. I mean all the old rubbish and all the sewage from the pigs and everything, it all went in that moat. It didn't smell very good at times as you can imagine. There was evidence of there being two ponds right round the back at the end of the churchyard. I know it used to be pretty bad round by the Dutch barn, I mean just mud and water. Then eventually it was concreted. This is where the main track down to Thorley Street used to be, down the Valley, it used to go straight down, across to Carpenters, and come out where the off-licence used to be and Mrs Groom's Post Office.

I first started working at Thorley Hall when I was a house boy aged 11. I was at school but I used to work every morning and every night and even Saturdays – the only free night I had was Sunday night. My jobs included cleaning shoes, chopping wood for the fires and doing the fires. I was paid about 7 shillings a week, which was quite a lot of money in those days. This would have been about 1930 and that was for the old Mr Tinney, Mr John Tinney, he used to be at Hatfield Heath, chapel man, and they always used to have bus loads of children come up here for their Sunday school treat. We used to give them a party, I mean he was very good with the church, people and children in the village. I can't remember his age, but he died quite youngish, he was quite a short man and very stout and I remember as a boy I often had to get down to do his shoes up or take his shoes off, he couldn't get down, you know, that was another job if I was there.

Jane Timmis who, with husband Richard and family, still lives in Thorley Hall:

We came to Thorley in 1976 and I think looking back over the years some of the happiest memories we have were [of times] spent with the Whitworths, the Lofts and Mrs Wolfson.

We usually spent part of Boxing Day at Moor Hall with Compton Whitworth, Isobel and Rodney. Isobel had a large box of postcards cut in half which she hid all over the house, and the children and Cynthia, their housekeeper, would race around trying to match them all up!

Bob and Anne Lofts always had a huge party after Christmas at the Old Rectory, with enormous amounts of food, and hundreds of people both local and professional, which was always a fun occasion. During our early years in Thorley there used to be events to look forward to. At Thorley Hall we used to host a Christmas and Summer Conservative party, and Mrs Wolfson used to hold the church fête at Thorley House. Later, Bob and Anne hosted the church fête at the Old Rectory for many years.

Another memorable occasion was not such fun. On October 24th 1979, we had a fire at Thorley Hall. The house was empty at the time and the poor painter was stripping paint off with a blow lamp when a spark went up in the parapet. Everyone on the farm was on hand to help. Mick Hill called the fire brigade which came I believe in four minutes, Tony Pigram went ahead of the fireman to show them where the fire was in the house. They all had breathing equipment, but of course poor Tony didn't and consequently got a lung full of smoke. We were extremely lucky and lost very little in the fire thanks to Tony, Liz, Colin and Mick. The fire brigade were there for three days trying to put it out, and we had tarpaulin on quite an area of the roof for a year. But fortunately no one was hurt.

The Pig Barn (St Barnabas)

Tom Camp, in words paraphrased by Liz, described the pig barn as it was before it was converted. After describing how the corn was reaped, tied into sheaves, stooked, pitched and carted to the barn, he went on:

The barn had two pairs of large doors opposite each other, so that a cart could be driven in, unloaded and driven out the other side. I remember my grandfather saying that all the corn was threshed on the floor (using flails), but in my time the threshing tackle would arrive and be set up in the barn with the elevator outside. The straw would be used for animal bedding, or the chaff-cutter would chop the straw into short lengths, to be used as part of the ration to feed the horses and cattle.

The barn was originally thatched but in my time it had tiles until these were replaced by corrugated tin when they became too much weight for the wooden beams. Later the tin was replaced by corrugated

Left: *The old pig barn at Thorley Hall Farm, Church Lane.*

Below: *St Barnabas Centre, 2000.*

aluminium – a very good rain indicator as you could hear the lightest shower.

There were other open barns across the yard from the main barn which housed the cattle in winter. These were later occupied by pigs. The barn at one time was also used to store implements, and it was later converted to a fattening house for the pigs. The adjoining low brick buildings which are now offices were the chaff store and stables for the cart-horses.

The other large barn in the yard was where the corn was stored after threshing and housed the grinder, which produced the wheat and barley meal used in the animal rations. There was also a mangel grinder which clipped the mangels for feeding to the cattle in winter.

When I was about 17 or 18 there was a plague of fleas on the farm. They were everywhere. We had two sets of clothes so that we could change before going home. I wasn't bitten much by them, but my mother was. We tried everything to get rid of them. The stables were lime washed, lime put down on the floors, and the barn was scrubbed down and treated with a mixture of creosote and paraffin. Then they all suddenly just decided to go away and they never came back!

Thorley Hall Cottages

These are two farm dwellings situated in Church Lane opposite St Barnabas. No. 1 Thorley Hall Cottages used to be inhabited by Mr Clark, who worked as horseman for the Pattens at Thorley Hall, and lived with wife Sarah Ann (Granny Clark) and children Ester (who later married Frank Monk's father Herbert) and her twin sister Ethel, Clara, Andrew (Drew) and Tom. When Mr Clark died, his family had to go to Thorley Houses, where Sarah Ann adopted the three Warman boys – Eric, Ernie and Frank. After them came the family of Harry Camp, who was a cowman at the farm.

Sarah Ann Clark at Thorley Hall Cottages, early 1920s.

Later, No. 1 was occupied by the family of Ernie Barker, who was farm foreman and whose son Gordon also went to the Village School. Afterwards in No. 1 came the Wick family: Dick Wick, farm foreman, with wife Dorothy, daughter Liz and two sons John and Tony (half-brother to John and Liz). Until recently, John Hammond lived at No. 1. He had to have part of both legs amputated, which obliged him to move to a sheltered home in the town, where he very happily resided until he died in April 2003.

In No. 2 Thorley Hall Cottages lived the family of Tom Clark, son of Sarah Ann Clark. He married Margery Hammond in 1938, worked on the farm in the 1940s, and lived in No. 2 until he retired to the London Road. Margery died in 1995, and is buried in the churchyard by the hedge next to Granny Hammond, who was buried on the same day. Her son Derek died in Linton in 2000.

No. 2 became the pig man's cottage. John Clark lived there with his wife Maud, son Stephen and daughter Sue. After the pigs were sold, Liz Eldred (née Wick) lived in No. 2 with her husband Dave until 1999 when they moved into White Cottage.

John Wick remembers life in Thorley Hall Cottages as a boy and young man:

Winters at Thorley Hall Cottages were long, dark and cold, the only heating being the living-room fire. Bedroom windows had to be scraped on the inside in order to see out, and the outside loo found by torchlight after dark.

Home entertainment was a radio. We also had a telephone, a party line with the farm, because of father's position, but as Liz recalls, often it was quicker to run across to the farm with a message than to try to wind up the instrument in order to tell the farm there was an incoming call.

Transport was 'shanks' pony' or a bicycle. Two things opened up our cloistered world – television and the motor cycle. Colin Sampford was the first to get a 'motor bike'. As soon as I had reached the legal age of 16 and had saved £75 I bought an AJS 350cc. The instant freedom of movement and stretching of horizons were wonderful.

My father having remarried quite soon after arriving in Thorley, to a local girl, Dolly Hammond, I gained a younger brother and soon a sister. My brother Tony [Pigram] and I grew up together and enjoyed the rural freedoms of the time, but Tony always seemed fated to be the one returning home the worse for wear. He got covered in wasp stings when retrieving a cricket ball from a ditch; found he had a Wellington boot full of blood during a knife-throwing contest; and one Christmas was hit by a gallon can serving as the target during an improvised clay-pigeon-shooting contest, which resulted in his head running with blood.

My full-time association with Thorley ended in 1955 when Her Majesty required my services in the RAF. Thorley has changed enormously but, as is often the case, the church is a bastion against change, and I find that if I sit quietly in the churchyard I can still indulge my nostalgia and conjure up the people and events that enriched my early years.

Liz recalls her own early life in the Uplands of Thorley:

Thorley Scouts marching past Thorley Hall Cottages.

When Mum was at work on the farm potato picking or bale carting, and before I started school, I would spend my days across the fields at No. 4 New Cottages, the home of my grandmother, Annie Hammond, known to everyone as Aunt Daisy. There I used to play in the garden and visit Mrs Lawford who lived next door but one in No. 2.

Mrs Lawford used to let me play for hours with her treadle sewing machine (after taking the needle out). I used to accompany her up to her allotment garden, where I remember masses of aquilegias growing, or 'granny's bonnets' as I called them. She kept chickens in hutches, and if I got impatient and opened the doors to see if there were any eggs, she would tell me 'snout ointment, tuppence a tin at Woolworths!'

I can remember washdays at my Nan's. The fire would be lit under the copper in the scullery, and the washing boiled up in it, with a 'Dolly Blue' washing cube, stirred occasionally with a copper stick (part of a broom handle) kept specially for the purpose. Then the washing was rinsed in a sink (one of the old white butler's sinks) before being taken out into the yard, roughly folded and put through the mangle to remove excess water.

All the cooking was done on an old kitchen range. It made the best toast ever. This is also where the flat irons were heated to do the ironing. No ironing-board, but a blanket and clean cloth spread on the kitchen table. I used to have my own miniature flat irons with which I was allowed to iron the handkerchiefs.

Nan kept chickens at the bottom of the garden, mostly for eggs, but occasionally a cockerel was dispatched for the 'pot'. I can remember seeing my Nan mending a cockerel's broken leg with a splint made of firewood and string.

My Nan was 'stone' deaf but always knew when there was a thunder-storm coming and would cover all the mirrors and take a chair and sit in the cupboard under the stairs until it was over.

Each afternoon she would sit me on the table and fetch a bowl of water, flannel and Lifebouy household soap, and I would have my face and hands washed and my hair brushed. The smell of that soap always takes me back to those days.

When I was home with my Mum, I would spend my time playing 'dressing up' with my friend Jane Barker, who lived just down the lane, or dressing up the cats in doll's clothes and pushing them around in my doll's pram.

Most of all I liked to 'go up the farm', and I grew up roaming the fields around Thorley Hall Farm. I enjoyed nothing more than helping out Dad with the sheep or being with my Mum when she was working there. It may sound like a lonely childhood but I loved it and wouldn't have changed it for the world. The men who worked on the farm were my friends, and later on my workmates.

That has all passed now, since there are no longer any sheep and there are no longer any farm workers residing on the farm. Life can be lonelier now.

The Croft

Before leaving Thorley Hall Cottages, we should note the white house, prominent at one end of the road bridge that Church Lane has now become across the bypass. The house was built for Mick and Hope Hill, when Mick arrived in Thorley as farm manager for the Tinneys. Mick died soon after he retired, although Hope still lives at The Croft.

And now we take the farm track behind the church to walk further on into the Uplands and arrive at Moor Hall. This is the sister farm to Thorley Hall.

Above: *The wedding of Marjorie Hammond and Tom Clark, with bridesmaids Joan and Jean, 1938.*

Chapter 7

The Uplands Farms

Moor Hall Farmhouse, 1900s.

Here we visit the Tinney and Streeter farms in Butler's Hall and Moor Hall Lanes, and the cottages that house their tenants and farm workers.

The Uplands

The Uplands are the farming areas around and beyond the church to the west and the north, also taking in Thorley Common. There were a good many Upland farms at one time, but at the time of writing there are only three working farms: Moor Hall and Thorley Hall, which are owned and managed as one by the Tinney family, and Butler's Hall, owned and managed by the Streeter family.

Moor Hall Farm

Rose Monk and Liz Eldred together recall the tenancies of Moor Hall:

The tenant of Moor Hall before the Second World War was Reggie Newman, who afterwards moved to Butler's Hall. Then came Captain and Mrs Elliott, who kept very noisy peacocks and hens. They had two daughters, Elizabeth and Ann, and a son Richard, who all went to boarding-school. The girls played the

violin. Mrs Elliott ran the WI group and held the afternoon meetings in Moor Hall, but as she always only put one piece of coal on the fire at a time, in wintertime it was very cold and the meetings were short! In the holidays, Richard used to play cricket in chicken field, and on one memorable occasion hit Phil Akers in the mouth with the ball.

After the Elliotts moved to Somerset, the Hall was let in 1947 to two ladies, Mrs Budd and companion, who kept open house for American officers when they were on leave.

Then came farm manager, Roy Money, until 1956, and afterwards, Mr and Mrs Brooks, followed by Compton and Isobel Whitworth with their two sons, one of whom sadly died young, and with housekeeper Cynthia Knott. After many years in Moor Hall, the Whitworths moved away to Suffolk in the mid-1990s and then came a brief stay in Moor Hall by the Beer family of Black Cottage. John Tinney's son David then moved into Moor Hall with wife Sally and carried out extensive renovation to house and gardens where the tennis-court was once located.

Cynthia, always a familiar figure on her bicycle in the village, accompanied the Whitworths and

85

Above: *Mr Newman senr* (middle row, third from left), *Revd Procter* (middle row, fourth from left) *and Reggie Newman* (back row, far left) *with farm workers at Moor Hall.*

Left: *Compton and Isobel Whitworth, in the yard of Moor Hall, 1990s.*

Below: *Cynthia Knott in Moor Hall kitchen, 1990.*

their dachshunds, Fergie and Hervey, to Walsham le Willows, where sadly Isobel died shortly after the move.

The Whitworths were very public-spirited and quintessentially English, and they lived in charming old-fashioned style. Compton was chairman of the Parish Council during the awful years of village confrontation with planners and developers intent on building thousands of new houses south-west of the town and a ring road through the parish. Although of advancing years, Compton fearlessly takes cruises and travels afar to see his many friends.

Roy Money lists the names of the Thorley villagers working on the Tinney farms and recalls the time when his family was part of village life:

We moved to Moor Hall in 1947 as manager of the Thorley farms, on the death of Wilfrid Tinney's brother Edgar. Working on these farms at that time were many villagers I got to know well.

On Thorley Hall Farm there were Ernest Barker (foreman), Ted Threadgold, John Clark, Horace Barnard, Tom Clark, George Chappell and George Clark. On Moor Hall Farm there were Alf Camp, Nathan Bird, Jack Bird and Harry Prior. On Piggott's Farm there were Frank Vale (foreman), Ernie Vale and the Owers family, father and two sons, Fred and Ron.

Ernest Barker retired in 1948 and was replaced by Dick Wick. Colin Sampford joined the staff when George Clark left. Frank Vale retired in the early 1950s and was replaced by Ernie Vale, and Colin's future father-in-law joined Piggott's staff.

Doll (Liz's Mum) and Bubbles (Gordon Barker's wife) also worked on the farms, mostly picking peas

and harvesting and grading all the potatoes that were grown.

The land for the extension to the church graveyard was given by Mr Tinney (senr) shortly after the end of the war. The main water-supply pipe to the Uplands area was installed in about 1950 going across the fields from Thorley Hall to Moor Hall and on to Butler's Hall.

Thorley was a very pleasant quiet village to live in in those days, with a thriving Men's Club in the Village Hut next to the school. We had a very good football and cricket team.

The village fête was held annually in the field by White Cottage, and when the village school closed we used it to play badminton in. My wife Mary was secretary of the WI for most of the years we lived at Moor Hall, with Pam Finch's mother (Dorothy Wolfson) as president and Gladys Warboys as treasurer.

Moor Hall Cottages

Along the lane are two tied cottages, occupied at the time of writing by Tony Pigram with wife Molly in No. 1, and Colin Sampford with wife Margery (née Morton) in No. 2. Both Tony and Colin have retired from working on the Tinney farms.

Tony, half-brother of Liz, is married to Molly, called the lady with the white dogs since she started keeping samoyeds in 1955 on the Twyford Park estate before her marriage. Colin was born in Millers Cottage in Pig Lane and went to the Village School. His mother Mary, aged 90, still lives in Thorley Street. One anecdote about Colin, as recalled by Mary, is that as a child Colin did not like Dr Newman who had a bald head, and he would always hide under the bed during Dr Newman's visits.

This picture: *Tony Pigram, mechanic at Thorley Hall Farm.*

Right: *The wedding of Colin Sampford and Margery Morton at Thorley Church.*

Alfred Camp, Albie's father, with horse and cart.

Below, left: *Nathan Bird with his horse at Thorley Hall Farm.*

Below, right: *George Camp with a horse on the farm, and Albert Camp in the background* (left).

The farm workers in Nos 1 and 2, before Tony and Colin, were respectively the Camp and the Bird families. Albie Camp remembers his childhood as 'living like the Victorians':

We had a three-bedroom cottage, there were five of us, three boys two girls. My brother Tom slept in a single bed, next to my brother George and I... we slept in a double bed.

We never had electric lights or gas; at night we had oil-lamps or candles to see, and at bedtimes we would take a little oil-lamp or candle upstairs to bed, or sometimes a torch. Water was fetched from a pump 100 yards away in buckets which were kept in the pantry. The water was replaced when required as it was used to wash with, also to make hot drinks. We had an old kitchen range fire stove, and if the wind was in one direction, it would not draw to heat the oven.

Washdays my mother shared with her neighbour Mrs Bird, using an old copper for boiling the clothes. Mrs Bird would always start first and sometimes she would be finished by 5 o'clock and call my mother that the copper was ready. Wood and coal had to be dry, kept nearby. They had an old fashion mangle which would soon get the water out of the clothes.

The wireless was run by accumulator and battery, which had to be charged up quite often.

As children we used to have to fetch milk for our parents; some went to Brook Farm, but we had to go to Thorley Hall Farm, which was over one mile by road, less by the fields. In winter I've known the snowdrifts to reach six feet high on the roads when we were cut off completely.

We all served in the war. Tom went into the Home Guard and I went into the Army and did six weeks' training on the Isle of Wight, and transferred to several different regiments. I was in Portsmouth on D-Day, and saw service in India, Singapore and Malaya. My brother George left Thorley at 21 to go into the Army Service Corps Tank Transport, and served in India and Burma. He came down to Poona but I missed him. My sister Dorothy went into the Land Army, and my other sister Clara was in the Army. Two bombs dropped near us at home, one in Mead Field behind the house, and one in Barn Field in front.

My brother Tom worked at Thorley Hall for Tinney, polishing boots, etc. He went at 7 o'clock until 8.45 when he went to school, then back at 2.45 till 5 o'clock. On Sundays he went an hour later and took Sunday clothes, changed and went to church. Tom left school at 14.

Mr Elliott lived in Moor Hall. He was head of a London hospital and used to bring home a jar of malt extract. Tom loved it and George didn't!

George was always getting up to mischief and getting other children in trouble. I remember when I first started school, I was always eager to get there. As I was younger I went to bed before George and in those days bedrooms were always cold. George went to bed one night and said to me 'It's time to go to school', so I jumped out of bed and started dressing. George undressed quickly and jumped into the warm part of the bed! On the way to school once, from Moor Hall to the church between the Twin Ponds, George stirred up a wasps' nest. George didn't get stung by the chasing wasps, but we did!

One day, grandfather Morton was hoeing beet in the field in front of the cottages with another chap. Someone had recently died in the village and they were chatting about it when grandfather said 'Well we're here today, but we don't know what might happen, we might not be here tomorrow.' The other chap said 'You don't mean that do you?' 'Yes' he said. 'Coo' said the other chap, 'I hope not. I've just made four and a half gallons of wine!'

Newmans the baker used to deliver provisions in a horse-drawn cart and kids used to hang on the back. He'd cut them across the backside with a whip. When they asked why, he said 'If you don't deserve it now, you will later.'

From Albie's sister, Clara Camp:

I cannot remember much of my school days and I left very soon after I was 14. Between 13 and 14 years I went to Bishop's Stortford where we were taught how to do washing, then domestic tasks, then cooking one day per week.

Albie's neighbours, Nathan and Mrs Bird (Jack's parents), lived in No. 2 Moor Hall Cottages. Nathan had a brother, who used to bring his grandson Grenville across the fields (now Thorley Park estate) to visit him. The Birds took in Edie and Gladys Pallett as 'home children', then they had their son Jack, and later became guardians for Don Powell.

in 2003 at the Rogation Day fête, Albie, at age 80, was persuaded to play the part of Sir Richard Whittington in the pageant written and performed by his fellow villagers some 50 years ago and re-enacted by local children. The children were adeptly directed by Alison Mitchell, a local mum and enthusiast in amateur dramatics, and Albie looked every inch a well-pleased Sir Richard!

The Old Thatch (Formerly the Nook) and Clay Cottage

On a bend in Moor Hall Lane, before reaching the five-arm roundabout on the bypass, there used to stand five small cottages, three known as the Nook and two as Clay Cottages. Clara Camp recalls:

The Nook in Clay Lane used to be three small attached thatched cottages. My grandparents Mr and Mrs Morton lived in the middle one, which had a tiny back door. Mrs Philpot and Mr Crabb lived each side. I, with my sister and brothers, called in

Above: *The Akers family outside Clay Cottage in 1937. Left to right, back row: Hilda Mary, James Henry, Sarah Ann (née Rand); front row: Lilian Florence, Maisie Esther, James Philip Henry.*

Below: *The wedding day of Maisie Akers and Bob Crisp.*

The Old Thatch and Clay Cottage, 1938.

daily. We've known times in the summer when my grandparents' pump ran dry and water had to be carried a quarter mile... it was a great relief when after the Second World War electric and mains water arrived and improvements made to the cottage.

Later, in 1970, the Old Thatch, as the Nook had by then become known, was occupied as one residence by the Shutes family. Mrs Shutes had been Diane Porter, who had lived as a girl with her family across the fields at Castle Farm. Then came Vic and Janet Haste, who kept rescued donkeys in the adjoining field. Vic continued to live there after Janet's sad and untimely death.

Next door stands Clay Cottage, a detached building that used to be two tied cottages. Harry and Olive Prior lived in one of the cottages, and later their son Fred lived there with wife Joy for 18 years. Bill Parrish, who had two daughters, Yvonne and Yvette, both attending the Village School, lived in the other cottage, followed by the Akers family. It was converted into one cottage for Jack and Rene Bird, after Jack's retirement from farm work for reasons of ill health. Its name evokes the time when Clay Lane was that part of the lane leading to the fork for Butler's Hall, but the details of its route are unclear.

Liz Eldred recalls, with Peggy Robinson and other villagers, an eccentric family living years ago opposite Clay Cottage. Harry and Mrs Longman lived in a hut up Moor Hall Lane just outside Jack and Rene's house. It had huge shed doors instead of a front door of normal size. Liz remembers her Nan frequently taking her to have tea with Mrs Longman. She had lots of plastic flowers everywhere and was very hospitable. The hut has long since gone. There is bunding on the site, intended to give Rene protection from the noise of bypass traffic.

Brook Farm

Having crossed the bypass at the new roundabout, we walk past the St Michael's Mead houses on the left to reach Brook Farm. This was a dairy farm owned by the Streeters. Billy Fuller was the first dairy man to live there, followed by the Hunt and then the Hatchett families. Brook Farm was where the Hammond twins, Jean and Joan, and the Harris sisters, Peggy and Audrey, used to have to go to collect the milk for the hamlet before going to school. Teddie Kent remembers helping head cowman Fred Hatchett with the milking, all done by hand. The cowshed was where Teddie met Joyce, later his wife.

The 20-acre dairy farm was sold in the 1950s to the Collins family and in 1962 to Peter and Deirdre James, who increased the inherited 400 laying hens to 2,000 and reared 400 turkeys in the first year. They made substantial improvements to the farmhouse, barns and gardens. Deirdre writes:

We supplied family butchers in Bishop's Stortford and Hertfordshire with turkeys for many years, and up to 50 people including children used to help pluck them in December. We then inherited two donkeys from Peter's Irish mother, and bought a pony for daughter Amanda. In 1972, I gave riding lessons to help with the cost of shoeing, and when pupils wanted to continue, the Thorley Riding Centre started up.

I was a founder member of the Riding for the Disabled Group in Farnham, which moved its activities in 1976 to an all-weather arena built at Brook Farm. The pony numbers grew to over 20 and large numbers of children, able and disabled, enjoyed riding the lanes and bridle-ways of Thorley. It was the only centre in the area specialising in riding lessons just for children. In the 1990s, Riding for the Disabled moved to Much Hadham's indoor

Brook Farm, 1962.

Brook Farm, 1992.

facilities, but riding for other children continued until 1997, when the fields were sold to Countryside Properties for the development of St Michael's Mead housing estate. Now a few ponies for grandchildren are kept in a paddock in the park land created by developers across the road from Brook Farm.

The balancing pond for the development has been created as an attractive lake, where Peter feeds the ducks every morning before going to work and has provided a raft in the reed bed for ducks to nest. There is no doubt that there have been tremendous changes here since we came in 1962, but then 40 years have seen changes around towns all over the country, although most have not been as dramatic as those here in Thorley.

Butler's Hall Farm

We now turn back to the bypass, cross it again at the roundabout and walk along what used to be Butler's Hall Lane to reach the hamlet of Butler's Hall.

Butler's Hall is the largest concentration of Uplands dwellings, with some ten previously tied cottages clustered around one side of the farmhouse. Meadow Cottage was once two cottages, as was Black Cottage, which was originally known as Old Cottages. The terraced row of four cottages, built in the early 1900s by the Streeter family, with dormers and frontage deliberately intended to ape the style of Twyford House, is called New Cottages, but was also known as the Barracks. The semi-detached houses named Kimbers and Firtrees were originally Nos 1 and 2 Butler's Hall Cottages. All the

hamlet houses were tied cottages for the farm workers, and the renaming took place when the Streeter family started to sell the houses in 1969.

Andy Streeter, son of Tom Streeter, recalls the characters who worked at Butler's Hall Farm:

Butler's Hall Farm was originally tenanted by Reggie Newman, who passed the tenancy to his nephew Tom Seabrook, who left in 1963, and I have been farming there ever since. Reggie Newman, with his wife Muriel, continued to live in Thorley, at Finch Croft, until he reached the very great age of 101. He took a keen interest in all local affairs, played cricket, and was a churchwarden and parish councillor.

I remember several of the men who worked there – Jim Day, who first used to look after the chickens when

Butler's Hall hamlet across the Mead from Moor Hall Lane, showing Meadow Cottage to the left, 1970s.

This picture: *Butler's Hall hamlet from the air, 1972.*

Below: *Butler's Hall, 1960s.*

he left school and then became a shepherd. We won a gold medal for the chickens (which I still have) and also many 'fat stock' prizes in the local market at Bishop's Stortford. He followed the sheep to Harp's Farm at Great Hallingbury. He was also a very good thatcher. He told me once that he remembers digging himself out at Butler's Hall through the snow, where they dug a path with walls of over six foot down the lane and it stayed like that for over two months.

Ernie Warman was another employee – he was the estate carpenter and lorry driver. He used to make wonderful oak gates in his workshop in the Thorley Place garages and would repair anything in wood. He was not so good at driving the lorry, but he used to take peas, potatoes and sacks of corn from the farm. The peas went to Covent Garden – when I was old enough I took on the job of driving them up to London.

There was a wonderful retired worker at Butler's Hall, Mr Clark. I don't know how old he was but he would never stop working and was always out trimming ditches, planting trees, helping in any way he could, and looked after the farm as if it was his own. He had been there all his life and when he passed on it was a very sad day. The only reason we knew he had died was because he didn't come to work that day. I am sure he was over 100 years old.

Geoff Ashwell, close family friend of the Newmans and owner of Warren Farm adjoining Streeter farmland, has many memories of this time, about which he has written in his own book.

After Tom Seabrook left, the farmhouse was rented to schoolteacher Eric Scrase who lived there with his wife Win and three children. Sadly, Win and her youngest daughter Roz died young. The house was eventually sold to a number of different buyers, and when the Frains finally arrived with their very large young family the hamlet started 'humming' with the open spirit of old. Doors were not locked, families celebrated 'occasions' with each other, and children were still safe to roam.

But change was happening in the Uplands as well as elsewhere in the parish. The consequences of excessive urbanisation of the countryside all around and material interests were beginning to take hold. In the hamlet, the wooden and Dutch barns in the stack-yard have gone, having been replaced by a large steel structure designed for storage; the farmhouse is behind high walls and gates and 'beware-of-dog' signs; ill-maintained bunding looms over the hamlet, obscuring views to the church; the lane and its hedgerows have disappeared with the fields; and the bypass and stopping up of lanes encourage isolation of parish settlements.

Michael Teitz, a wartime evacuee child billeted in the hamlet, recalls the route he used to take to the Village School, and in doing so reminds us of what has been forever lost:

In memory, the walk to school remains as powerful as school itself. Butler's Hall was about one mile away, along a winding and wonderfully varied lane. Every day, we walked each way, usually in our group – my brother Peter David, Mick Marns, Reggie Jay (nephew of the Clarks) and I. For the first 100 yards or so, the lane ran between fields. To the right lay the large ploughed field in front of Butler's Hall Cottages, separated from the lane by bank and a substantial ditch that was satisfyingly full of water much of the time. However, the ditch was off-limits because it was also the place where dishwater from the sinks in the cottages ended up. The lane was generally below the level of the fields because of centuries of use, so we would make our way as children do, frequently climbing out of it. To the left, we first passed the stackyard, with its two nearly dead, ivy-covered trees, then we came to the twin fields, separated by a baulk and footpath that sloped down to the brook. This field was the first place that I saw a mole drain in action, towards the end of the war. The heavy clay soil overlaying chalk was probably suitable for this economical form of drainage.

Just beyond that field, the lane joined with the branch that led to Moor Hall, but before the intersection, on the left-hand side, was the meadow in which cows from the dairy grazed. This was the first point at which the lane was bordered by thick hedges, in which all manner of things, from hazels (very good for nuts and straight sticks for bows) to wild flowers could be found. A small and very private gap allowed us to climb into the field for exploration or to avoid people on the road. The meadow led to the dairy, which lay a little further down the lane, just before it crossed the brook. Often in the afternoon, we would go to the dairy to pick up our milk in a small metal can. The dairy farmer wore a brown coat and a skullcap to protect his forehead as he leaned into the cow's side. He would sit on his three-legged stool, milking as we watched. Sometimes, a jet of fresh milk would fly in our direction as he laughed. The dairy always had a wonderful aroma of cow, fresh milk, and dung, together with the trickling sound of milk pouring over the corrugated surface of the cooler. It was a special place.

Besides its name, each field had its own character and its own part in my history. The field opposite the dairy was the first place I saw kale growing, the first silage preparation that I saw, and the site of the most beautiful double rainbow ever. The latter astonished me, but making silage was an amazing mystery.

The walk to and from school never lacked in interest. We dawdled or ran as the spirit took us, and I relish in memory the freedom that very few modern children experience, despite their wealth of material possessions.

Meadow Cottage

Meadow Cottage was owned by the Streeters, and was originally used as two dwellings, with one dwelling a 'one-up one-down' barn on the end of the main cottage.

In the early 1900s, Susannah (known as Granny Harris) lived in the one-up one-down barn with her husband, William John, who was brought up in Castle Farm as one of the sons of great-grandmother Jane Harris (née Fisher). Susannah had nine children. Hugh died in 1919 after a leg amputation as a result of war wounds. George was the father of Peggy and Audrey and lived with his family in No. 2 New Cottages. William Charles (Charlie) married Agnes Abigail Chappell, thus linking two of the well-established Thorley families. Albert was a policeman and the father of Geoffrey Harris, who has researched the family history and can correct what memory recalls here. Susannah died in 1945. In 1946 Violet, the youngest, married Frank Crabb who served with the 8th Army in North Africa. They lived in Corner Cottage throughout the 1970s and '80s. Peggy as a child remembered going to Sunday lunch with her grandmother every week, and wet or fine all year round they would eat apple suet pudding made in a dish.

Meadow Cottage, possibly in the 1920s.

Another of great-grandmother Harris' sons had four children, one of which was Fred, father of Jack Harris who married Gwen and eventually also lived in Butler's Hall hamlet at No.1 New Cottages, he and his father having lived previously in Thorley Street.

Later, in the 1940s, came the Hammond family, and it was Granny Hammond's son Len who was the horse keeper for the Streeter family and lived with his wife Annie Harriet (known as Aunt Daisy) at No. 4 New Cottages. They were the grandparents of Liz the shepherdess. It was another of Granny Hammond's sons, William John, who married Sarah Georgina and lived in Old Cottages, where they had a family of eight, the youngest being the twins Joan and Jean. On marriage, Joan moved into No.1 Butler's Hall Cottages, so the hamlet became a real family complex at this time.

Meanwhile, in the main part of Meadow Cottage lived farm worker Ernie Warman, who had married Edna, daughter of the pub landlord, Nat Graves. During the Second World War, the house was rented to the Marns family who came from London. The Hammonds still lived next door at that time.

After the war, Meadow Cottage was renovated by Andrew Streeter's brother John, who lived there for a while before the property was sold to the Reece family, and then to a stockbroker who filled in the pond, and eventually in the 1970s to David and Edith Herbert.

Old Cottages (now Black Cottage)

Old Cottages were two joined cottages behind Butler's Hall Cottages (now known as Kimbers Cottage and Fir Trees). Farm worker William Hammond and his wife Sarah Georgina used to live in one of Old Cottages and then in both as the family grew to nine children. Frank Monk's uncle Drew (Andrew Clark) lived next door to the Hammonds until the family got too big. There was a pump outside for water and the front room at the end was always damp because of the well.

Jean and Joan, the Hammond twins, were the youngest of Sarah Georgina's children and tell us of their six brothers and sisters:

Dora and Ada both worked in service for the Freres and the Tinneys, and later married and moved away. Sid also married and moved away. Ernie was Frank Kinge's assistant gamekeeper and died at 31, Marjorie married Tom Clark who worked for the Tinneys, and Bert died at 47 years old on a Tuesday and Joan found him.

The twins also remember that after the Hammonds, Mrs Clark, who was considered rather 'nutty' and had no children, lived in one of the Old Cottages until 1969, when it was sold as one of the first three tied dwellings to go to private owners. There have

The Harris family at Meadow Cottage, possibly in the 1930s. Left to right, back row: *William Charles, Susannah, Harold (Bidge), Agnes (née Chappell), William John;* front: *Violet and Lois (daughters of Susannah).*

Inset: *Meadow Cottage, 1980s.*

Above: *Old Cottages, 1950s.*

Above, right: *Sarah Georgina Hammond outside Old Cottages, 1950s.*

Right: *Ernie Hammond outside Old Cottages, late 1930s.*

The wedding of Ada Hammond and Fred Turner, and bridesmaids Jean and Joan, 1939.

William Hammond in the garden of Old Cottages, with No. 4 New Cottages in the background, 1950s.

Joan Kimber (née Hammond) and son Stephen in the garden of Butler's Hall Cottages, with a view of the barns in the stack-yard in the 1960s.

since been five owners, including Canadian Paul Bristow and wife Wendy, whose two daughters were born there, and John Beer (renowned champion trampolinist) who came with wife Penny and two daughters, one a very keen horserider at Brook Farm.

Butler's Hall Cottages (now Kimbers and Firtrees)

Joan Hammond, on her marriage to Joe Kimber in 1953, moved from Old Cottages to live in No. 1 Butler's Hall Cottages (now Kimbers Cottage) and in 1969 moved again to Great Hallingbury after her marriage to Joe Brace. Joan's twin sister Jean had married Les Sage in 1956 and already moved to Great Hallingbury near Harp's Farm, the Streeter home.

Before 1953, No. 1 had been occupied by Fred and Jean Simmons, who had three children. And before that, as Peggy Robinson recalled, Aunt Lucy and Uncle Will lived in No. 1 Butler's Hall Cottages. They were possibly the son and daughter of Peggy's grandfather's brother, William Harris. If so, their brother was Fred Harris, who later lived next door in No. 2 with his son Jack, Peggy's cousin. No. 1 (Kimbers) was sold in 1969 to the MacMillans and then to the Freer family.

Peggy also recalled that Aunts Jane and Polly lived next door in No. 2 (now Firtrees). They were probably the sisters of Susannah's husband William John (grandfather of both Peggy and Geoffrey). In the 1950s, Fred Harris and his son Jack came from Thorley Street to live at No. 2, before Jack married Gwen and later moved across the Dall to No. 1 New Cottages. Ned, the proud owner of a Morgan and a frequent visitor to the Green Man with Richard Freer, lived in No. 2 at one time with wife Sue. Afterwards a local businessman, Mr Ashpole, lived there, and it was eventually sold to Tony Drath, who has since moved and lives with

his new family in St Michael's Mead.

New Cottages

The alignment of New Cottages was planned, it is said, so that the view of the church spire would not be impeded for Butler's Hall farmhouse. The first tied cottage to be sold was No. 4. The others were sold subsequently, as they became vacant and were no longer needed for farm workers.

No. 1 New Cottages was occupied up until the end of the Second World War by Henry (Harry) and Sarah Clark (née Gilbey). Harry worked for the Streeters as horse keeper and was keen on growing standard roses. Sarah was described as a 'dear lady' by Peggy Robinson who remembered that she had put a milk pudding on her doorstep every day when Peggy was carrying her son. All their four children were born in No. 1. Dick went to work for the Birds and kept ferrets. Kathleen (or Kit) married George Chappell and went to live in 1 Sunset Cottages until George died and Kit eventually moved into town. John married Maud and lived in Glen View in The Street, and George (Titch) started working for the Tinneys at age 14, before later going into the Army, where he served as a Desert Rat fighting at El Alamein and later met Phil Akers in Tripoli. He was wounded at Cassino, and after the war he married Betty Sapsford, whose father was the postman, and worked at Millar's.

After the war, Albert Clark moved into No. 1 from two doors down at No. 3, where he had lived with Annie and billeted the Teitz boys. Details are unclear about relationships between branches of the Clark (or Clarke) families in Thorley. After Jack and Gwen Harris in the 1970s/'80s, the house was sold to the Robins, who moved in with son Andrew and daughter Charlotte, and assorted animals including the family pony.

Annie Harriet (Daisy) Hammond and dog Gyp, at No. 4 New Cottages, 1960s.

Len Hammond, Daisy's husband, 1930s.

In No. 2 lived the Wood family. John Wood worked as gardener for the Streeters, and later moved to Thorley Place Cottages (known as Laundry Cottages), which was situated opposite Thorley Place, the Streeter family home at the time. In 1924, No. 2 was occupied by George Harris and his wife Dorothy, who as a widow later married Jock Lawford and remained in the cottage where she brought up her two daughters, Audrey and Peggy Harris. Audrey moved away on marriage to 'Ginge' Sayers, and Mrs Lawford stayed on in the house with Peggy and grandson Gerald.

Peggy started to retell many stories about school and about the postwar years when she and her friends were young adventurous people, but the next meeting we looked forward to didn't happen. Some of the stories Peggy recalled were that she and her sister Audrey were the only children in the school with long hair in ringlets, and she had five. The Camp girls always wore pinafores to school; Don Powell always wore a velvet suit; and the Brewster girls, who walked from Latchmore Bank, always came with white gloves on and would have shoes to change into from their Welly boots. Mrs Smith wore pink woolly knickers, and because she didn't like Dolly Hammond, she would make her write out lines such as: 'disrespectful and deceitful girls are not wanted in this world.' Peggy told of pea picking and 'spud' lifting, which wasn't to her liking at all. She used to hide potatoes in the ditch to bring home for the whole hamlet. She preferred to spend her free time going up to London to see Arsenal play home games or to wander in Battersea Gardens or to go shopping. She had taken

Betty Brewster to London to buy a winter coat one year and was going to take her up again the very day Betty died. Peggy never missed an Arsenal game. She described her journeys to London in detail, the times of the trains she caught and the cost of the tickets, the streets she walked along, the Lyons Corner Houses she stopped at, and riding home at night on her bicycle which she had left at Fyfe's. She recalled how her mother used to get mad about Norrington's men who collected insurance, allegedly 'doing Aunt Daisy out of pounds' because she was stone deaf. Peggy's was a 'larger than life' personality, and her mother was a lady who 'knew her own mind'. Peggy's son was highly intelligent and the apple of their eye. All are now deceased, but well remembered.

No. 2 was eventually sold to a young couple, Richard and Dorothy, whose daughter was born there and who, with the Beers and McDonalds, spearheaded the Old Thorley villagers' fight to stop the new housing and bypass road development. No. 2 has changed hands several times since.

At the time of the war, No. 3 was the home of Albert and Annie Clark, with whom Michael and Peter David Teitz were billeted. After the war, Michael Clark moved in with his German wife Hilda and her rather unpopular dog, and in 1953, a dated ration book shows that William Day lived at No. 3. We know from other reliable postal evidence that William was formerly of Rumbolds [sic] Farm and before 1912 of 7 Thorley Street (known then more fully as 7 Pump Yard). He moved to No. 3 with his son Jim, who worked for the Streeters. The house was eventually sold after Willie died in 1958 and Jim went later to Harp's Farm, the Streeter farm in Great Hallingbury, where he tended the sheep. He later went to Beldams Lane, where the Streeters had converted pig barns into sheltered homes for farm workers.

No. 4 was occupied before the war and until 1951 by Annie Harriet (Aunt Daisy) and Len Hammond, the grandparents of Liz the shepherdess. They had five children: Dolly, whose daughter Liz is from her second marriage to Dick Wick, foreman on the Tinney farms; Henry Thomas (Tom), who died in April 2002; Arthur George (known as Ben); Walter (known as Pimp); and Ellen (Nelly) whose son was John Hammond (who died in hospital in April 2003). Daisy moved to No. 2 Moor Hall Cottages and later to Glen View in Thorley Street. Peggy Robinson, who died in May 2003, recalled that for a while a 'rough and ready' family, employed as labourers, lived at No. 4 before it was sold to the McDonalds, who live there at the time of writing.

Before leaving the hamlet, we should reminisce briefly with Michael and Peter David about New Cottages. Michael writes:

Butler's Hall, a small cluster of cottages and houses adjacent to a modest tenant farm, was the centre of our world. New Cottages was actually a dark brick row of four connected houses, three stories tall. They stood facing across the fields and were reached by a short, dirt path (called the Dall) from the lane that led up to Butler's Hall from the school and church, about a mile away. The paved lane ended at this point, giving way to cart tracks out to the fields, where we roamed freely.

There were four boys in our gang – my brother, who was David to the family and Peter outside, Mick Marns, Reggie Jay, and me. There were others, such as Ronnie and Freddy Owers, who lived near the Green Man and joined us from time to time. Together we played, explored, got up to mischief, scrumping apples in the orchard near Thorley Place on the way home from school, eating peas from the fields and, of course, we played war. It was on everyone's mind most of the time.

Mr and Mrs Clark were quiet, undemonstrative country people. Mr Clark was a farm labourer, working at Streeter's Farm, near the Green Man. I wondered why he did not work at Newman's, but it was never explained and I did not ask. He had been gassed during the First World War, losing flesh around the nostrils, which gave him a frightening appearance at first sight to a child. In fact, he was a very kind and thoughtful man, who talked with us and showed us how to be comfortable in his world. Like all farm workers of his time, he could do many things. He repaired our boots and shoes, when leather or studs could be found, putting the nails in his mouth as I watched, fascinated. I still know how to handle a pocket knife and to chop kindling safely, among other things that he taught me. He responded to our questions about the war – how many soldiers in a battalion? – though, like so many of his tragic generation, he did not speak of what they endured. In the evening, after tea, he read the Daily Express but said little about politics.

The house had three floors. One entered always by the back door on the ground floor into a tiny scullery, then two steps up into the living-room/kitchen, and from that into a front room, where no one ever ventured. From the front room, a 'front door' led into the garden that had no access from a public path or road, which led me to wonder why it was there. Up a very narrow and steep staircase were front and back bedrooms, and on the third floor, two rooms under the roof with dormer windows on each side. The toilet was outside the back door, its spotless wooden seat covering a bucket that Mr Clark emptied into a cesspit well away from the house. Square pieces of newspaper on a string served for toilet paper. Water was carried in buckets from the pump, a few yards from the back door, on a path that led to the other houses. Later, I would help to pump and carry water.

Mrs Clark cooked on a coal stove in the living-room, where we ate, played, bathed and did our reading. In that small room, we would lie on the floor, playing or reading while she worked, stepping around and over us. Her pies, especially blackberry and apple, were delicious. I would watch her make them in a deep, oblong ceramic dish, with a small chimney-like, earthenware support in the centre to hold up the crust and let out the steam.

I did not know what the war being over might really mean. What I did know were the fields and paths, the stack-yard, and life in the hamlet that I was loath to leave when that time came.

But we readers shall leave, crossing Double Gate where in wartime a bomb fell and a Spitfire crashed, to take the bridle-way to the Green Man.

Doris (Dean) Saville at Thorley Houses, 1928.

Fred Harris on horseback, Thorley Hall, c.1945.

Violet Harris, aged 20, on horseback near Butler's Hall, c.1934.

Right: *Jim Day with his bicycle and flat cap, 1930s.*

Bottom right: *William John Harris, with a spade over his shoulder by the pond (now filled in) at Meadow Cottage, c.1920. In 2002 grandson Geoffrey was in possession of William's spade.*

Below: *Doris Saville in the garden at Thorley Houses, 1928.*

Left: *Joan and father 'Pedlar' Hammond, outside the Green Man, early 1950s.*

Below: *Doris and Leslie Threadgold, 1940s.*

Right: *The Akers sisters. Left to right: Hilda, (aged 14), Maisie (12) and Lilian (10).*

Left: *Joan Hammond in Butler's Hall stack-yard, 1950s.*

Emily Day (leading the horse) *and Alice Day in* **the tumble cart at Rumballs Farm, early 1930s.**

Frederick Bird (Molly's grandfather) in front of the cartwheel, and sons Frank and Bert (far left), Hither Farm, c.1906.

Right: *Mary Monk and her father Herbert in the Thorley House pageant, 1951.*

Colin and Margery Sampford with their first car, a Morris Minor, 1960s.

John Hammond, late 1960s.

Jim Knight at Harringtons, early 1960s.

Adrian Taylor, who lived in the schoolhouse, in his Scout uniform, 1950s.

Chapter 8

The Edge of Thorley Common

Having now reached the Green Man, we are in the vicinity of Thorley Houses. Its history is a source of confusion.

Thorley Houses Settlement

Today there is a single dwelling, called Thorley Houses, located near Castle Farm and the Green Man. The people of Thorley, however, recall that at the beginning of the twentieth century there used to be five or six dwellings at this location around two ponds. Behind and close to the Green Man there was a row of three terraced cottages seemingly referred to on the 1923 Ordnance Survey map as Thorley Houses Farm, since demolished. The single building that exists as Thorley Houses used to be two black-boarded cottages, later converted into one. Some villagers recall a fourth cottage near the row of three. We know that at the beginning of the century Teddie Kent lived in the end cottage of a row of three and that his grandfather lived next door to the Owers family in a black-boarded building of two adjoined dwellings. Moreover, the OS map from around 1921 shows clearly the buildings and ponds behind the Green Man at that time and confirm what villagers recall. Mr Whalley's research suggests that much further back the cottages were castle crofts of Waytemore Castle.

Teddie Kent, a pupil of the old Village School, gives the most comprehensive account of the history of Thorley Houses:

I was born at the Uplands of Thorley nearly 75 years ago

in 1928. Then it consisted of the Green Man public house, three cottages behind the pub, then a pond, and a drive down to a farmhouse which had been made into two cottages. I was born in one of the three cottages behind the Green Man. On the other side of the road was Castle Farm, where the farmhouse had been made into two cottages and there were various farm buildings in the yard.

On the road to Much Hadham, past the farm on the left-hand side of the road, was a lane leading to Butler's Hall. Further down, on the right-hand side of the road, was a lane to Bury Green, and a little way down this lane was a TB or fever hospital, which was pulled down when I was about five or six years old.

When I was about four or five, the three cottages behind the Green Man were condemned and pulled down, and we then moved into one of the Castle Farm cottages, next to Mr and Mrs Speller. Castle Farm was owned by Mr Tom Streeter. My Dad worked for him as horse keeper. I was the only child living there for some time and then a family moved into one of the

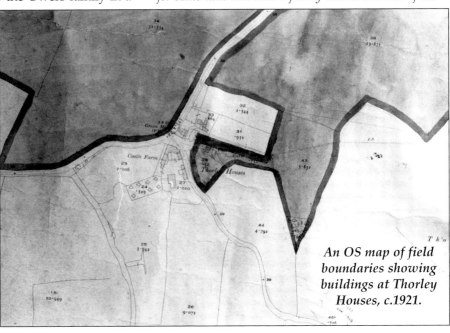

An OS map of field boundaries showing buildings at Thorley Houses, c.1921.

two cottages down the drive from the pub. They were Mr and Mrs Owers, and their sons Fred and Ron. My grandfather lived in the other cottage.

Teddie continues with his account of life in Thorley, which is written here in full because it so simply 'says it all' and fittingly gives us a breather on our 100-year walk around Thorley. Would that the Green Man were still open! Teddie writes:

I remember before I started school that my mother and some of the other women in the village used to go into the fields pea picking and potato picking. As I grew older I used to be interested to see the fields being ploughed with the big horses, and then by tractors. It used to be fun when the big steam ploughs used to come and plough and land-ditch the fields. When they did land-ditching they used a thing called a mole to pull holes under the ground, a process which enabled them to drain the ground.

I used to meet the other children and we walked to school every day and twice on Sunday, to go to church in the morning and to Sunday School in the after-noon. Quite often in the winter the lanes used to get blocked with snowdrifts and had to be dug out.

Further along Thorley Lane towards the school there were two cottages and Rumbles Farm, all owned by Mr Streeter, and then the butcher's shop, where I sometimes called on the way home to buy brawn or a basin of pork dripping. Round the bend in the lane was Thorley Place and Stone Hall, where Mr and Mrs Monk lived.

At school our teachers were Mrs Warboys (then Miss Eagling), Miss Hummerstone, Miss Moorhouse, and Mrs Smith. Sometimes the students from Hockerill used to come and teach us. The rector used to come into school to take morning prayers.

In the summer holidays, some of us used to help get the harvest in, and also with pea picking and potato picking. I can also remember helping to stand the sheaves of corn up into stooks (or shocks), and when the sheaves were dry I often used to lead the horse and cart round for the men to load the sheaves into the cart and take them to be stacked up.

Teddie Kent, with evacuee Kathleen Hutson, outside the Green Man, 1939.

At night during the war we could see the glow of the fires in London. There were quite a few evacuees in Thorley. We had four living with us at one time, but their mother did not like the country and returned to London.

I used to help Mr Knight look after the heating of the church. On Saturday afternoon we used to light the boiler, and go back at night and early on Sunday morning to stoke it up, to make sure that the church was warm.

When I left school I went to work for Mr Streeter, and later I worked at Brook Farm with Mr Hatchett. We milked the cows by hand, and the milk churns were picked up by lorry and taken to Allen & Hanbury's in Ware.

The Hut near the school was the Working Men's Club, where we used to play cards, snooker and table tennis.

Thorley was a lovely old village until they decided to build houses over the land. There is not a lot of Thorley left now as I used to know it. But I still like to think of it as my home village. We traced the Kent family living near the Green Man public house as far back as 1780.

The Green Man

Jim Morton, brother of Margery Sampford, recalls happier times for the Green Man:

The Green Man public house was a very busy 'watering hole' for the locals and also several customers from Bishop's Stortford who would come by bicycle on Sunday mornings to meet up with old friends and enjoy a pint and a talk together. The landlord at the time was Nathaniel F. Graves. As children we had several arguments about what the initial 'F' stood for, but alas we never knew. Mr Graves was a white-haired be-whiskered elderly gentleman who with his wife ran the place for years. As a child I would go into the passage to buy crisps, and I have a clear picture of seeing men playing dominoes and darts.

The Green Man is thought to have had another resident more ethereal than the landlord and landlady. Footsteps and noises were heard and it was said that these belonged to a child who was no longer alive but seemed reluctant to go.

Three workers in caps outside the Green Man, 1950s.

Frank Monk and Frank Warman in Thorley Lane outside Stone Hall, 1930s.

Grenville Bird and Rose Monk add:

The Green Man was at one time run by the Palmers, then by Mr and Mrs Graves. Nathaniel Graves was a railwayman and because of the war kept working beyond normal retirement age to help the war effort. He walked into town from the Green Man to Stortford station every morning and after a day's work back home at night. His wife looked after the pub during his absence, although of course trade was quite light. They remained at the Green Man until about 1958, and were followed by the Dales. After the Dales came Dick Speight, brother of television-script writer Johnny Speight, who created Alf Garnet in 'Till Death Us Do Part'.

Colin Sampford recalls that the drinking hours while Dick was landlord were 'from daylight to daylight' and it was not unheard of to get Dick up in the morning and help wash up. After Dick came Don and Peggy Hayden, and later, in the 1970s, Sid and 'Bo' Hardwidge, who eventually moved to The Falcon in town.

Peter and Jean Cullen then took over the tenancy, and set out to attract passing trade and a wider family clientele, holding bonfire nights and petanque competitions, as well as providing a stop on the way home for local commuters! When Peter and Jean moved to the Hop Poles in Great Hallingbury, the brewery let the pub go downhill, and it was boarded up for many years. The, in September 2003 it was razed to the ground by property developers.

Thorley Houses (a farmhouse converted into two cottages)

John Savill worked at Piggott's Farm and lived with his wife Emma and family in Thorley Houses from 1925 until 1932, when they moved to Much Hadham. They had five children, and three of them (Horace, May and Doris) attended the Village School. It is intersting to note that the children put an 'e' on the end of their surname when they went to school. It is possible that the family lived in the whole house. There are steps visible in the pre-1933 pictures, but not the pretty wooden porch that Jim Morton recalls from 1951.

Ron Brett, grandson of John and Emma Savill, tells us some of the family history:

My mother, Doris (who was called Dorinda) was an assistant to Miss Hummerstone, headmistress of the Village School, and later married Walter Brett. My brother Horace married Hilda Akers, whose family lived down the lane from Thorley Houses, and they had three children, one being Jean (now Wharbey). All the Savill children were taught to swim by Miss Frere in the cold mill pool. The family has kept its interest in Morris men and folk dancing that came from those early Thorley days.

I remember that during the 1950s my father did some maintenance work on the Old Rectory for Revd Robinson.

105

Certainly Thorley Houses was two dwellings after 1932 when the Savills left, because we know from villagers that Ted's grandfather William moved there in about 1933 and that Fred and Lottie Owers brought their sons Ron and Fred to live there next door to him in what Peggy called the Uplands Barn, also in 1933. Mr Owers worked at Piggott's Farm. Ted recalls that he walked with the Owers boys to school, and Peggy remembered that Ron would run off to see where the bombs dropped, on one occasion finding marks of shrapnel on a tree on the Common where a plane came down. So the family was living there, in the right-hand side of the building, during the Second World War.

Jim Morton recalls that the Owers left in 1947, when possibly Mr Poulter, pig man for the Tinneys, moved in before Mr and Mrs Ken Newland took up residence. They left in 1950, at which time William Kent was still in occupancy next door but shortly afterwards died in hospital. In early 1951 it was converted into one house. Jim tells us about his life there:

This picture: *Emma Saville and daughters Doris and May, on the step of Thorley Houses Farm, 1929.*

Top: *Thorley Houses, 1930.*

On 9th November 1951, just before my 10th birthday, my parents Tom and Eva Morton moved from Albury to Thorley. Bert Outlaw drove the lorry to move our furniture. The family was seven children between 16 and 4 years of age. Joining us were some chickens and our dog Rover. We moved into a large house, black-boarded, which originally was two cottages. It had several rooms and a large garden. At the front and the back of the house were two very deep ponds where moorhens used to nest and bring up their chicks. One pond was to the east side of a remaining brick wall and the other was about 10 yards from the corner of the house, across the boundary hedge of Finchcroft garden. There was a pretty wooden porch to the front, alas no more. Also gone are the blackboards of the house, now under pebble-dash. In the winters of 1950 through to 1956 we used to skate on the ponds, as it was so much colder in winter then than now. We also had snowball fights between ourselves. The house has been occupied by the Trill family since the 1970s.

Four Cottages Behind the Green Man

Rose Monk tells us:

There used to be four cottages, a row of three and one on its own, behind the Green Man. Sarah Ann Clark (Granny Clark) lived one of the three terraced houses by the pond. The Vealeys, who had a consumptive daughter, lived in the cottage standing alone. Sarah's husband had been horse keeper for the Pattens at Thorley Hall Farm, and afterwards for the Tinneys. When her husband Richard died in 1913, she had to move from Thorley Hall Cottages to Thorley Houses. In 1916 she became guardian to the Warman boys Eric, Ernie and Frank, aged eight, six and four. Frank Warman eventually married Jane Kent (Jane's father was Teddie Kent's grandfather). It was Ernie who married Edna Graves when she left the ATS and then moved from Meadow Cottage to Rectory Close. He died in the 1980s.

From conversations with Peggy Robinson and the account Bob Crisp gives of his family's history, it seems that Bob's grandfather, when he took up work for Mr Fowler at Piggott's Farm, moved his family into one of these cottages at the rear of the Green Man at the beginning of the century. The family had to move out of the tied cottage when Bob's grandfather lost his job at Piggott's. Peggy recalls that also living in these cottages were Aunt Jane (who could have been the sister of Peggy's grandfather William John Harris) and Uncle Ike (who could have been the Francis William Harris who Geoffrey Harris tells us sported a long white beard and wore a skull cap).

Castle Farm

Castle Farm was once two dwellings owned by the Streeters. Peggy Robinson recalled that her great-grandmother lived there (in 1900s) with two sons.

In the 1930s and '40s, Willi Speller lived in Castle Farm, and Teddie Kent's father Jim (known as Jimma), who was horse keeper for Tom Streeter, lived with his family in the cottage next door. Stories have been told of how Grandad Willi chased the Land Girls, and how his house was found full of bottles of home-made wine when it was cleared.

Jim Morton recalls:

Castle Farm was sold to Mr and Mrs Harry Porter, who ran it as a turkey farm and lived there with son Alan and daughters Pamela and Diana. Mr Porter used to cycle every day into Bishop's Stortford, where he also owned a ladies' hairdressing shop, and then come home to work on his farm. I used to help Alan and Diana with their horses. I learned to drive the Ferguson tractor, and would plough, cultivate, harrow and drill. At harvest time I would be placed on the back of the binder. In those days, children had to earn their pocket money and not just hold their hands out.

Mr and Mrs Sparrow, who were well-known towns-people and ran a large store in North Street, lived in Castle Farm just after the war, before it was sold to the Whalley family in 1960. Mr Whalley recalls:

It was a very dilapidated collection of buildings. When we first lived in Castle Farm I was going to change the name. However, whilst selling Red Cross badges in the village I encountered an old lady who said, 'You cannot change the name. I am 90 years old and it has been Castle Farm all my life.'

Castle Farm was eventually sold by Mr Whalley to Bevan Clarke who played as number Eight in England's rugby squad. It was then sold to the Gibbs, who have made many improvements to the house and outbuildings. They keep horses and have rescued the favourites amongst the sheep that Liz the shepherdess had to lose when David Tinney ceased sheep rearing. Sandie's pony riding at the 2003 Rogation Day village fête was a hugely welcome attraction.

Isolation Hospital

The isolation hospital for infectious diseases, run by the Bishop's Stortford Guardians until 1897 (when it was taken over by the local Urban and Rural District Councils), had been the only prospect for the seriously sick, and it was always full. Grenville Bird recalls the existence of the isolation hospital:

It was a wooden building which was on the bridle-way which leads from the Great Hadham Road (just past the Green Man) to Bury Green. It was only used when there were cases of diphtheria, etc. It was certainly in use until the early 1920s. My mother's sister used to have to go there from Haymeads Hospital, where she normally worked, to assist the nurse at the fever hospital.

By the late 1800s there was such concern about the lack of health care for the people of the town, living in abject poverty and dying from disease prevalent in such conditions, that local families, including the Freres of Twyford House, met in 1894 to discuss the founding of what became Rye Street Cottage Hospital (now closed). In the event, Laurie Frere and his sisters, in memory of their father who had instigated the idea with Sir Walter Gilbey, paid for the building, designed by architect Eustace Frere, on land donated by Sir Walter.

It was, however, to the Hertford isolation hospital that local schoolchildren were sent for examination when Ben Hammond, Flossie Hutchin and Denis

Castle Farm in the 1900s.

Prior contracted diphtheria, possibly, it is thought, owing to contaminated water at school. Grenville recalls seeing the remains of the old hospital when his grandfather took him for a walk down the bridle-way at the beginning of the war.

Finch Croft

Jim Morton:

Just down Thorley Lane from the Green Man, Jack and Dora Knight lived at Finch Croft and had a son Michael and a daughter Pat, who became a hairdresser in Much Hadham. Michael was a keen photographer and took many photos of Thorley. Mr Knight was a church-warden at Thorley Church and also owner of a five-acre field in which he kept pigs and chickens. As a boy I used to help look after them in my spare time and at weekends. At the age of ten I learned to drive a Ford 8 motor car and ride Mr Knight's 350cc Royal Enfield motor cycle.

After the war the Knights left the area, and Reggie and Muriel Newman moved from Butler's Hall Farm to Finchcroft, where they lived until they died at a good age. Muriel was driving well into her eighties, but Reggie never did drive, and after Muriel's death, his friend, farmer Geoff Ashwell from Warren Farm, would visit him to chauffeur him about.

Reggie Newman's 100th birthday at Finchcroft, with Geoff Ashwell of Warren Farm, 1987.

Chrysanthemum and Fairview Cottages

Jim Morton:

Further down Thorley Lane there were two terraced cottages, Chrysanthemum and Fairview. Ron and Winnie Barker lived at Chrysanthemum Cottage. They had almost half an acre of ground on which they kept goats, rabbits, chickens and ducks. Mrs Barker was a widow for many years and her pleasures were simple – to walk around the fields with her border collie, following all the old footpaths that she knew so well. Win watched all the wild flowers, trees, birds and animals as the seasons came round. In particular she was fond of the foxes who used to call to see her. I remember one evening about a year prior to her death I dropped by to see her. She was sitting by the back door, and she motioned me to be quiet. Before long, just as it was getting dusk, there appeared a semicircle of five foxes waiting for their supper. It was a nightly ritual; they always called for supper and never missed it.

Curiously, Winnie was a keen supporter of the hunt, and huntsmen would call greetings across the field to her. She loved the countryside of Thorley and stood her ground with the developers, telling them that the road and housing would go ahead over her dead body. These were prophetic words. She died before it had all taken place, and her ashes are scattered in Matham's Wood. Next door in Fairview lived the Akers family: parents Sarah and Jim, and children Phil, Hilda, Maisie and Lilian, all pupils of the Village School. As a boy their father lived with his parents Jim and Esther in White Cottage, Church Lane. Jim senr had been the pig man's help at Moor Hall Farm, and Esther died in 1927, the year grandchild Lilian was born. Lilian tells us:

Our mother, Sarah Ann (née Rand), was head cook for the Frere family in Twyford House before the First World War, and she was often called upon by Mrs Streeter, along with her friend, Sarah Georgina Hammond, to help cook and serve for the parties of guests from London that the Streeter family entertained.

Left: *Winnie Barker at Chrysanthemum Cottage.*

Far left: *The wedding of Horace Saville and Hilda Akers. Left to right: John and Emma Saville, Lilian Akers, George Saville, groom and bride, Maisie Akers and Sarah and James Akers.*

Sarah Georgina was Auntie Georgie to the Hammond twins, Jean and Joan, who lived across the field in Old Cottages at Butler's Hall.

Our father, Jim, worked as chauffeur gardener to Captain Elliott of Moor Hall until Capt Elliott left Thorley in around 1938. He later worked as a van driver for Collins Cross laundry until he retired. I remember he used to cut all our hair on Saturdays.

At school, I was thought of as mischievous and a bit 'dizzy', but Teddie Kent was my 'boyfriend' at school and we always sat together, and Gordon Barker stood up for me when I put a frog in Miss Smith's desk, making her scream! I liked singing, and later I was in TADS. And I still sing in the Bishop's Stortford Choral Society and Little Hallingbury village choir.

Phil used to work for de Havilland; he is married with four children. Hilda married Horace Saville, who lived back along the lane at Thorley Houses, and they have a daughter Jean (now Warbey). Maisie married Bob Crisp, whose grandfather had also chanced to live at Thorley Houses, and they too have a daughter. Lilian has two daughters. Jean Warbey tells us:

My mother Hilda at 16 years old worked as a kitchen maid for the Freres at £1.10s. per month. Beryl Frere paid for her to have her eyes tested by a London specialist because she was having trouble with her vision, and Beryl Frere put down lino so that my mother wouldn't have to scrub floors, but it made the cook pick on her because she was favoured. She told Hilda that she wasn't bright enough to get into the WAAF, but my mother met her once in her WAAF uniform – sweet revenge. After two years, my mother went to the Wolfsons as cook general for £2 per month. She cooked for everyone and the work was harder, but the people kinder. As soon as she was 17 she worried her Dad to let her go into the WAAF, and although not old enough she didn't need a birth certificate for her medical, and she reported for duty in 1940.

Bob Crisp tells of his family's association with Thorley and the Akers family:

My great-grandfather and his family fished the Norfolk and Suffolk Broads, but my grandfather came to Thorley to

start a new life at Cox's Farm, later moving to Piggott's Farm and going to live with his family in one of the cottages at Thorley Houses, which chanced to be close to my future wife's grandparents.

The 1914–18 war came along, and my father Albert joined the Army, as did Jim Akers. When the last war broke out and the Home Guard was formed, Jim joined and became a member of the Platoon that used Twyford Mill in Pig Lane near to the Frere mansion. At 15 years, I also joined the Home Guard and was sent to the Mill to join up with Sgt Field's Platoon to train with Jim Akers and other local people.

After my demob from the Army I met up with Maisie (one of Jim's daughters) and we were married in December 1949.

Rumballs Farm (or Rumbles or Rumbolds Farm)

Next we come Rumballs Farm, but only after crossing the bypass and finding our way along what used to be Thorley Lane. It has been stopped up and is now a featureless track alongside wooden fences enclosing back gardens. In the 1950s Rumballs Farm was a pig farm and was divided into two dwellings, where two families lived – the Days and the Browns – both working for the Streeters. The Days used the back door and the Browns used the front.

Little has come forward about the Browns. In the Browns' half of Rumballs Farm lived Bertha Warwick (née Griggs), who had married Mr Brown and had a son named Tom, and had later married Mr Warwick who worked at Millar's. Bertha was the sister of Winnie Griggs, who lived with her aunt Mrs Hudgell in a house next to Rockdale in The Street. Ted Kent recalls that she was his mother's best friend.

Rumballs Farm, 1920s.

Alice Day.

Richard Doe, whose mother was Alice Day, recalls his visits as a child to Thorley, where he had many relations on both sides:

My grandfather, Dick Doe, was raised in Hope Cottage on the London Road at the northern edge of the parish.

Dick and Mabel Doe had five children: Margaret, Frank, William, Tony and Gerald, all of whom were baptised in Thorley Church. Mabel (1894–1983) was a very gifted needlewoman, making clothes for her children and later items for exhibition at local and county WI, of which she was an active member. She became a good friend of Pam Streeter, sister of Tom, and later spent years as a resident companion to Mrs Blanche Streeter at Thorley Place. Mabel and Dick are buried in Thorley Church graveyard.

My mother was born at Rumballs Farm in 1919. Her parents, Willie (Jack) Day and Sarah (née Crabb), who took on the tenancy of the farm in 1912 when they married, had three other children – Emily (Cissie), Joe and Jim. Her father William had been raised at No. 7 Pump Yard by Joseph and Emma Day. He moved from there to Rumballs Farm in 1912, and from there to New Cottages in 1953, when I was ten years old. Sarah 's mother was known as Great Granny Crabb, who had four other children: Walter, Emily, Alice and Lizzie. My mother's sister Emily, who died at the end of 2002, was married to Ron Corbyn, and had a daughter Pat (now Birch). She was a great friend of Beattie Stoakes.

I particularly remember Jim. Born in 1913, he was a likeable, quiet character. During his early years he suffered an accident while playing with a fire, and one side of his face and hair were burnt. I remember that Jim was often to be found at the Green Man, scanning the paper for tips for the weekend horse races. On days off he would don his best flat cap and catch the train to Newmarket, enjoying the spirit of the races. Throughout most of his life he would cycle to his sister Emily Corbyn (my aunt) in Nursery Road for Sunday lunch, using a moped in later years. One Sunday, Jim didn't appear and he was found near the Green Man sleeping it off in a ditch! He was known for always giving really good Christmas presents, and he would always buy good clothes. He would bring his latest purchases in a brown paper parcel tied with string and show them to his sister and then take them back home on his bicycle.

Willie Day.

During the '50s my father would drive us in his Austin 7 from Cambridge to visit family in Bishop's Stortford and Thorley. I can remember the cold air coming in through gaps in the canvas hood. We would sometimes stop first at The Lodge to see Mr Kirk, organist at Thorley Church. The Lodge was on Thorley Lane at the entrance to an avenue of fir trees, planted by Sir Walter Gilbey who thought that evergreen was supposed to be a cure for TB.

The farm was eventually sold by the Streeters to Martin Sortwell, whose wife Brenda ran a craft shop for a number of years, until the new housing enveloped the farm and the Sortwells moved away. Brenda Sortwell writes:

Rumballs Farm Craft Centre was opened in October 1984 as a craft centre selling traditional English crafts set in a traditional working farm setting. The centre was an instant success and the teashop followed in 1988. Visitors came from miles away and once a year local craftsmen came and demonstrated their skills. Eventually the centre became a needlecraft centre and workshops were held. It was a special place to a lot of people, including myself.

Jubilee Cottage (Crow's Croft)

Rose Monk recalls:

Crow's Croft is a thatched cottage located just past Rumballs Farm and near the spinney at Thorley Place. The 1901 census gives its name as Jubilee Cottage. Early in the 1900s it was a pork butcher's shop, run by Lew Reed. His pork sausages and brawn were well known, and he would deliver his meat by pony and trap to all the villagers. The shop itself was alongside the cottage, and the horse was tethered on Thorley Common.

A Mr Parris and Mr Alderson lived at Crows Croft in the war and worked in London. Jean and Joan's mother used to do housework for them. She was also caretaker at the school and made the tea at all the jumble sales held there. The cottage has changed hands many times.

Piggott's Farm

Piggott's Farm was situated on the northern town edge of Thorley Common and was once owned by Edgar Tinney and later by Wilfrid. Ernie Vale was foreman, as was his father.

When the Thorley Park estate was built, the farm was sold and converted into the Harvest Moon public house. We shall not go there; instead we shall continue along Thorley Lane to Corner Cottage.

Painting of Crows Croft by Mrs Reed, 1920s.

Piggott's Farm, with pigs in the foreground, 1930s.

Left: *Frank and Violet Crabb are pictured* (fifth and sixth from left) *in a wedding group at Thorley Church.*

Right: *Corner Cottage, with sash windows. The building was demolished and rebuilt in July 1995.*

Below: *The wedding of Dorothy and George Wood at Thorley Church.*

Chapter 9
Where the Lanes Meet

Corner Cottage

Rose Monk recalls:

Corner Cottage [which is shown as Burnthouse on the 1921 OS map] *was owned by the Streeter family and was once lived in by Mr and Mrs Alford and their family of boys Reggie, Alfred and Billy. Mr Alford was chauffeur/gardener to Tom Streeter, who lived in Thorley Place along the lane. Then came the Harris family from Meadow Cottage, and later Frank Crabb lived there with his wife Violet (née Harris) until her death. Frank was a widower for quite a number of years. Violet used to plant snowdrops in the spinney across the lane and there they still bloom in profusion every spring as a memory to her. The house has since been taken down and rebuilt, and has had several owners.*

Thorley Place Cottages

These cottages were located in the grounds of Thorley Place, the Streeter family home, and at one time were called Laundry Cottages. The two Misses Archer (sisters) ran a laundry at No. 1. One of them had a daughter; the other stood only a few feet high. At some time, Freddie and Ellen Brewster (née Carter) moved into No. 1 from the White Cottage. Betty, their daughter, a friend of Peggy at 2 New Cottages, was ill and died of cancer aged 26.

Probably in the early 1920s, John Wood, who was the Streeters' gardener, moved from No. 2 New Cottages to No. 2 Thorley Place Cottages. His wife Cis was the sister of Freddie Brewster and Alice Gilson who lived in The Street. Cis and John's son George married Dorothy Cornell when both were in the employ of the Freres at Twyford House. George proposed marriage under the mistletoe one Christmas when Dorothy was working in Twyford House as a kitchen maid and George was cleaning boots and the silver. Dorothy was a great friend of Kit Clark of No. 1 New Cottages, who had always herself had an eye for George but eventually married a different George, son of Grandma Chappell and brother of Frank and Peter. Dorothy herself had been a girlfriend of Eric Warman.

The cottages have since been sold to different buyers, the owners of one of them at the time of writing being the Loadmans who moved from Pig Lane.

Thorley Place, The Cottage and Premier Court Nursing Home

Thorley Place, like the other 'big' houses in the parish, was where village gentry lived and hosted village 'occasions'. Bought by the Streeter farming family in the 1890s, it was set in park land and spinneys, and remained the home of widowed Blanche Streeter until 1966, when it was bought by Bernard Mulvany and became the Thorley Place Hotel. Bernard's father, 'Pops', used to be the groundsman.

All the Streeter children, except Pamela, married and moved away. The eldest son, Tom Streeter, continued to run the family's Thorley farms from Harp's Farm, Great Hallingbury, where he and his wife Nesta brought up their family. Mr Tom Streeter was lord of the manor at Thorley and also a churchwarden. Peter Warboys recalls that his mother's Aunt Carrie had been nurse to all the Streeter children, and then to some of the grandchildren, the Chester-Masters who lived at Cirencester. Some villagers say that they have heard tell of the story that the ghost of one of the children would be seen walking down the spiral staircase. Rose Monk's earliest memories are of Mr and Mrs George Streeter giving the village Christmas parties held in the Village Hut, and she recalls that Thorley Place was where Mrs Blanche Streeter would hold the WI meetings, run by Marjorie Robinson of the Rectory, as well as other village events.

As an hotel, Thorley Place at first prospered and was the venue for wedding receptions, club dinners and seminars, with businessmen sometimes arriving by helicopter, but it declined and Bernard Mulvany moved with his father to a nearby cottage in the grounds, where Pops died, having reached his 100th birthday. The gardens, bordering on Thorley Lane and having become very overgrown, were sold in the 1990s for the development of Premier Court Nursing Home, and Thorley Place itself has since been sold

Thorley Place, 1930s.

and restored as a family home.

Premier Court is where Gladys Warboys resides at the time of writing, and for Rogationtide celebrations in 2003 Richard Doe assembled a team of Morris men in honour of Beryl Frere and Tom Camp. They performed at the fête taking place on the cricket field and then crossed the lane to dance for Gladys and other residents at Premier Court, where they were received with enthusiasm.

Stone Hall

Rose recalls:

Stone Hall is the oldest building in Thorley. Centuries ago the Defoes lived there, and a pane in one of the windows was scratched with the name of Daniel Defoe [1660–1731]. The front hall floor was laid by a Defoe on the occasion of a wedding and a Defoe is buried in the churchyard.

Stone Hall used to be owned by the Streeters. Earlier tenants, we understand from older relatives, were the Batt family, Lady Clark, and Mr and Mrs Maber. Mrs Maber was the Under Matron at the then Rye Street hospital. Mr and Mrs Eagling and family stayed there for a spell in the 1920s, and then there were the two Misses Mavrojinis. The Franklins, who were connected with the French family of butchers, also stayed there.

While Stone Hall still belonged to the Streeters, Herbert and Esther Monk (my future in-laws) went to

live there with their family in 1937. In 1961, after the Monk children had left home, it was sold to John Tinney, whose niece Daphne moved in with her husband Mr House. Mrs Claire Hewitt, widow of Dr Patrick Hewitt also lived in Stone Hall for a while, and then the house was sold to Mr and Mrs MacGregor and family. At the time of writing the MacGregors live in Walsham le Willows and are neighbours of the Whitworths, who at a later date moved there from Moor Hall.

In the wartime, when the unexploded 500lb bomb landed on the cricket field opposite, the Monk family was evacuated. Mr and Mrs Monk stayed

Stone Hall in the 1920s. Left to right: *Phyllis Eagling (now Want), Doris Eagling, George Chappell.*

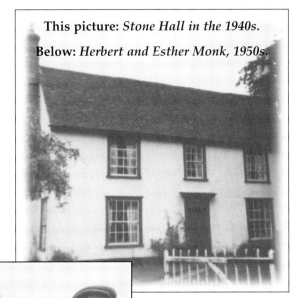

This picture: *Stone Hall in the 1940s.*

Below: *Herbert and Esther Monk, 1950s.*

with Horace Barnard, sons Noel and Vic went to Miss Moorhouse at the schoolhouse, and Mary, John and Dennis went to Aunt Ethel (their mother's twin sister) at Farnham. Mr Piper, who ran an antiques shop in town, gave Mr Monk a job moving furniture for the eight weeks it took to detonate and dispose of the bomb, during which time schooling was set up temporarily for the 'Lowlands' children in Thorley House.

Sunset Cottages

As the reader already knows, Gladys' grandparents, the Watsons, lived in No. 1 Sunset at the turn of the twentieth century, and she and her family moved into No. 2, where the Warboys family stayed throughout the wartime, next to 'Uncle George' Chappell in No. 1. Peter and Frank Warboys describe their family's home in the 1930s and '40s:

We were five children – Frank, Peter, Cecil, Barbara and Michael. We lived from 1931–48 at Sunset Cottages, a pair of semi-detached cottages in the centre of Thorley, about 100 yards from the school. The cottage had two downstairs rooms, a kitchen and a 'front room', and three bedrooms. There was no electricity, no running water, an outside bucket loo, a pump at the back of the house drawing water from a well (shared with next door), and no bathroom or sinks in the house. In some summers the pump ran dry in common with other wells in the village. The only water to be had then had to be fetched from a horse-drawn water tank on wheels, which was parked by the council outside the school in long dry spells. We children were sent down with buckets and jugs to fetch

water back to the house with the inevitable spillage and accidents. Beyond the pump was a wash-house with a copper and a shallow stone sink and incorporating the loo at the back. There were coal fires, and lighting was oil-lamps downstairs and candles upstairs. Electricity was installed in 1947, but there were no running water, bathroom or toilet facilities, even in 1948. We kept chicken for both eggs and meat and bred rabbits for the table. One of Frank's abiding memories was the constant job of finding greenery for the rabbits from the roadside verges.

In No. 2 lived George and Kit Chappell. For a while George had been engaged to Doris Eagling, Gladys' sister, who was heartbroken when George split up with her in order to marry his first wife Lily. About two years after Lily died in 1943, George married Kit Chappell, who stayed on in the tied cottage after George's death, until the Tinneys took on farm worker Derek Bradnick, who then moved in with his family.

At the time of writing, Colin Selwood and his wife Heather live in No. 1 Sunset. He is a tailor and photographer.

Peter Warboys recalls childhood memories of the traffic going by Sunset Cottages in the 1940s:

Vehicles passing the house were few and far between. The milkman, baker, butcher and coalman called regularly, but the most exciting was when the agricultural steam engines went past. These were always in pairs called Darby and Joan, Prince and Princess, etc., and towing large reversible ploughs, cultivators and the caravans in which the men lived. A particular memory was the doctor's car, as when visiting Mrs Streeter he dropped his dog off at the bottom of the lane and left it to run behind the car. He would go past at about 15mph and the dog would follow about five minutes later.

Alison Bradnick, another child, but from a time 50 years later, also writes about the traffic going by:

One of my memories is when my Dad asked me and my sister if we would do him a favour, we thought like tidy our rooms or something, but it was to do him a traffic survey. We did it for about two hours out of our living-room window. There were very few cars, lorries or vans, but there were lots of people going for walks. If we were to do it again now, there would be about ten times more because of the old people's home and also

Sunset Cottages, with Rectory horses in the paddock.

young teenagers racing up and down from the new estate. But an exciting memory that has stuck in my mind is when a Sainsbury's lorry ended up in the cricket field along the lane. When we saw it go by, we thought that it was probably going to turn around in the car park on Thorley Lane. It didn't, it ended up blocking part of the road and most of the cricket field entrance. My Dad had to get a tractor and chain from Thorley Hall Farm where he worked at the time, and he towed the huge lorry around the field and fetched it out the other end. My Dad got a round of applause.

I have seen lots of changes in Thorley, but I'm glad to say though that they have mainly been happy ones and only one or two sad ones.

Harringtons

Harringtons.

Below: Simon Knight in Scout uniform at Harringtons.

Left: Children in the garden at Harringtons. Left to right: Sheila Robinson, Adrian Taylor, Philip Robinson, Andrew Taylor, Jane Knight, Richard Robinson.

Harringtons is set back in gardens between Sunset Cottages and the one-time grounds of the Old Rectory, where Revd Sydney Robinson and his family lived as neighbours of the Knight family. Jim Knight, a mainstay of the Thorley British Legion, lived there with Dorothy, daughter Jane and son Simon.

The Old Rectory, Church View (formerly the New Rectory) and Pendle

At the turn of the twentieth century the rector, Revd John Procter (senr) and his wife were living in the

Old Rectory with their three children, all of whom remained unmarried. It is believed that a previous rectory had existed in the grounds of the Old Rectory, which had been completed in 1854, the date scratched on one of the bricks. The architecture is impressive and one of the interesting features is an ancient kitchen-garden wall. The gardens and grounds of the Old Rectory were extensive, and many villagers recall the rooks settling in the tall trees that were a feature of the landscape seen from across the fields all around. Then came Revd Sydney Robinson, who lived with his wife and family in the Old Rectory until a newer building, the New Rectory, had been erected further away in the rectory grounds.

Lawyer Bob Lofts then bought the Old Rectory and lived there with his wife Anne and their family until Bob died, when it was sold to Elliotts, property developers, and later bought by Mr and Mrs Bailey who lived there with their extended family until 2000. Anne Lofts, who was a Girl Guide Commissioner, retained one of the fields for its continuing use by the Thorley Scouts and Guides.

After the Robinsons retired, the next rector was provided with a church house on the newly built Thorley Park estate, and what was known as the New Rectory was renamed Church View and sold to Michael and Maura Newman, who still live there with their family at the time of writing. Pendle was built in the rectory grounds in the late 1960s and the first residents were the Bulloughs, with Lofty the sausage dog. In 2003 it is occupied by Fred and Jean Townsend, who have lived there for many years.

In these excerpts Sheila Dutton, daughter of Revd Sydney Robinson, shares her memories of rectory life:

The Old Rectory had 18 rooms. When my parents, Sydney and Marjorie, arrived there was enough furniture to occupy one room, and bedrooms for themselves, one child and a baby.

Rosa Monk and Mrs Peter Chappell assisted my parents in the cleaning of the Rectory. The only sources of heat were a Rayburn oven in the kitchen, and a coal fire in the lounge.

Winter was nearly always an expensive time for my father, as the pipes would always freeze up, and then burst. We often had water dripping through ceilings. On one occasion father missed his footing and came crashing through the ceiling of the bathroom, leaving a gaping hole and a dint in his pride, so that was also extra expense.

During winter, as others will recall, the lane would not be passable, and this meant a day off school to build snowmen, or have snowball fights with Jane and Simon Knight, who lived in Harringtons, and other villagers. This unfortunately also meant that milk and bread deliveries were delayed or not available, and I have known my father walk down the lane and collect milk in a wheelbarrow.

The Old Rectory in the 1930s.

Inset: *Marjorie Robinson with the family – Philip, Sheila, Michael and Richard, 1955.*

At Christmas a fire was lit in the dining-room, as we children virtually lived in there over that period. Getting in the Christmas tree was very exciting, as my father would go into the woods and saw off a suitable-looking yew tree branch, followed closely by all of us. Christmas dinner was traditional. The turkey was given by the Streeter family each year, and this would be hung for several days. My father plucked and drew it on Christmas Eve.

Carol singing was also a wonderful part of Christmas. Myself and Jane Knight (daughter of Dorothy and Jim Knight, who was the churchwarden) had the privilege of collecting the money and wishing everyone a happy Christmas. My earliest recollection of carol singing was when Pam Streeter's mother was still alive at Thorley Place. We would all be asked in to sing in the hall, and the old lady would listen, aided by an ear trumpet, which sent myself and Jane into hoots of laughter (afterwards, of course). We were also invited into Castle Farm, when Mr and Mrs Sparrow lived there (they ran a shop in Bishop's Stortford), but the finale was at the home of Reginald and Muriel Newman, who gave us mince pies and drinks.

To help with income, the top storey of the Rectory and one of the bedrooms and a downstairs bathroom were let out to various people. The people I remember were Mr and Mrs Keegan, who were Scottish, and who stayed there for a long time, until the new Rectory was built. Charlie Sargent, who was a founder member of the Thorley branch of the British Legion, also lived at one time in the flat with his wife Kathleen.

My father let part of the field to some families with caravans. One such caravan was owned by Mr and Mrs Smith who kept several wire-haired terriers. I loved to go down and visit, and when she was baking, my treat was to lick out the cake-mixture bowl. Ponies were always a feature of the Rectory. A field and glebe at the back of the Rectory were used. The first pony was bought with a trap from Cambridge for my mother to go around the village. Another source of income was the rearing of pigs. This came about because at my parents' first garden party there was bowling for a pig, which of course my mother won.

The Working Men's Club or Village Hut (Scout Hut)

Having turned into Church Lane at the Village School, we pass the Village Hut on the right before arriving at Rectory Close. The Hut was given to the village by Tom Streeter after the First World War. It was for use by the local men returning from war as the Working Men's Club, and as the reader by now knows,

The Village Hut.

The wedding reception of Beatrice and Edward Lloyd in the Village Hut, 1939. Pictured are: 1. and 2. George and Rosa Stoakes (Beattie's parents), 3. Jimmy Eames, 4. Mrs Eames, 5. Lil Chappell, 6. Eileen (Lil's niece), 7. George Chappell, 8. Win Candy (later Barker), 9. Ron Barker [obscured: Kate, Charlie and George Blackman], 10. Cyril Adams, 11 and 12. Mr and Mrs Lloyd (Edward's parents), 13. Barbara Lloyd, 14. Tom Lloyd (Edward's brother), 15. Groom, 16. Bride, 17. Rose Stoakes (Beattie's sister), 18. Molly Lloyd [obscured: Mary and Hilda Reed], 19. Mrs Reed, 20. PC Reed, 21. Harry Bailey (Cyril's brother), 22. Meda Dean, 23. Cyril Bailey (Dolly's husband), 24. Gladys Oliver, 25. Dolly Bailey (Beattie's sister), 26. Yolande Frost.

the Village Hut became a focal point for the villagers' small gatherings, meetings and entertainments for two or three decades. It is now the Venture Scouts' Hut, and is in dire need of renovation. A planning application has been granted and funds are being raised for this work.

Nos 1-6 Rectory Close

The six houses in Rectory Close were built as a crescent of council-houses in Church Lane after the Second World War. At No. 1 lived Connie and Jack Williams, who had three children: John, Clifford and Mary. Connie's father was Bill Seabon, who was the road sweeper and lived in Thorley Street. Living at No. 1 at the time of writing, with his wife and sons, is Ron Cox, a retired policeman who was involved with the tracking and apprehension of criminal Harry Roberts. In No. 2 live Rose and Frank Monk.

Over the years the Rectory Close council-houses, as with the houses built as the Blocks in The Street, have been purchased by residents or sold after tenants have left. Betty and George (Titch) Clark, with son Ian, used to live in No. 3, which is the only house to remain a council property at the time of writing. Ernie and Edna Warman (née Graves) lived in No. 4. Liz remembers that she and Dave were out early during lambing time and spoke with Ernie in the lane on the day that he died by drowning in the river. Then came Ian and Pat Bateman, who sadly lost one daughter Laura in a road accident. In No. 5 there used to live Bubbles Barker and husband Gordon who was a pupil at the Village School. The house was sold to Sheila Hewitt and Robin Lumsden, who arrived just before the farmland behind Rectory Close was built up with bunding and tree planting as park land adjacent to the new St Michael's Mead estate. And No. 6 was where Gladys lived until 2002.

White Cottage and Penningtons

After leaving Gladys' old house, we turn back towards Thorley Lane. Rose Monk recalls:

Opposite the Village Hut there is an old farm cottage, once lived in by Mr and Mrs Malyon, and earlier by great-grandparents of the Akers family, Jim who was the pig man at Moor Hall, and Esther who died in 1927. Then came Freddie and Ellen Brewster, who later moved to Thorley Place Cottages and whose daughter Betty, Peggy Robinson's friend, sadly died of polio aged 26. After the Brewsters came Horace Barnard, with his sister Emily Debnam and little terrier Binny, and until 1999 it was the home of Mr and Mrs Bailey, who both lived to a good age. Ex-shepherdess Liz and husband Dave now live there.

Next door there used to be a thatched cottage called Penningtons, which was destroyed by fire. Beyond this, in the early 1900s, were two joined cottages which also burned down.

From here we continue walking down Thorley Lane past the Old Rectory, with its driveway securely fenced and gated, and on through a spinney to reach the Whittington Way roundabout, which gives access to the Thorley Park estate. We cross the roundabout and continue past Bishop's Avenue which gives access to the Twyford Park estate until we reach the T junction at Hither Farm.

Above: *White Cottage in winter.*

This picture: *Penningtons, which was destroyed by fire.*

Above: *Frank and Rose Monk outside No. 2 Rectory Close, 2003.*

Inset: *Bubbles Barker with daughters Jane and Jacqueline, 1950s.*

Above: *Fred Bird (Bert's father) in a pony trap outside Park Gates,*
leading from The Lodge in Thorley Lane, c.1910.

Below: *Cox's Farm, in Havers Lane, 1950s.*

Chapter 10

Where Village Meets Town

The Gilbey Lodges

Thorley Plantation in the first half of the twentieth century was mostly open country or woodland, with gravel pits on the lower ground to the south. Sir Edward Gilbey, before the First World War, had plans to build a mansion on the higher ground in this area, with tree-lined driveways leading to it from Thorley Lane and the London Road. He did not realise his ambitious idea, but three lodges were built as part of this scheme.

The Lodge in Thorley Lane was once owned by nearby farmers, the Cox family, who farmed on the site of what is now Great Havers School at the top of Thorley Hill. An avenue of trees was planted from The Lodge, the intention being to create an impressive tree-lined drive extending northwards and reaching as far as the top of Thorley Hill, where the proposed mansion was to be built for the then Sir Walter Gilbey, a well-known benefactor of the area.

There were large wrought-iron gates at the entrance to the drive, but the project was never completed owing to the outbreak of the First World War in 1914. Early residents of The Lodge were Mr and Mrs Cyril Kirk.

As part of the same Gilbey design, two additional lodges were intended to lead up to the Gilbey mansion from the east. South Lodge is situated on South Road leading into Bishop's Stortford, alongside a definitive footpath. It would have given access to the planned Gilbey mansion at the top of Thorley Hill near Great Havers School. A second lodge at the bottom of Thorley Hill was to serve as a third driveway to the Gilbey mansion and had at its entrance large white double gates for this purpose. This lodge still exists, but is now part of the Thorley Hill and the Havers estate housing.

Joe Brace, husband of Joan, recalls that Cox's farmhouse used to be near the site of Great Havers School, and the farmland used to stretch as far as The Lodge in Thorley Lane and border Bird's Farm. Harry Cox was the farmer and Tubby Brace used to deliver the milk. The farmhouse was purchased by John Tinney and converted into one house and four flats. Fred Owers, who worked at Piggott's Farm and later Thorley Hall Farm, lived in the house with wife Stella.

Millar's Machinery

This factory was first called Featherby's, then Thorley Works and later Millar's. It was here that many of the villagers found employment, particularly women during the Second World War when everyone able was called up to fight or to take up some form of war work. It was demolished in the 1990s.

One of the villagers, Vic Monk, recalls working at Millar's:

The day started by clocking in by 7.30a.m., putting on overalls ready to start working your machine. I was a Centre Lathe Turner in the Machine Shop. I worked a 48-hour week, and [you] had to clock off at dinnertime if you left the works and in the evening when day's work was finished. At one time there were about 250 employed there.

The foundry made castings of all the machine's parts from wood patterns in sand inside square boxes for cement mixers, trench pumps and tarmac-laying machines known as chip spreaders. The plate shop cut steel plate to shape for the parts. The machine shop machined the parts by boring holes and turning diameters for exact fit. The fitting shop assembled finished parts to complete the machines.

They were then all tested before being loaded onto flat trailers and towed by a road tractor from Millar's to the railway siding opposite the Tanners Arms public house on the London Road. From there they went to various road-working sites in England, and many others were exported to countries abroad.

Left: *Millar's workmen. Left to right: ?, John Eldred, Charles Sargent, Sid Hammond, Des Ramsey, Arthur Peck, Bert Hammond, 'Ginger' Snapsford, George Clark, Ken Milton, Jack Partridge, Frank Monk.*

Right: *A tarmac mixer made at Millar's, with Frank Monk driving the engine.*

Edward Miller recalls:

Millar's Machinery Works which manufactured heavy plant and equipment was a major employer in the town, employing perhaps 200 staff. Work would start at 7.30a.m., with lunch break between 12.30 and 1.30p.m., and finished at 5.30p.m. Saturday work was between 7.30a.m. and 12.30p.m

Manual workers in the town were warned of the time by the 7.20a.m. hooter which was heard all over the town and I think was sounded again to signal 'knocking off' time. Millar's Works broadcast 'Music while you work' throughout the factory in both the mornings and afternoons and, living in Park Lane, we could hear the music with ease. When work finished the roads were filled with staff making for home on their bicycles.

Adjacent to Millar's Works were Browns Timber Yard and the Snap factory, which made snaps for Christmas crackers. From Brown's yard would be heard the whine of the circular saw as it cut through the timber. Many of the workers at the Snap factory were ladies from London and Burley Road who might be seen hastening to work in the morning with hair in curlers covered with tucked-in scarves.

Barrett's (Dawn's Stores)

This village shop in London Road on the corner of Nelson Street served the village for the whole of the last century. Originally called Barrett's, and run by the Foremans, it is now owned by Dawn Ashraf (née Prior) and her husband, who purchased the house and shop in the 1960s. Pam Finch (née Wolfson) recalls:

My mother got her shopping at the store run by Jimmy Foreman, who had a marvellous baritone voice. We had an Austin Seven in those days when it was rare to have a car, and I used to go to Foreman's for lighter fuel to run it on. Half a gallon (not purchased all at once) would be enough to take us to Hatfield Heath.

Thorley Terrace and the Mission Hall

The 1901 census lists the names and occupations of families living in the parish of Thorley at that time. In Twyford Road there was a row of 18 houses known as Thorley Terrace. Mention should be made of Adelaide and Robert Pigram who lived in No. 8 Thorley Terrace and had ten children. They died in 1914 and 1922 respectively and are buried in St James' churchyard. Very many of their descendants have close connections with Thorley, a number of them staying in the area. Ivy Pigram tells us that Hazel Upton (née Pigram) remembers her Uncle Fred, one of Robert's grandsons, telling her about relatives who came from Thorley. Also, Dolly Hammond, mother of Liz the shepherdess, was first married to Robert Pigram, Tony in Moor Hall Cottages being Liz's half-brother.

Further along towards the river were the Church Mission Hall and the level crossing at Twyford. It is known that James Hale, who ran the Post Office in The Street around 1900, built an outpost for Thorley Church in Twyford Road called The Mission Hall in 1892. Incidentally, James also built a barn for Francis Newman at Moor Hall Farm in 1896 for £40. Richard Doe recalls:

My grandfather Dick Doe, met his wife Mabel (née Smith) when attending a Sunday afternoon meeting of the Lads Bright Hour in the Thorley Mission Hall. They spent their early married life in Southmill Road, and after moving to Hallingbury Road they converted their front room into the Boundary Stores. Mabel ran the shop after Dick died. Mabel's father, James Smith, lived with his family in Twyford Road, and ran the Bishop's Stortford railway engine depot,. He always insisted on wearing white trousers to drive the locos to Liverpool Street Station.

Grenville Bird remembers that on the Stortford side of the railway level crossing in Twyford Road there was a Church Mission Hall. It was a wooden building lit by oil lamps, and Sunday school classes were still being held there when he first moved to Thorley parish in 1958. Edward Miller tells us:

We young people in the parish used to meet with the rector at the Sunday school held in the Mission Room in Twyford Road, memorable amongst other things for an organ of considerable age which stopped playing when it thought it would! In 1953 a number of us attended Confirmation classes there before being confirmed by the Bishop of St Albans.

Jack Phillips recalls:

Although I was brought up as a Nonconformist and living on the fringe of the parish, we were still within the parish boundaries, and I remember we used to attend evening services on occasion in the Mission Room in Twyford Road, when the Revd John Procter used to conduct a short service. Here again he used to cover a lot of mileage as he used to walk everywhere. He was very popular with the parishioners and on Rogation Days he used to conduct services on the various local farms to bless the growing crops. These visits used to attract quite a lot of attention from the local people, who used to follow him from field to field.

Twyford Rail Crossing

Near Southmill Lock there was a vehicular level crossing over the railway at the end of Twyford Road. It is still a crossing at the time of writing, but only for pedestrians. Grenville Bird recalls:

Beside the railway was the crossing keeper's hut and cottage. The keeper was a disabled railwayman, Mr Moxom. I believe he was wounded in the First World War and given this 'light' job as crossing keeper. Mrs Moxom was renowned for never stopping talking if you met her at the gates.

John Pigram, of 8 Thorley Terrace, Twyford Road, c.1910.

Level crossing with Mr Moxom, the gatekeeper.

Bryan South reminds us that the level crossing keeper who kept the crossing south of Thorley Wash at Spellbrook was Mr Bright, who lived in the Blocks in Thorley Street. The road becomes Twyford Lane once over the pedestrian level crossing at Twyford. This leads past Twyford Bury and its farmhouse to join Pig Lane.

123

Twyford Bury, 1930s.

Above: *Frederick George Warboys, with his prizewinning tandem team, at Twyfordbury Farm, 1926.*
Left to right: F.G. Warboys senr, F.G. Warboys junr and his wife Dolly, ?.

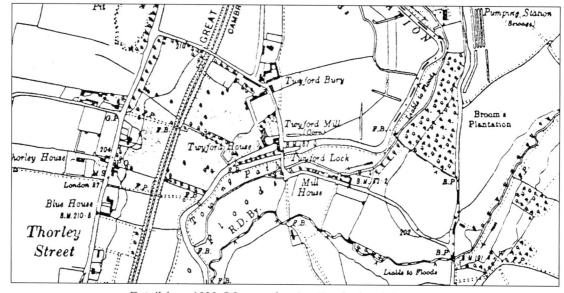

Detail from 1923 OS map, showing Twyford and the estate.

Chapter 11

Twyford and the River

Twyford House, 1939.

We will walk along Pig Lane from Twyford Bury to Latchmore Bank and back.

Pig Lane leads to the riverside settlements in Twyford. The significant dwellings in this area are Twyford Bury, Twyfordbury Farm, Twyford Mill, Twyford Mill Farmhouse and Twyford House. All of these properties, their stables, barns and outbuildings, as well as the surrounding fields and park land, belonged to the Frere family who lived in Twyford House and rented out farms and property until just after the Second World War. Alfred George Boyd Gibbins purchased the estate, split it up to sell or rent as plots of land or converted properties, and he himself lived at Latchmore Bank, keeping Twyford House in trust for his daughter. None of this former magnificent country estate is recognisable at the time of writing.

Twyford Bury

Twyford Bury was once lived in by Eustace Frere, an accomplished architect, then the Misses Prior, afterwards Patrick Frere and family, and then the Maxwell family, followed by Dr Ian Paterson, whose wife received an award in the Queen's Honours List and became Dame Betty in recognition of her work in local government as chairman of Herts County Council. After the Patersons, in about 1987, came Geoffrey Thurley who was an accountant for Elliotts; his wife continued living there after her husband died.

Twyfordbury Farm

At the time of the First World War, Twyfordbury Farm used to be worked by Frederick George Warboys and later by Tony Klyusse, who eventually purchased Thorley Wash Farm after the sale of the Frere estate properties. It was the son, Frank Bertie Warboys, from Twyfordbury Farm, who married Gladys Eagling, the village schoolteacher. Both Frank and Peter Warboys and Molly Lambert (née Bird) have too many stories to tell here of the people of Pig Lane and the village during the time of the Freres.

The farm is no more, and its three buildings – Twyfordbury Farmhouse, Twyfordbury Cottage and Twyfordbury Barns – are now owned separately. The first occupant of the farmhouse was Mrs Ellis Eadie, CBE, whose work at one time involved the drafting of parliamentary bills. After she moved out in 1972 came Edward Stoneman and his French wife, who had connections with a vineyard in France. In the 1980s Colin and Jacqueline Arnott (née Ursell), whose parents lived in Ashdene in The Street, moved in with their three boys. In the cottage, for many years before his wife Beryl died from lung cancer, lived Cmdr and Mrs Cunningham and their three daughters. Gillian went into the Royal Navy, Annabel took up a career in the Army and was married to an SAS colonel, and Sarah, who used to play as a child with the Woods' son, Andrew, in Twyford Lodge and later became head girl at her school, went into the Bank of England. The barns were occupied by Mr Kluysse, who unsuccessfully tried to buy the farmland for housing development. His son, who replaced Jo Wood on the Parish Council, then bought and farmed at Thorley Wash in The Street, and the property in Pig Lane was bought by a sculptor who used the outhouses at the back as a studio and was very eccentric.

Twyford House (Twyford Mews)

Twyford House was a magnificent mansion, the home of Laurie and Maud Frere, and their four children, Phillis, Ursula, Beryl and son Bartle who died, the last of the male line, in the war. During the Second World War, Twyford House was taken over by the War Office as a maternity hospital for pregnant women evacuated from London. Afterwards, for a short while, it became an hotel that failed, and then flats. Boyd Gibbins had financial worries at this time and when the sale of flats fell through, Twyford House was bought by local property developers, Elliotts, who restored it as a listed building and converted it into offices. To help finance the costs, Elliotts built maisonettes and flats in the grounds. The occupants, apart from the two ladies in Nos 4 and 10 Twyford Mews, tend to be transitory. One feature of Twyford House, holding almost as much significance for the village as the church bells, used to be its

chiming clock, which could be heard on the hour all the way down Thorley Street when the wind was in the right direction. Lawrence Karthauser, a protégé of Miss Beryl, tells us that the clock had to be wound up and had long weights running from the loft. It is pleasing that Elliotts the builders retained the clock as part of the planned restoration.

Twyford Lodge (Converted Stables, Coach-house and Gardener's Cottage)

Jo and Peter Wood, who have lived in Twyford Lodge since 1962, are at the time of writing the residents who have lived longest in Pig Lane. Jo recalls what happened after the sale of Twyford House. Many of the Freres' tenants had problems when Boyd Gibbins broke up the estate, and there were a number of court cases. He sold the outbuildings of farms separately and built new houses in smaller pieces of land.

In the old swimming-pool at Latchmore Bank he kept two lions, Josephine and Napoleon, which had been given him as cubs by members of royalty with whom he played polo. Workmen engaged on alterations to Twyford Lodge in 1972 were concerned about the roaring of hungry lions, and eventually they were given to Whipsnade Zoo on his death. They did not settle and had to return to Latchmore Bank until Mrs Boyd Gibbins took them with her to live in Guildford, where they were kept in a tennis court.

Twyford Lodge was sold by Boyd Gibbins as a property comprising the Freres' coach-house, stables, gardener's cottage, kitchen and lean-to wash-house in four acres of park land. The first purchasers were Sue and John Cullver, then for five years Jean Asquith who rented out the field to horse owners and later sold the property to Jo and Peter in 1962. Peter, originally from Cambridge where his father was a don, and Jo, from Shropshire, had met in wartime when both were serving in the Forces. Peter commuted to London until 1983. Jo brought up their son Andrew and took part in village activities, becoming president of the Guides for the Eastern District, and serving on the Parish Council for 15

Jo and Peter Wood at Twyford Lodge, 1990s.

years, having taken over from Jean Asquith.

The four neighbouring properties are Twyford Orchard, Clappergate, The Chase and Chester Cottage. All are in what used to be the grounds of Twyford House. Boyd Gibbins turned a potting shed into a tiny bungalow, Chester Cottage, where Col and Mrs Hammond lived, until it was purchased by Herts County Council then Christopher Poole, who built on five rooms. The Freres' walled garden and fruit gardens were sold to Mabel and George Woodcock when Boyd Gibbins was in financial difficulties, and George built The Chase and his workshop. Clappergate used to be the piggeries, and was first owned by Percy Stevens who had a music and china shop in town before he sold it to Marks & Spencer a few years before he died. The Pages then bought Clappergate. Boyd Gibbins built Twyford Orchard for his foreman, who later went to Australia, and the property was then sold to Bryan and Doreen Piggott. The chauffeur's cottage was also sold separately.

Jo particularly remembers the Woodcocks as family friends:

Our son Andrew was fascinated by George Woodcock. He had a miniature railway going round his garden and in his workshop he could mend anything at all that was broken. He was a good friend, and he would come whenever we needed him. I remember how he saved our Xmas in 1962, a particularly bad winter when our roof began leaking. About 30 years ago he had just gone home after repairing our larder when Mabel fetched me because he felt ill, and he died in my arms. Mabel too was a good friend, a dressmaker, and she would babysit for us.

Twyford Lock and Canal Boat Octrine

Grenville Bird remembers the barges laden with timber that used to be drawn by horses on their way to Hughes timber yard frequently passing through Twyford Lock. He does not recall there having been a lock keeper's cottage at Twyford and wonders if his great-grandfather who was lock keeper at Southmill

Twyford Lock, 1906.

lock and lived in the cottage there, was lock keeper at Twyford too. Jo Wood recalls that at one time George Woodcock used to be the lock keeper at Twyford.

In recent years, two young people, Charles and Suzy, lived by the lock on their canal boat, *Octrine*, which they moored in the spur alongside, bringing a welcome atmosphere of life to the waterway.

Twyford Mill

In the early 1900s, Colin Sampford's grandfather was the miller. Jack Phillips recalls that Twyford Mill was still in operation as a working mill up to the early 1930s, and his memory of it was seeing Mr Lane, who was in charge, spending hours on his knees, chipping away at the huge grinding wheel. Mr Lane used to live in London Road, and his assistant was Reg Saban of Twyford Road. The owner of the mill was another well-known character, John Lawrence, who lived at Latchmore Bank. Jack recalls that he was a nice man who always had a word for everyone he met. He used always to walk down through the fields on a Thursday to attend Stortford market, appearing as a typical Dickensian character in his manner and the way he used to dress.

Frank Warboys recalls a Billy Poole who lived in Millers Cottage (which used to be two cottages) and worked at the mill in the 1940s.

Twyford Mill Farm

From 1926 until the break-up of the Frere estate in 1947 the Bird brothers, Bert and Arthur, farmed Twyford Mill Farm. Bert Bird lived at Twyford Mill Farm where daughter Molly (now Lambert) was born. Molly tells her story:

In 1901 Frederick and Fanny Bird were living with their young family in Sparrow's Nest. They had previously held the tenancy of Butler's Hall Farm and Castle Farm from the Streeter family, but this had not worked out well, and in 1902 they signed deeds entitling them to become, for the price of £66, the tenant farmers of Hither Farm, a dairy farm owned by the Frere family. They had 11 children. Two of their sons, Arthur and Bert, later farmed in partnership both Bird's Farm and Twyford Mill Farm, for which the tenancy rights had been purchased from the Frere family in 1926.

In about 1930, my father went to live in Twyford Mill Farm, on his marriage to Doris Eagling, sister of Gladys Warboys. I was born there and lived there until my marriage to Clarry Lambert in 1955. Soon afterwards my father retired through ill health to the farm he had eventually managed to purchase from Boyd Gibbins, who was experiencing financial problems at that time. Earlier in 1947 there had been a case brought to court to resolve the dispute between Boyd Gibbins and the Frere estate tenant farmers.

Left:
*Twyford
Mill
Farmhouse,
1940s.*

The rear view of Twyford Mill Farm, 1911.

*Molly Bird and her father Bert at
Twyford Mill Farm, c.1949.*

*The meadow opposite Twyford
Mill Farm, 1940s.*

The wedding of Molly Bird and Clarrie Lambert at Thorley Church, 1955. Left to right: Brenda Perry, Peter and Mrs Lambert, groom and bride, Bert and Mrs Bird, Barbara Warboys.

Bert Bird, with Gilbert the cart-horse, late 1940s.

The farm has gone, and the farmhouse is occupied in 2003 as two separate dwellings, Twyford Mill Farmhouse East and West, in one of which, at the time of writing, lives Robin Dromard, who runs the Stort canoe club at Southmill Lock. East Mill House, Mill Stream House and The Piggeries are conversions of outbuildings or are new dwellings built on the river side of the lane opposite Millers Cottage. Further along the lane are four houses set back from the road, called The Willows, Wragglers, Brookside and Heronswood. Roger and Sandy Halford in Heronswood are keen environmentalists and campaigners against the leaving of litter on the canal tow-path that runs through the parish and Pig Lane gardens.

Valley Riding Stables

The Streeter family owns land alongside the tow-path and has rented out fields to owners of riding stables since the 1960s. The Valley Stables horses bring back a welcome reminder of the rural atmosphere of earlier times.

Millers Cottage

Millers Cottage, which is now one dwelling, is situated on a footpath leading away from the mill, but strangely it falls just outside the Hertfordshire county boundary. Colin Sampford, a pupil of the Village School who has worked all his life on the Tinney farms, was born in one of the two cottages in 1937. His mother was Mary (née Barker), whose father Ernie Barker was foreman at Thorley Hall Farm.

Mr Sammy Barker was chauffeur to the Freres and lived in one of the cottages. He married Fanny Chappell, daughter of the Chappells in The Street, who was in service for the Freres at Twyford House. Sammy Barker later became chauffeur to Major Leach of Millar's.

Colin and his mother Mary are related (details unclear) to Emily Glasscock (née Turner), who remembers visiting, with her sisters Daisy and Lil, their Aunt Cis in Pig Lane during holidays. Emie's Aunt Cis used to make the caps and aprons for the Freres' maids, and do the laundry, as well as make school uniforms for the Streeter girls. Through her aunt, Emie became very much part of Thorley village life during the time of the Freres and has many stories of people and events. Since the 1980s Mrs Cooke has lived in Millers Cottage, which she used to let out as bed-and-breakfast accommodation.

Latchmore Hall

We now reach the T junction of Pig Lane with the Hallingbury Road, at Latchmore Bank, where Harry Brewster's daughters Joan and Margaret, pupils of the Village School, used to live and from where they would walk the two miles to school every day, down the lane and across the park stepping-stones, to join up with school friends in The Street.

Along the road to the right is Latchmore Hall, where Beryl Frere went to live after leaving Twyford House. Lawrence Karthauser, who was looked after by Miss Beryl as a child, tells us:

I have known Auntie (Beryl Frere) for most of my life. She lived in a big house in four acres of ground, with her housekeeper, Miss Lawrence. She had several people working for her; I remember a gardener Mr Death, her cook Mrs Luff, Mr Luff and Mr Brewster. She used to call them all in with a handbell that she rang exactly on the hour for refreshments at 11a.m.

Sally Brewster, from Pig Lane, came to live with us when she wasn't yet six, and also Malcolm Morris, who was a ward of the Spastics Society. Auntie had two horses, Billy and Rocket, and Sally eventually had a horse called Smokey.

Auntie was full of energy. She loved her garden and helped a lot in the village. She taught country dancing, and had her piano on the lawn at Latchmore Hall, and had a wind-up gramophone that she used to take around with her. She taught at Little Hallingbury School, where there is a painting of her on the wall and a plaque in commemoration. She was very keen on swimming and made sure that we were all proficient. She had a dog, a terrier called Bobby, and fostered several cats. She also had a pony trap and we used to go round the village in it, pulled by Billy.

Eventually I moved to Kent in 1970, Malcolm returned to the care of the Spastics Society, and Sally left later. Auntie moved to sheltered accommodation in Dorking, near her sister Phillis, and she died in Abbeyfield Nursing Home in Bishop's Stortford in 1975.

It is time now to retrace our steps back to the London Road and turn south into Thorley Street.

Chapter 12

The Street

The Street, looking north from the Post Office, 1920s.

The last stretch is along The Street from Hither Farm to Thorley Wash.

The Street in 2003 is no longer the leafy lane seen by Virginia Wade Bain from her Greenline coach, or the quiet road remembered by villagers who as children from the Blocks let their balls roll across the road, or as farm workers let their cattle cross to grazing pasture on the other side.

The 'elders' of The Street, not to mention the 'youngsters' of the Blocks in The Street, have put their minds to the task of recalling which Thorley families lived when and where in the village. Helped by clues in the 1901 electoral roll given to us by Mrs Curnow, we will try to bring some of the villagers back as we walk.

6 - 9 Pump Yard Cottages (Park View Cottages)

At No. 6 there used to live a plumber called Mr Byrne, about whom nothing more is known. It is thought that in the 1930s Alice Bird (aunt of Bert and Arthur Bird of Hither Farm across the road) lived there, possibly with Clara Bird, and then later, after the war, Mrs Reynolds, a nursing sister at the hospital, came to live there with her mother.

At No. 7 lived Joseph Day with wife Emma and family before they moved in 1917 to Rumballs Farm. After the Day family there lived an elderly man at No. 7, and then came the Hutchin in the 1930s, prior to their moving across the road to Parkside Cottages. In the 1920s Arthur Hills, who worked on the railway, used to live in No. 8. Later came Grace Ashpole who lived there until her death in the 1990s, possibly followed by Mr and Mrs Hector Prior. In 1965 Peter Ashpole (Grace's son) came to live there with wife Anne.

It is recorded that Ernest Chappell with his wife, Abigail, lived at the turn of the century in Thorley Street, presumably in No. 9. Much later, in the 1950s, came Janet Rolph's aunt, Fanny Barker (née Chappell) who stayed at No. 9 until her death in 1990. Fanny would be seen with her bicycle everywhere, always pushing it up a hill and free-wheeling down!

Hither Farm (called Bird's Farm)

The Bird brothers, Bert and Arthur, were tenants of two farms, one in Pig Lane as Molly Lambert, daughter of Bert, has told us, and Hither Farm in The Street. Bert also rented the Twyford House meadow

131

Hither Farm, with Bert and Arthur in Bird's Lane and Florrie in the garden, next to Parkside Cottages, 1920s.

land, called the Park, that lay opposite Hither Farm on the other side of the London Road, for the dairy cattle to graze. On marriage, Bert went to live at Twyford Mill Farm, and meanwhile brother Arthur remained living at 'Bird's Corner', where his wife Isobel, who suffered from consumption (and eventually needed to spend time resting in a revolving greenhouse set up in the garden), started up a farm shop in the building that is now a veterinary surgery. Isobel used to keep Great Danes.

Rose Monk, who worked for the Birds, recalls:

When cows were driven from the barns across the main road into the park opposite, on a wet day, you can imagine the road was very muddy with manure! Florrie Bird (sister of Bert and Arthur) ran the dairy in those days. Inside were the milk pans; some would be for fresh milk, others for skim. As youngsters we fetched the milk from the dairy and before school delivered the milk to various villagers in the Street. We would have quart cans and pint ones. I remember having three in one hand and three in the other, and in the winter my fingers were frozen!

Parkside Cottages

There were two cottages adjoining Bird's Farm, in which lived the cowmen and their families. James (Jim) Hutchin, with his wife Florence (née Gilbey) and daughters Flossie and Cicely lived in the cottage next to the farm. Jim and his sisters, Martha, Emily and Annie, all attended the Village School, as did both of Jim's daughters. Cicely Eadie (née Hutchin) writes:

I was born in 1933 and brought up at 11 Parkside, although it was opposite and not by the side of the Park. I lived there for 20 years. The school closed in 1947 when I was 14 years old, and since they put the school-leaving age up to 15 years, I went to a secondary modern school in town. Ina Bright, who lived with her brother George and family in the Blocks (now Highland Road), and I were great friends in our school days.

Her sister Flossie was born in 1928 at No. 7 Pump Yard Cottages.

Next door to the Hutchin family, in the end cottage, lived Harry (known as Skygo) Prior with his wife Olive. Their two sons Denis and Fred, both pupils of the Village School, did not leave school to work on the farm. Denis (who passed away in 2003) worked for Sparrow's in town and Fred worked for the Lea Conservancy Board. On marriage Fred went to live in Clay Cottage for 18 years and then moved with wife Joy to The Street. Tom Camp moved into the cottage from Sparrow's Nest in the 1970s and stayed there until he died in 2000.

4 and 5 Post Office Cottages

Rose recalls the time when Thorley had a Post Office in The Street:

Two sisters, Annie and Alice Hale, used to live in the cottage (No. 5 Post Office Cottages) where their father James Hale had set up the first village Post Office in 1854. Annie married John Watts and when her father

The Hale sisters, Alice (left) *and Annie, c.1900.*

Above: *Mr Clark, father of Ruth and Joyce, c.1945.*

Left: *Milestone on the garden wall of the Post Office, 1910.*

died in 1902 they took over the running of the Post Office until 1933. We all remember how Mrs Annie Watts was a real gossip! She would glean every bit of news, good and bad, which then spread in no time around the village!

A church magazine article written by Bill Hardy tells us:

The Post Office had been a small community sideline for the Hales, as James was also a builder and carpenter whilst his wife Eliza ran the laundry for Twyford House in a wash room at the back of their cottage.

Rose continues:

The first Thorley postman I remember was Mr Bayford, who was another character who could recite all the news to everyone by reading the postcards! Then in 1916 came Mr Albert Brewster until he retired. When the Watts retired and passed on, the Post Office was moved in 1933 to Spellbrook just opposite Thorley Wash Farm, and at first the Hadaways ran the Post Office from their off-licence store, and then during the war Mrs Groom, a little further down the London Road, was the postmistress for a while until she retired.
The Post Office then came back to Post Office Cottages in The Street, and Miss Ruth Clark, who lived next door with her sister Joyce, ran the Post Office until her bad health in 1967, when it then closed. Miss Joyce Clark retired as an SRN to look after her sister until she died, and Joyce still lives in No. 4 Post Office Cottages in 2003.

Joyce, who has many memories to recall, thinks she must be the resident who has lived the longest in the same house in The Street. Her older sister Ruth was born in the house in 1907, and her father, brother and two sisters all attended Thorley Village School, as did Joyce. They are all now deceased. Outside the house against the wall of her garden is an old milestone showing the distance to London, and further along her garden wall is the rare pinch gate already mentioned.

Janet Rolph, who belongs to the old-established Chappell family and has very many stories to tell of characters in The Street, recalls:

After the Hales' Post Office closed in 1933, George Wood whose mother was Albert Brewster's sister, lived in No. 5 Post Office Cottages with his wife Dorothy. My aunt Kit was bridesmaid to Dorothy and very good friends with her. Most recently it has been the home of Paul and Catherine Newman for the last eight years.

Thorley House

Rose recalls the early occupants of Thorley House:

The first people to rent Thorley House from the Frere family were a Dr Hardigan, next Dr Dockray, then Dr and Mrs Newman with their son John and daughter Betty, followed in 1938 by Cmdr and Mrs Wolfson, with their daughter Pamela and son Mark, who later became the Conservative MP for Sevenoaks in Kent.

A tragic and fatal accident happened to Cmdr Wolfson when, a few years after the Second World War, he was flying back from the island of Elba to England with war correspondent Chester Wilmott, and the plane crashed. Pamela married and moved away, but in the 1970s returned with her husband Allan Finch to live with her mother who had sold Thorley House to Mr and Mrs Mouser and moved into Sparrow's Nest. For a while the church fêtes continued to be held in the grounds.

Thorley House figured significantly in the lives of the villagers of Thorley while the Wolfsons were there, as many can recall. Mrs Wolfson herself wrote in 1969 about her feelings for Thorley:

[When we began] *to search for a permanent English home, we were in no doubt as to what we wanted... I came to Thorley Houses and I wandered through the village. There were meadows with fat sheep and lambs grazing; the church spire in the distance; a footpath leading to it; a wood and, across the road, the River Stort. I phoned my husband in his city office and said, 'I think I have found the very house', and he said, 'Clinch!'*

Suddenly then, everything seemed an enchantment – a dream come true. Here were great elm trees and green lawns, and a majestic oak at the front door, and a cottage at the front gate – Sparrow's Nest – over 300 years old. There were friendly and helpful neighbours and moving in was a wonderful event. I never seemed to tire.

For 32 years now I have lived in this house – most of the time in deep contentment, shared in the village life and grown deeply attached to it and to its people.

In 1944, Thorley Women's Institute came into being, and we formed our first committee in the drawing-room of Thorley House. Later the Women's Institute Choir came there regularly for practice. Each year our church fêtes have been held in the garden, as well as fêtes in aid of the C of E Children's Society's Thorley Branch, of which I was secretary for many years. There have been Scout rallies and jumble sales also in the garden and the house, and the first Thorley tennis club also started on our lawn court. A happy and lovely village existence. But with the war came great changes.

The men of the parish made big sacrifices in the First World War, and in the Second World War Thorley men and women served in the Forces – no less than 103 in all. Their names are commemorated in Thorley Church. We had our share of evacuees and also our share of the bombing. An unexploded bomb landed in the field near the school, and this resulted in the entire school coming to Thorley House for a week. We held

Thorley House, 1940.

Cmdr and Mrs Wolfson and their daughter Pam at Thorley House, 1951.

Left: *Vera Camp and son Michael at Sparrow's Nest, 1951.*

was a cousin of Albert Brewster and the brother of Harry Brewster of Latchmore Bank, was chauffeur to Dr Newman at Thorley House. After the Brewsters came Tom and Vera Camp, with son Michael. Tom continued as chauffeur gardener to Cmdr and Mrs Wolfson, when they took up residence in Thorley House.
He moved across Thorley Lane into Parkside Cottages when Mrs Wolfson needed to move out of Thorley House. Pamela and husband Allan continue to live in Sparrow's Nest in 2003.

lessons in the cellars when the sirens went, and upstairs when the 'all-clear' sounded.

Most of us took a turn at fire-fighting practice, drew rations for our neighbours, helped the gypsies and their children, and grew fond of our Land Army girls. A Boys' Bible Class was held once a week in Thorley House, led by Revd Harding-Wood, and our garden provided all the vegetables for the school dinners throughout the war.

In 1951 we organised a Pageant in the garden – the biggest event up to that date, for practically everyone in the village took part in it. We attempted in tableau form to give the history of Thorley from 1051–1951, and on a perfect June day, in the Festival of Britain year, it proved an enormous success. As a result we were able to raise a large sum for our 'Welcome Home Fund' for the returning servicemen and women. I have had endless requests throughout the years for a repeat performance. The rector, the Revd Sydney Robinson, wrote up the historical record and my husband was the commentator.

Maurice Hockley, along with his sister Brenda and other villagers, remembers the events taking place at Thorley House during the years of his youth, the fêtes and special occasions, taking part in a historical pageant around 1950, the sad occasion when Commander Wolfson did not return after a fateful air crash, the friendships with the Wolfson children, and Tom Camp the gardener who lived in Sparrow's Nest. Brenda recalls many happy hours at Thorley House with Pam, who kindly taught her to ride her pony Georgie, featured on this book's front cover.

Sparrow's Nest

Rose recalls the early occupants of Sparrow's Nest:

One of the first families to live in Sparrow's Nest was that of Mr and Mrs Matthews, whose son Leslie was well known for his singing. After the Matthews came Herbert and Mary Brewster. Herbert, who

Blocks 1 and 2 (1–8 Highland Road) and Blocks 3 and 4 (1–8 Hawthorn Rise)

The Blocks, as they were originally known, were built in 1935/6. There were 16 houses, in blocks of four, facing each other in pairs. These form two little streets, later named Highland Road and Hawthorne Rise.

The families who lived there in the wartime and postwar periods knew each other well, and their children played together. Two of the fathers, Percy South and George Reedman, died in the war, the only two men of Thorley not to return. Some of the sons and daughters still live in the area, and for them and because of the binding community spirit there used to be in the Blocks, it seems appropriate to give a brief run down of occupants, as far as is known, during the wartime period and since.

In Highland Road lived the following families:

No. 1 (Block 2/1): Arthur (Smudger) and Edie Smith (daughters Iris and Maureen, who married an aircraft engineer and went to America); now Det.. Insp. Ian and Lucy Baker.
No. 2 (Block 1/1): Mr and Mrs Tucker (daughter Barbara); Mr and Mrs Jack Prior (two daughters); then Mr and Mrs Walker (two sons, one daughter); now Andrew and Julie Wise.
No. 3 (Block 2/2): Ted and Lily Shorter (daughter June); now Mark Dedman.
No. 4 (Block 1/2): Mr and Mrs Chappell (children Dawn, Coral, Valerie, Arthur); then repeatedly sold.
No. 5 (Block 2/3): Mr and Mrs Hockley (children Maurice, Brenda with whom George and Win

Above left: *Brenda Hockley and Bill Pleasance on their wedding day, February 1955.*

Above right: *Bryan South, with a donkey, 1951.*

Below: *Len Wood with Mr Wood and Uncle Fred, 1958.*

Brewster lodged for two years); now Maddams.

No. 6 (Block 1/3): George Newman (ex-London copper) and wife (who took Tom Camp as lodger before he married Vera); now Jane and Paul Grace.

No. 7 (Block 2/4): Bert Bright (son George and daughter Ina); now Doris Webb.

No. 8 (Block 1/4): Gladys Dedman (son Eric, daughter Diane Knight) still lives there.

In Hawthorn Rise lived the following families:

No. 1 (Block 4/1): Mr Wood (sons Len, David, Philip); then Dorothy and Michael Clark (sold up).

No. 2 (Block 3/1): Percy and Mrs South (daughter Phyllis (Pookie) and grandson Bryan); then sold to builders Bray; now Barry and Pauline Mascall.

No. 3 (Block 4/2): Mr and Mrs Roberson (adopted son Kevin); now Martin and Pauline Cockman.

No. 4 (Block 3/2): Cath and Fred Eldred (Fred used to live two doors away); now Brian and Caroline Coles.

No. 5 (Block 4/3): Doreen and Dai Griffiths (Doreen (Griff) still lives there).

No. 6 (Block 3/3): Mr and Mrs Reedman (sons Ian and Trevor); now Colin/Christine Ross, many years.

No. 7 (Block 4/4): Mrs Wright; now Alan and Evelyn Whale for last 24 years.

No. 8 (Block 3/4): Daisy and Fred Eldred (brother and sister); then Jack and Daisy Davidson (née Eldred); then empty for a long time.

The Reedman, South, Wood, Hockley, Bright and Chappell children of the Blocks have between them so many memories that here can only be given a short conglomeration of a child's perspective of living in The Street during the time of change heralded by war. They recall:

We had two water pumps, one at each end of The Street. Our water-supply was driven by a windmill at the top of the field near our house. During the war when there were no men around, if this windmill broke down, Mrs Reedman would have to go and fix it.

Milk was delivered from a horse-drawn wagon, and bread was brought round daily in a huge basket. The Post Office was in Miss Clark's front room. Most of the children went to Sunday school on foot up Bird's Lane and came back over the fields.

The bicycle was the primary form of local transport. The bus service was the 396 from Epping to Bishop's Stortford with conductors on board with tickets on racks – the fare was one old penny. The first car to be owned by a family in the Blocks was an Austin 6 belonging to our neighbours, the South family, which we greatly admired.

My memories as a boy in the early 1950s are of the cart-horse derby held in the fields by the Coach and Horses pub.

A particularly enjoyable occasion [says Len Wood] was the Hayter's fête when Harry Radley's band played and my father loaned them an amplifier.

Most children would engage in carol singing at Christmas to get some pocket money. I can remember one occasion being unceremoniously rebuffed by the Misses Hale as 'you are coming round far too early – come back in two weeks'. But a carol singing visit to Thorley House would often result in an invitation inside.

Harvest time was laborious but very entertaining. It was all about stooks, stacking and threshing. As the combines got closer to the middle of the field, guns would be produced to slay the rabbits, which inevitably ran for cover at that stage. Some of these unlucky creatures found their way into our shed where they were skinned and drawn ready for the oven.

Television arrived but only in a few houses in the mid-1950s. My parents [says Maurice Hockley], not known as instigators of fashion, had to my amazement a Bush installed in time for the coronation in 1953. Everybody came in to watch this new wonder.

In 1944 at the age of five [says Coral Gray, née Chappell], I started at Thorley's old school, with my two elder sisters, Dawn and Valerie. Teacher used to stand our small bottles of milk round the big open fire in winter to warm. We had to walk a good two miles to school in all weathers. At the school we had chickens, rabbits, and at one time a goat. During the school holidays we took it in turns to come and feed them all.

The school was given a large piece of ground in the Rectory gardens [recalls George Bright] and this was divided into three for us to grow brassica, root vegetables and peas. We had a gardening teacher in school one day a week, and our vegetables were cooked and served in the Village Hut for our school dinners.

I remember the two Misses Hale. They used to make these little dolls from the wishbone of a chicken, and they used to dress them in little dresses with tiny white aprons and little caps. The head was made of material, and a verse was tied on with cotton around the neck. The verse went like this: 'Once I was a merry thought, Belonging to a hen; Now I'm just a little slave To wipe a dirty pen.' Of course it was a pen wiper, and as a small child I thought it was lovely.

Local farmers would come and ask us children to help either with pea or potato picking. As an adult I did potato picking for John Tinney. It was as good as any health farm today. Clean fresh air, birds singing, and plenty of exercise when the tractor with the spinner on the back came up the rows of potatoes. Everyone worked hard, and we used to enjoy the friendship of all the people working the field.

In wartime [remembers George Bright], children did ten days' farm work a year, as whole days or 20 half days. The whole school used to walk up to the Streeters' field behind Crows Croft, near Rumballs Farm, to pick up potatoes. Streeter would pay 10d. an hour. We would also go up to Reggie Newman's farm at Butler's Hall, where he would pay 6d. a bag.

Newman would harrow the field first and we would pick up the harrowings. I can remember him kicking the soil with his foot and saying; 'Potatoes under there boy, start again, I'm not paying you for nothing!' When we went potato picking at Thorley Wash Farm, the Patten brothers would also pay 6d. a bag. Another job was putting turpentine down chicken's throats to stop feather picking.

I remember gleaning for corn to feed our chickens in the back garden, and the Blue Café opposite us which was burned down.

I remember too Miss Frere, who lived over in the Park and taught us children to swim in her mill pool. Every Wednesday we would swim in the mill pool with Miss Frere, and we'd also swim in the Stort by the Roley Croak. We'd buy ice-cream in the Blue Café on the way home.

The Wolfson family had fêtes in their big garden. And there was a little general shop [Barrett's] that sold different things, including Smith's crisps, but they would only let us have one packet at a time.

Miss Beryl Frere rode in a pony and trap and came around the houses selling National Savings stamps, usually on a Monday, which was washday and when my mother did not want to be disturbed!

We had the Valleys to play in, and it was a very happy time.

George Bright (Bert's son), who in every photo is seen wearing a tie because as he says he has worn one all his life, has very clear memories of his life in Thorley, both as a child and later. His account adds to his schoolfriends' stories:

As a boy, I worked for Mrs Bird at Bird's Farm, and for half a crown I worked from 9 'till 12, cleaning boots (lots of them!), gardening, shopping, getting wood in, cleaning chickens, helping in the dairy, and at harvest time driving a tractor. I once ran over an Italian POW's jacket and Arthur Bird tore me off a strip. I remember Mrs Bird kept Great Danes, and there were two cowmen at the farm, Jim Hutchin and a Mr Dobson, who both had several daughters.

One thing that the schoolmistress, Miss Hummerstone, insisted we all do was to go into the schoolhouse to learn how to use a telephone. I had an electrical bent, so I did the stage lighting for school productions. I didn't want to learn Morris or sword dancing – I've no sense of rhythm and not a musical note in my body. I could only play a washboard or shake a tambourine.

My good friend was David Teitz, an evacuee from London, and I remember how we used to tease his younger brother Michael on the way home from school. Another friend was Arthur Chappell, Coral's brother, who was keen on motorbikes and whose father, Jack, was a 'mystery man' who would travel in and out of London.

I suppose as boys in the 1940s we got up to normal pranks. We had catapults, which one of the farmers would take away from us; we put a 'Beware of Snakes' notice in the fruit that used to be sold in the Blue Café; and we would toboggan down the Highland Road slope straight through whatever traffic there was on the London Road.

Blue House

In 1901 it is recorded that Thomas Evans lived at the Blue House, which is one of the oldest houses in Thorley. During the 1930s and '40s it was owned by Mr and Mrs Avery, who had a daughter Mary and son Billy. They used to keep goats and Rose Monk remembers how The Street children loved to watch them being milked.

Blue Café (Thorley Motors)

In the grounds of the Blue House were a number of barns, one of which was a wooden structure with a thatched roof, owned by the Avery family and run as a café by Miss Riddle, who was aunt to Mary and Billy Avery. This café very much figured in the life of The Street, being frequented by children out on walks and cycling groups from round about.

Many people recall the accidental burning down in 1942 of the Blue Café. It was not restored afterwards. Instead, the Avery family began its motor repair business on the site initially under the name of ASM (Avery, Somerville and Marriott). The business still exists at the time of writing, and one of the workers there is Simon, the son of June Fuller (née Darnell) who was brought up in Wood View at the other end of The Street.

The Blocks boys, Ian Reedman, Len Wood and Bryan South, saw what happened. A spark from a passing steam engine used for ploughing at nearby Thorley Wash Farm ignited the thatch of the café. Len and Bryan sat on the bank opposite watching what went on. Fire hoses were laid down to the River Stort – under the railway line. Baths and buckets, including soapy water, were commandeered. The heat was intense. Ian's mum went in to rescue the refrigerator with Mrs Avery, as this was a valuable

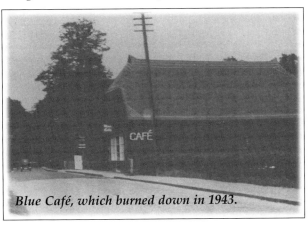

Blue Café, which burned down in 1943.

Mary Avery (right) with Connie Briers in the garden of the Coach and Horses.

piece of equipment in those days. Ian had to be an official witness to the event. Grenville Bird recalls being taken by his parents the following evening to see the still smouldering embers.

Saxons

Saxons was built after the war. Among the families to become residents were the names Rigby, Kent, Gough and Percy. The Percy family, who had a double-glazing business, had moved from Bishop's Avenue, but did not like living in The Street, and so moved back. The Doherty family moved there c.1992.

Ashdene

Janet Rolph (née Chappell), who was born in The Street and has lived there all her life, recalls that there used to be a cottage just beyond Hill Cottages where Mr and Mrs Collins had lived before it was destroyed by fire in the 1920s.

Rose Monk (née Stoakes), who was also born in The Street, recalls that in the space where the cottage stood, the ground was left empty for some years. It was said that Mr Collins would be seen for a long time afterwards foraging in the debris looking for any valuables.

Eventually a new bungalow, Ashdene, was built on the site. Geoffrey Brewster lived in Ashdene

while he was in the process of building the new house called Owletts next door. Afterwards, came Tony Sturgeon, then George Lyus, then Nora and Derek Ursell whose married daughter lives in Pig Lane. Tony and Margaret Dedman, whose son Mark lives in Highland Road, moved there c.1999.

Owletts

Geoffrey Brewster sold Owletts to Peter and Nan Davies in c.1962. Peter was well known by everyone as Dobbets or Dob, the barber in Station Road, Bishop's Stortford. Dobbets, now sadly deceased, knew everything and everyone!

The *Herts and Essex Observer*, featuring Thorley Street residents in March 1989, reported as follows:

What is perhaps Thorley Street's most sporting house-hold can be found at Owletts, for 27 years the home of Peter and Nan Davies. Mr Davies (68) played for Bishop's Stortford Cricket Club for 15 years, and the Davies Cup for which local village teams now compete every year was donated by him. He also played football for the town and is a former vice president of the club. In 1938/9 he was the town's table tennis champion. Now he spends much of his time playing bowls.

During the Second World War Mr Davies was an armourer in Fighter Command's 29th Squadron based at West Malling in Kent. The first pilot he worked for was Guy Gibson, the future leader of the Dambusters. Douglas Bader was also in the squadron. He remembered persuading Max Bygraves to play the piano by buying him a drink when he was part of the RAF gang show. He said that on one occasion three German Fokker Wulf got lost while testing new navigational equipment and landed at West Malling by mistake.

1 and 2 Hill Cottages

Grandma Chappell lived in No. 1 Hill Cottages, with her large family of eight children. She may have been the Julia married to George, who is recorded as living in Thorley Street in 1901. There are stories to tell of five of her children: Frank (the father of Janet Rolph) who brought up his family in Rose Cottage in The Street; Peter (father of Jean Humphries and Thorley's First World War Military Medal holder) who married Hilda Collins and brought up his family next door to his brother, in Laburnum Cottage; George who married Kit (née Clark, deceased) and lived in 1 Sunset Cottages near the school; Bob who during wartime went to live with his wife Jessie and daughter Kathleen (Bunty) in No. 7 Pump Yard Cottages, but eventually moved back into 1 Hill Cottages and stayed there until 1978; and Fanny Barker, who lived with her

adopted son John in No. 9 Pump Yard Cottages.

Grandfather Ernie Chappell may have had a brother Charlie, and it may be that Jack Chappell, who lived during the war with his wife and family of four children in the Blocks, was the son of this brother, but this is not clearly known.

After the Chappells in No. 1 came Mr Davies, followed by Louise and Dave Perrill, who was a parish councillor until his ill health and their consequent move to Cambridge.

Albert Brewster, the village postman, lived in No. 2 Hill Cottages with his wife Ada and three sons, George, Ron and Geoffrey and daughter Joan. George tells us:

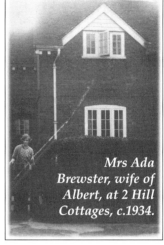

Mrs Ada Brewster, wife of Albert, at 2 Hill Cottages, c.1934.

Albert Brewster, my father, finished his working days as the village postman. He was wounded in the First World War and was discharged with a pension for

George Brewster's wedding, 1943. Left to right: Kathy Painter, Geoff Brewster (best man), groom and bride Winifred, Joan Brewster.

Sid Oxborrow and Spot the dog, c.1943.

Above: *The wedding of William Charles (Charlie) Harris and Agnes Abigail Chappell, 1920s. Left to right, back row: ?, ?, ?, Harold (Bidge) Harris (brother), Queenie Chappell, ? (far back), George Harris (brother), Violet Harris (sister), John Harris (brother); front: Fred Harris (brother), William John Harris (groom's father), Susannah Harris (groom's mother), groom, bride, Mrs Chappell, Mr Chappell.*

light duties, so he became a postman in 1916 in Bishop's Stortford. In those days he was an early-morning starter. On several occasions he felt unwell at 4.30a.m. so he would wake me to walk into the office and report him as sick. During the coldest weather he never used gloves, too fiddling.

When I was 14 and about to leave school, he got me a job at the garage in town. The motor trade went dead in 1939, so I and a few others were dismissed. I was due to go into the Army for six months' training. I got another job with a haulage contractor, and I was called up in May 1940 to the Royal Corps of Signals. In November I was released for work of importance, class WT Reserve. I used to drive lorries with jerry cans of petrol during the night to London Wall. My headlamps had masks on. I married in July 1943; my wife's work at the time was making parts for tank tracks at Millar's Works.

Albert Brewster had a brother Fred and two sisters Alice and Cis. Alice married Arthur (Sonny) Gilson, publican of the Coach and Horses. George remembers that during the First World War they billeted 14

soldiers in the bar. He also recalls that the land behind the pub was called Gilsons Meadow. Later, the Gilsons lived across The Street at Rainbow Cottage. Alice Gilson was the cook at the Village School and some former pupils remember having to go her to do the washing-up as a punishment. Cis married the Streeters' gardener John Wood and they lived first in the hamlet of Butler's Hall and then in Thorley Place Cottages, where she did the laundry for the Streeter family. At about the same time Fred moved in next door with his wife Ellen. Both Fred's wife and Albert's wife worked as maids for the Streeters at Thorley Place. After the Brewsters there were quite a few new occupants of No. 2 Hill Cottages, including the Hickey family, who later moved to 6 Park View Cottages.

Two Brewster brothers celebrated their 60th wedding anniversaries in 2003: George with wife Win and Geoffrey with wife Hilda.

1 - 5 The High

Five houses were built in 1959, set back from a small

service road in front of them called The High with a letter-box in it. In No. 1 lived Frank and Elizabeth Chappell, parents of Janet, who lived next door at No. 2 with husband Jimmy Rolph. On the death of her parents, Janet moved with Jimmy into their house. Other residents in The High have come and gone quite frequently, with only the Ellis and Newman families staying in Nos 3 and 5 respectively for some while.

1 Thorley Street (Rockdale)

In 1937, Charlie and Agnes Harris lived with their daughter Joyce in Rockdale. Joyce continued living there with husband Bill Parsons until c.1960. Later came Vic Monk and wife Flossie (née Hutchin), who still live there in 2003. Vic served in 403 (Four 0 Three) Flotilla Landing Craft Crew, Combined Operations Sea Service RM, and Flossie remembers before they were engaged being very confused seeing him cycle by in The Street dressed in both khaki and blue uniform.

2 Thorley Street (Listohill)

From 1937 until 1957 Winnie Griggs lived in No. 2 (Listohill). In 1949 Ron Oxborrow moved there on his marriage to Vera (née Adams). Ron is one of the longest-lived Thorleyites in The Street. He recalls:

I was born and brought up in Thorley and have lived in The Street all my life except for three and a half years' service in the Royal Navy. I served in minesweepers in the Mediterranean as seaman/ gunner/helmsman. I remember coming home on leave to be met by Mum and dog Spot who ran and leapt into my arms. Before call-up I was apprenticed carpenter to Cannons and afterwards worked for Boyd Gibbins for over 20 years, and then for Elliotts.

I remember ploughing matches with one horse held on the farms, when Ron Barker [Winnie's husband, who lived in Chrysanthemum Cottage] used to win most prizes. Some did say though that Ted Threadgold's furrows were straighter than Ron's.

I used to be in the church choir with George and Geoff Brewster, Gordon Barker and Phil Akers. Miss Eccles played the organ which had to be pumped by hand, with the boys taking turns. Thorley school swimming team used to compete against other schools at Bishop's Stortford swimming-pool, where Gordon

Barker won three first prizes and I won three seconds.

As a schoolboy I remember going beating and being given half a crown, a piece of bread and cheese and a bottle of ginger beer, with extra if we boys went early to go round keeping the birds in the wood. We used to get smothered in mud! The shoot used to go through Thorley Wood in the mornings and across the fields in the afternoons, with hares and rabbits as game as well as pheasants. Rooks nesting at Thorley Rectory were also shot.

Ron met Vera at a darts match at the Eagle, Kelvedon. They both remember the Thorley cricket matches, and Ron also recalls playing football in the Thorley football team, which comprised Revd S.E.F. Robinson, Phil Akers, Sid Hammond, George Clark, Gordon Barker, Les Collidge, Roy Money and George Brewster.

Coach and Horses

The 1901 records show that Arthur and Emma Gilson were the publicans at the Coach and Horses, which is owned by Benskins Brewery. The Gilsons were followed by the Reids who had a son Bill and a daughter. Then came Mr and Mrs Powdrill who had a son. In 1938 the publicans were Connie and Charlie Briers. The old barn belonging to the pub and close to the road used to house a small-time engineering business run by Constable and Son from the neighbouring village of Spellbrook. Connie Briers, widowed in 1963, remarried and became Mrs Jack Constable. John Bradley then became landlord from 1963 to 1967, followed by Arthur Cook, Jane and Laurie Jenner, Angie and Andy, and then Tim and Sharon Metcalfe, who left in 2000 after a spirited local campaign failed to thwart the brewery's plans to turn the traditional village pub into an upmarket pub restaurant. Tim and Sharon moved to the Old Bull further along the London Road towards Bishop's Stortford.

Pat Martin (née Briers) recalls some of her mother's neighbours and also some of her customers at the Coach and Horses:

We used to have donkey derbies and games of football and cricket in our field for The Street children and the evacuee children who came to the village. Among them were the Herbert boys, Frankie and Robert, the Oxborrow boys Ron and Sid, and their parents'

Charlie and Connie Briers, landlord and landlady, 1941.

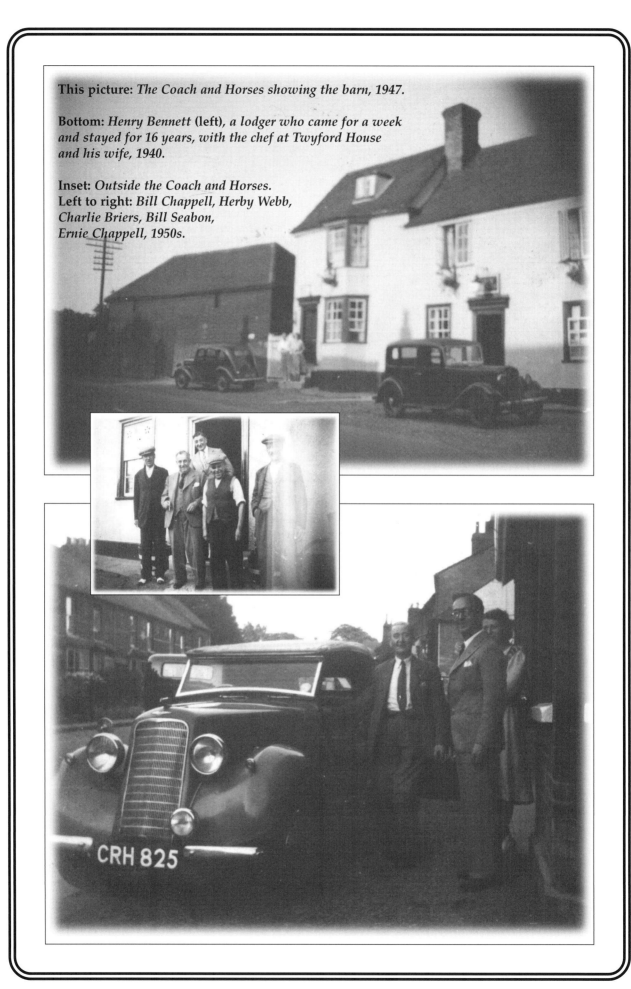

This picture: *The Coach and Horses showing the barn, 1947.*

Bottom: *Henry Bennett* (left), *a lodger who came for a week and stayed for 16 years, with the chef at Twyford House and his wife, 1940.*

Inset: *Outside the Coach and Horses.*
Left to right: *Bill Chappell, Herby Webb, Charlie Briers, Bill Seabon, Ernie Chappell, 1950s.*

evacuee Georgi Black, Mrs Watts' two nephews Harry and Tommy, and Harry Roberts who was an evacuee in the Blocks. Sid said he only asked my brother Peter to play with him because he had a full-size set of cricket stumps. Derek Jameson (the well-known journalist), who was an evacuee with the Elliotts of Maze Green Road, also used to come to the pub. Our lodger Henry Bennett, who stayed 16 years, only came to stay for a week.

Old Police Cottage

Rose, who was brought up in the cottage next door to the police station, can well remember her next-door neighbours:

In the early years, there were several policemen who lived in Thorley Street, in the cottage which was then the Police House. In those days we as a family lived next door, so we knew how to behave ourselves, specially as children! The first of

George Beatty Stoakes, private in Royal Army Service Corps, 1914–19.

the policeman I can only just recall was PC Eames. Before him there may have been PC Reeves, the grandfather of Betty Jennings who lives in Elm Trees. After PC Eames came PC Frost, PC Smith and PC Reed who had two daughters. This was fine for for my sister and me, because we all became firm friends. PC Shadbolt was the last of the village constables. PC Eames had a son Ivan, who also joined the police force, and in his turn Ivan's son John too became a policeman, keeping this in the same family for three generations.

The police gave up the cottage during the Second World War, and Mary Sampford (née Barker) has lived there since 1941. Her husband George was from a Thorley family, and had been brought up by a sister, with whom he lived after his parents died until he married Mary in 1934. They first lived in Millers Cottage, Pig Lane, where their son Colin was born. George worked in Millar's Machinery and also as a gardener. In their garden and on the allotments opposite, he and Mary grew vegetables and flowers, particularly chrysanthemums and dahlias, which people in The Street and passers-by would buy.

Hillside Cottage

This was the family home of Rose Monk (née Stoakes) for many years. Her parents, who came to Thorley in the early 1900s, had five children, the youngest being Rose (born in 1917). Rose and her sister Beattie both attended the Village School, and Rose later became engaged to Frank Monk. They married after Frank's miraculous return from a Japanese prisoner-of-war camp and went to live in Rectory Close.

Rainbow

The Threadgold family can be traced back in Thorley as early as 1750. In 1901 the electoral record shows that James and Alice Threadgold, who had been married in St James' by Revd John Procter, lived in Thorley Street presumably in Eastview (renamed Rainbow Cottage).

Alan Threadgold, great-grandson of Alice and James, and family archivist, tells us:

Since James died in 1904, Alice had to bring up their eight children alone. Daughter Minnie, who is Alan's grandmother, married Fred (Pop) Wright in 1920, and they lived in Southend Cottage next door to the Oxborrows in Northend Cottage. Minnie's two

Family group. Left to right: *Beattie Stoakes, Frank Chappell, George William Stoakes, Rosa Agnes Stoakes, Rosie Stoakes, George Beatty Stoakes (seated), 1925.*

Doris and Leslie (in uniform) Threadgold with his mother Alice and son Alan, 1941.

children, Leslie and Peggy, attended the Village School, where Leslie and Beattie Stoakes were inseparable – if one was absent, so was the other. Both Peggy and Leslie were clearly well thought of by Miss Beryl Frere and Miss Hummerstone, from the letters written by these ladies in 1940. Leslie (who took the name Threadgold) married Doris Stock and moved into the cottage that was to become Elm Trees. I was born there in 1937.

I attended Thorley School, probably during 1944/45 when my mother was seriously ill, and I stayed with Minnie and Pop, my grandparents. I remember at the time the Valleys being frozen, walking over crisp hoar-frost and breaking the ice on puddles on our way to school. I well remember that lunch was cooked and served in the wooden hut (now used for storage of Scout gear) – the smell of the paraffin used for those stoves is with me to this day. I remember that to get in and out of our classroom we had to climb five or six stairs, open a large window, and then go down the stairs the other side into the playground (I can't remember why). Finally I remember Gran Wright coming to the school Nativity Play and hearing for the first time the carol 'We Three Kings of Orient Are'.

Grandad (Pop) Wright was a keen gardener growing vegetables and in particular flowers with zinnias and sweet peas as his speciality. I'm sure that he and Mr Oxborrow were in keen competition.

I remember too the water pump in the front garden (which may be still there) was shared with the Oxborrows. Two galvanised buckets were kept full in the kitchen for daily use, and quite often it was my job to keep them filled.

Further to singing for our pocket money at Gran Wright's (Southend Cottage), we would persuade our parents, whenever we visited Thorley, that we had to visit Aunt Minnie (née Eldred) and Uncle Ted (Gran Wright's brother) across the road at Moorlands. Our obvious intention was to gain more pocket money by yet another rendering of 'Little Bird I Have Heard' to Minnie and Ted! The words were: 'Little bird, I have heard, What a merry song you sing, Soaring high Through the sky On your tiny wing (you've got)' – which we would always add at the end. We often had to walk past the cottages opposite the Coach and Horses where the Seabons and Mrs Watts lived in the 1950s, and we usually came upon Mrs Watts standing by her front gate. I've since come to believe that this lady was the Central Intelligence Agency of Thorley! In 1949 the Gilsons moved into Rainbow Cottage.

Glen View & Moorlands

Strangely, little has come to light so far about Glen View. We know from Ron Oxborrow that early occupants were: the Reynolds family, Sonny Prior, John Clark, Anna and Tony Swan, Daisy Hammond and family and Liz and David Eldred, who left in 1986. Until 1978 Moorlands was occupied by Ted Threadgold who married Minnie (née Eldred) in the 1920s and went there to live.

Malting Row

In the 1920s there used to be a row of eight small terraced cottages, with thatched roofs, located opposite the Coach and Horses. They were catastrophically damaged by fire in 1923, fortunately with no lives lost but with all possessions ruined. Memories of this disaster still live on. Philippa Woodall, daughter of Phillis Frere, remembers that her family in Twyford House gave all the families living in the Well Houses, as she called Malting Row, shelter until they could be found new homes. Rose Monk was at the scene:

In the year of 1923 I was a young child. We three, my sister, myself and one of the village children, were playing in our front garden and my sister and the playmate said they could smell smoke. They darted outside the gate and saw that the smoke was coming from the row of cottages along the road. We tore indoors and told our mother, who at the time had an elderly friend, Emily Martin, who lived in one of the houses. Meanwhile the fire was spotted by other people, and in a short time the fire brigades arrived and with help from the villagers they tried to save what they could. It was a hot and dry summer that year, so that the water pipes had to be laid over to the river.

A report in the *Herts and Essex Observer* of July 1973 tells us that:

The row of eight thatched cottages that disastrously caught fire on unlucky date Friday 13 July in 1923 was called Malting Row. Everything was lost, except – luckily – the lives of the villagers who lived there. These were Mr and Mrs F. Clark and their six children; Mrs Martin, Miss Martin and a nephew; Mr G.E. Chappell; Mr J. and Miss S. Clark; Mr and Mrs F. Chappell and a daughter; Mr and Mrs Threadgold; Mr and Mrs Anderson and their six children; Mr and Mrs Travers and their two children.

In 2000, the *Herts and Essex Observer* carried another article about the disaster:

The Bishop's Stortford firemen of 1923 attended a blaze at a row of Thorley cottages to find that the fire had taken a strong hold and the houses were beyond being saved. The pictures clearly show the devastation caused to the eight homes and how the salvaged furniture was lined up along the pavement opposite. The photos were sent to us by 81 year old Morgan Travers, who was aged just 4 when the disastrous fire struck. He lived in one of the cottages with sister Ada and parents Morgan and Edith and can remember with some clarity the events of that July day. 'I am convinced that my sister and I are now the only survivors of the event because I feel sure there were no other children in that row of cottages' he said. 'It happened just a week after my sister's sixth birthday and she was at school when the fire broke out. I was four

Furniture rescued from the fire that destroyed Malting Row in 1923.

years old and my mother took me to Bishop's Stortford for my first haircut. As we were re-entering Thorley in the bus, we were preceded by one of those Foden steam wagons that plied the roads in those days. It was belching forth sparks, and these were blown on to the tinder-dry thatch of the cottages, which in no time at all were reduced to a heap of ash.'

It would appear that there were four cottages on or near the site that were occupied between the 1930s and 1960s, of which the two nearest Thorley Wash were converted into one dwelling called Elm Trees. The end cottages were occupied by Charles and Agnes (Aggie) Harris who, before the Second World War, moved across The Street to No. 1 Rockdale. Then in the 1930s came Leslie and Doris Threadgold, whose son Alan was born there. In the 1940s came the Morley family who had a daughter. Mr Morley suffered from shell-shock from the First World War.

Next door lived Emily Farthing with her elderly father. After he died she lived there with husband Sid Herbert and sons Bob and Frank. In one of the other two cottages lived Bill Seabon with sons George and Ron and daughter Connie. Bill retired and died there aged 72 in the 1960s. Next door to them lived Mr and Mrs Bill Watts (née Firmin), with lodger Mr Ganley and his sons Harry and Frank. In 1927 Mrs Watts' cousins Harry and Tommy joined them.

Everyone knew Bill Seabon, who was the road sweeper, keeping The Street meticulously clean from Thorley Wash to Pig Lane. Colin Sampford recalls that he lost an eye from road chippings flying up and hitting him. He was the father of Connie, who married Jack Williams and then went to live in No. 1 Rectory Close. Ron Oxborrow, who lived opposite, tells us that Mr Seabon used a handcart, broom and shovel. When roads were icy he would also throw down sand. He was remarkable for the pride he took in his work. Ron also recalls that Mr Ganley always had a pipe in his mouth. It is thought his son Harry joined the RAF as a rear gunner in the Second World War and was killed when transporting a plane to another country. His brother Frank suffered from shell-shock.

Villagers living in The Street remember

Mrs Watts and Mr Ganley.

Mrs Bill Watts as a frightening character, who watched at her gate to see what everyone was doing. Pamela Finch, whose mother Mrs Wolfson used to ask her to call on villagers to see if they needed help in any way, was reluctant to talk to Mrs Watts. She remembers one time, when Mr Watts was unwell, Mrs Watts sent her back to get her mother to phone for the undertaker to come and measure up for the coffin. (Bill Watts was the brother of John Watts, who married Annie Hale, so The Street had two characters called Mrs Watts.)

Elm Trees

In 1954 Henry Jennings (who died in 2002) came to live with wife Betty in the cottages he converted into Elm Trees. The grandfather of Betty Jennings was policeman Reeves who lived in Police Cottages and had three children, Edith Mary, Elsie and Robert. Betty recalls that Edith was awarded a school medal for perfect attendance for two years. Edith had four children, one of them Betty's husband Henry. A newspaper article on The Street in March 1989 records:

If you brave the dangers of her geese you can meet Betty Jennings of Elm Trees Cottage. She and husband Henry have lived at Thorley Street for 35 years. They transformed a neighbouring plot of land into a garden after 60 years of neglect, and used to own goats and a Jersey cow. She had one reservation about Thorley Street – the volume of traffic, and said that she preferred the old days. They have four children, ten grandchildren and one great-grandchild.

Northend Cottage

Northend and Southend Cottages were built in 1921, alongside a footpath leading to the river. The first occupants of Northend were the Oxborrow family. Wilfred Edmund married Ethel Maud Howard and they had sons Ron and Sid, born 1923 and 1929. When Mr Oxborrow arrived to work on the railway in 1921 the family was considered well off by most neighbours who worked on the land.

Ron tells of one early excitement that he was told about, which was when the

Fred Wright, 1930s.

Left: *Fred and Minnie Wright with daughter Peggy in the garden of Southend Cottage, 1937.*

Below: *Mr Wilfred Edmund Oxborrow in the garden of Northend Cottage, with Elm Trees in view, 1950s.*

cottages opposite burned down in 1923/4 and his parents left him as a baby on the sofa while they went to help with the rescue.

Ron has only moved house once, to No. 2 Thorley Street (Listohill) on marriage to Vera Adams, a girl from Kerry.

Afterwards came Bert Mingay, who was well known locally in his retirement years for delivering newspapers, and was the brother of Jack Mingay, also well known in the town for his taxi service.

Ron recalls that a Mr Mascall and Bert Mingay both worked for the Pattens at Thorley Wash.

Jimmy Rolph from The High recalls:

In the 1950s Bert still worked for the Pattens. I used to see him there because, when I was at school, I used to go early to the farm to get the horses in from the field and into the stables in the Pattens' yard ready to take carts of girls up to the fields to do potato picking. Bert was a character; he used to keep his

149

money in the back of a clock and was burgled several times when he retired to live next to the Three Horseshoes in Spellbrook.

Southend Cottage

Fred (Pop) Wright and Minnie (daughter of the Threadgold family across the road in Moorlands) lived in Southend Cottage throughout the wartime. Fred used to cycle to the train and travel to London every day. He worked in Northgate House, office cleaning and fire watching on the roof. He would come home on the 3.30, and as a daily ritual the children would wave to him on the train with handkerchiefs.

Fred and Joy Prior live in Southend Cottage at the time of writing. They moved there in about 1958, having lived for 18 years in one half of Clay Cottages in Moor Hall Lane, at the time when it had been two cottages. Their neighbours in the other half had been Jack and Rene Bird, who continued living there after Wilfrid Tinney had made it into one. Fred had also lived next to the Hutchin family in Parkside Cottages when he worked for the Birds.

There used to be another cottage set back between Southend and Laburnum Cottages, where Winnie Griggs lived. It was her aunt Mrs Hudgell who was the old lady 'rescued' and pushed away from danger in a wheelbarrow by Charlie Harris of Rockdale, where a bomb dropped and didn't explode.

Laburnum

The Chappells, like the Harris', the Brewsters, the Birds, the Warboys and the Hammonds, are a long-established Thorley family with branches appearing in all corners of the parish. Only follow-up 'Chronicle Supplements' will allow family archivists to tell their stories. Peter Chappell, the only Thorley man to be awarded the Military Medal, married Hilda Collins, whose parents had lived in an old cottage near Hill Cottages that had burned down. Peter and Hilda lived with their family in Laburnum Cottage, where daughter Jean and husband Derek Humphries later lived until 1983. Peter had first been engaged to Alice Jennings. He was broken-hearted when, living away in service, she had died in a fire caused by a burning candle. The Cayfords, Derek and Jane, have lived in Laburnum Cottage for the last 20 years.

June Darnell (later Fuller) with her doll's pram, in the garden of Wood View, with Thorley Wash Cottages in the background, 1940s.

Rose Cottage

Peter Chappell's brother Frank lived in Rose Cottage with his wife Elizabeth (née Prior) and daughter Janet, who later married Jimmy Rolph and moved to The High. Frank, described as a lovely man and very intelligent, like many a man returning from war to a time of change, wanted to better the chances for his daughter, and he even gave up smoking to be able to send Janet to St Mary's School. When the Chappells eventually left Rose Cottage, it was purchased by builders Carpenters & Cross.

The Off-Licence and Sweet Shop (The Glade)

The shop and off-licence in Thorley Street was run by Mr and Mrs Hadaway, who had a daughter Ethel. Rose recalls that it was a popular place for children to visit, being the only shop nearby where they could buy sweets and ice-cream. Sweets were purchased for as little as a farthing, with halfpennies and pennies spent if more could be afforded. Rose thought to pop in and buy sweets was a real treat, although in later years neither Bryan South nor Len Wood liked going into Mrs Hadaway's shop.

Ron Oxborrow recalls that Jim Godman kept the off-licence after the Hadaways, and then Mrs Chastney (who used to run The Swan and had a son called Peter). The builders, Carpenters & Cross, purchased the properties, which are known as The Glade.

Wood View

June Darnell, whose grandparents were Ernie and Abby Chappell, lived with her parents in Woodview until she met and married Peter Fuller. Then came Mr and Mrs Moody. The old house was demolished and rebuilt in the 1970s.

Thorley Wash Cottages

These were two tied farm cottages when the Patten brothers farmed at Thorley Wash. In one lived the Jennings family and afterwards came farm worker Percy Abra. In the other cottage lived the Browns. Jack Brown was the foreman at Thorley Wash Farm, and his children, Des, Ron and June, attended the Village School. June was remembered as being very pretty. The Browns used to look after Percy, who was the son of a gamekeeper and had come from Broxted in 1939 to work at the farm. After Willi Patten's death in 1971, Percy moved into a caravan near Laburnum Cottage. Villagers recall that Mr Warwick, the farm worker who was killed in an accident involving farm machinery at Thorley Wash, also lived in one of the cottages.

Ernie and Abby Chappell (grandparents of June Fuller) outside Woodview in The Street.

The Pattens left the Browns' cottage to the family, and June (later as Mrs Clanford) converted all of the cottages into one house.

Thorley Wash Farm Cottage

In the mid-1970s, Tony Kluysse, who bought the farm and continued farming after the death of Willi Patten, sold Thorley Wash House separately from the farm, which he then farmed from a new cottage he had built in the grounds for his mother. In the late 1990s, following Tony's untimely death, Thorley Wash Farm was sold at public auction, the majority of the arable land west of the main road going to John Tinney, including the cottage, which became the home of farm manager Geoff Hayes and family. It is rented in 2003.

The names of the properties have become unclear in recent years, and to add to the confusion the barns at Thorley Wash have recently been converted for domestic and office use, but it appears that the Pattens' original farmhouse, Thorley Wash House, is now Thorley Wash Grange, and Kluysse's newer farmhouse is now Thorley Wash Farm Cottage, to distinguish it from the original Thorley Wash Cottages in The Street.

Thorley Wash House (Grange)

Thorley Wash House is situated on the boundary of Thorley with Spellbrook. Rose reminds us that it was the farmhouse for Thorley Wash Farm, the owners of which were one time Mr and Mrs George Patten (senr), who had four sons, Drury, William, John and Henry. When John and Henry married and ran their own farms, Drury and William remained bachelors and ran Thorley Wash Farm. Their farmland included Thorley Wood, and also the moors, through which there was a favourite walk crossing the railway line and the river, and leading to the Warbury Dells (Hallingbury).

Rose recalls that the Pattens had a horse and trap, and that Mrs Patten, widowed by then, sometimes walked through The Street going perhaps to the town of Bishop's Stortford. Her attire was a very long black skirt, a black coat and a black bonnet-shaped hat, the fashion in those early 1900s worn by elderly ladies.

Miss Beryl's pony and trap route leads us back across the Valleys to St James' Church, whence it is but a step to the Village School and Gladys who inspired it all.

Peggy Wright on bicycle, c.1937

Pam Wolfson in BOAC uniform, 1950s.

Left: *Wedding of Ron Oxborrow and Vera Adams, April 1949.*

Christmas 1950, the Coach and Horses. Charlie Briers (blowing coach horn) is pictured with *son Peter* (in RAF uniform) *and John Clark* (far right).

Family picnic at Roley Croak, 1938. Left to right, back row: *Cyril Hockley (Brenda's uncle), Mrs Broad, Nelly Hockley (Brenda's mother)*; front row: *Violet Hockley (Brenda's aunt), cousin Paul, Brenda Hockley.*

Inset: *Phillis Frere with goats at Twyford House, c.1930.*

This picture: *Charlie Harris outside Rockdale, 1930s.*

Above: *June Darnell* (left) *and Pat Briers on holiday in Weymouth, July 1948.*

Top: *Dorothy Stoakes* (left) *with her mother Rosa Stoakes at Hillside Cottage, early 1900s.*

Above: *More personalities from The Street, 1950s.* Left to right: *Alice Gilson (née Brewster), George and Kit Chappell (née Clark), Ellen Brewster (née Carter) and Ernie Warman.*

Left: *Ethel Oxborrow* (left) *with Minnie Wright* (centre) *and Annie Jennings, late 1950s.*

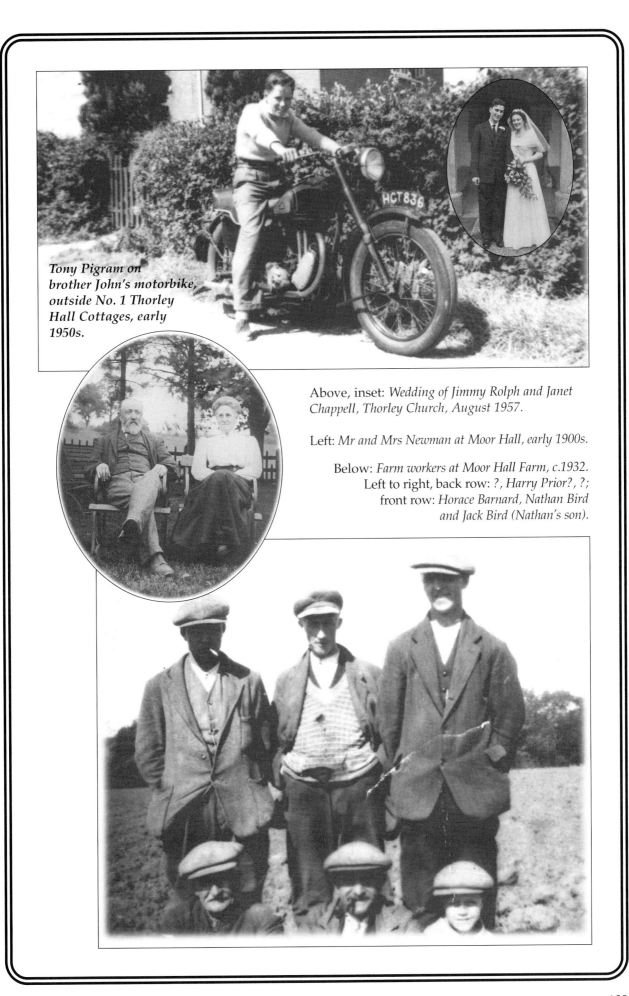

Tony Pigram on brother John's motorbike, outside No. 1 Thorley Hall Cottages, early 1950s.

Above, inset: *Wedding of Jimmy Rolph and Janet Chappell, Thorley Church, August 1957.*

Left: *Mr and Mrs Newman at Moor Hall, early 1900s.*

Below: *Farm workers at Moor Hall Farm, c.1932. Left to right, back row: ?, Harry Prior?, ?; front row: Horace Barnard, Nathan Bird and Jack Bird (Nathan's son).*

Left: *Mark and Pam Wolfson in the cart carrying chicken manure, c.1939. The horseman is unknown.*

Left: *Bert Bird in foreground with a Land Girl and Ernie Hammond at Hither Farm, 1940s.*

Below: *Margery Sampford with her brother Jim Morton at the door of his car, 1950s.*

Left: *Dick Wick and Thomas the cat at Thorley Hall Cottages, late 1970s.*

Right: *Dorothy Wolfson (left) and daughter Pam Finch in Sparrow's Nest, 1978.*

Epilogue

This untitled poem, written and narrated by Mark Wolfson OBE on the occasion of Gladys Warboys' 100th birthday, is an optimistic and fitting end to work done, or perhaps only just begun...

I remember, I remember, not the house where I was born;
But a Thorley in the forest long before historic dawn.
Then.. a clearing in that forest,
thatched homes of mud and clay;
And the people working slowly to build themselves a better day.
And after the dark ages
of strife and battles done,
The three great field system
of pasture, corn and fallow,
wide open to the sun.

Our church there at the centre,
under the wide East Anglian sky,
And around it in the churchyard, real history makers lie.
Both known and unknown people
of now and long ago,
lying there together in great unbroken line
Make a special piece of England, for us and them combined.
And that precious England, of town and countryside,
Forever in the memory of men
who fought and died.

Now here, you have determined,
through the battering winds of change,
To tell this Thorley story
of the last one hundred years,
of losses and of gains,
A story of its people and of much of Britain too,
Of wider lives and comforts for the many not the few.
And as the Village changes from rural life to town;
You it is who know
that 'Thorley's heart keeps beating
within its ancient Parish Bound.'

Subscribers

Joan Abbotson

Bery Abrahams

Barry, Chris, Tim and Pete Adams, Bishop's Stortford

Michael Adams, Bishop's Stortford

The Beer Family, formerly at Black Cottage, Thorley

Mary Joan Brace/Kimber (née Hammond)

Robert Britton, Bishop's Stortford

Mr D.J. Brown

Stan Brownridge, Bishop's Stortford

Alyson Carter (née Phillips), Halifax, N.S., Canada

John A. Challis, Bishop's Stortford, Hertfordshire

Anne Curnow, Bishop's Stortford, Hertfordshire

R.A. (Tony) Doe, Maldon, Essex

Kevin and Hilary Doherty, Thorley

Sheila Dutton, Northwich, Cheshire

The Flack Family, Thorley Park, Hertfordshire

June, Peter and Simon Fuller, Bishop's Stortford

Councillor Ralph Gilbert

Emie Glasscock

Dr and Mrs R.M. Griffin

Tom and Janet Hammond

J.F. Harris, Ilford, Essex

David M. Hickling

Allen Hilson

Maurice Hockley, Basingstoke, Hampshire

J.W. and L.F. Holme, Thorley Park

Mike and Hope Hill

Iain Hornett, Thorley, Hertfordshire

Frances Hornett, Thorley, Hertfordshire

Neil Hornett, Thorley, Hertfordshire

Paul James

Betty and Henry Jennings

Adrian Kimber, St Neots

Mrs M.A. Lambert (née Bird)

John and Lina Loadman, Thorley, Hertfordshire

The McDonalds, 4 New Cottages

Roy Money

John and Joan Monk

Rose and Frank Monk

Bert and Ethel Outlaw

Fred and Stella Owers

The Patterson/Roy-Chowdhury Family, Thorley

Janet Payne, Bishop's Stortford

Jack and Joan Phillips, Calverton, Notts

Doreen Pigott, Thorley, Hertfordshire

Brenda and Bill Pleasance

Patricia R. Pretious (Hollidge), Lincoln

Dawn Prior

The Reed Family, Old School House, Thorley

Trevor and Glyn Reedman

Colin and Christine Ross, Thorley Street

Georgia Chloe Samuels, Lauren Wick

Mrs Anne Saunders (née Warboys), Peterborough

Colin and Heather Selwood, Sunset Cottage, Thorley

M. Streets, Thorley

R. Fred Strong, Bishop's Stortford, Hertfordshire

Simon Taylor

The 1st Thorley Scout Group

Alan Threadgold

The Timmis Family

Hazel Upton (née Pigram), Bishop's Stortford

Mrs E. Vale

The Revd Alison Walton, St James the Great, Thorley

Elaine Warboys, Thorley Park, Hertfordshire

Frank and Molly Warboys

John S. Warboys, Solihull

Mr and Mrs Mark Warboys, Bishop's Stortford, Hertfordshire

Judy Wick and Dave Eldred

Dorothy and George Wood